Gender, Family, and Adaptation of Migrants in Europe

Ionela Vlase • Bogdan Voicu
Editors

Gender, Family, and Adaptation of Migrants in Europe

A Life Course Perspective

palgrave macmillan

Editors
Ionela Vlase
'Lucian Blaga' University of Sibiu
Sibiu, Romania

Bogdan Voicu
'Lucian Blaga' University of Sibiu
Sibiu, Romania

Romanian Academy
Research Institute for Quality of Life
Bucharest, Romania

ISBN 978-3-319-76656-0   ISBN 978-3-319-76657-7 (eBook)
https://doi.org/10.1007/978-3-319-76657-7

Library of Congress Control Number: 2018935696

© The Editor(s) (if applicable) and The Author(s) 2018
Open Access Chapter 9 is distributed under the terms of the Creative Commons Attribution 4.0 International License (http://creativecommons.org/licenses/by/4.0/). For further details see license information in the chapter.
This work is subject to copyright. All rights are solely and exclusively licensed by the Publisher, whether the whole or part of the material is concerned, specifically the rights of translation, reprinting, reuse of illustrations, recitation, broadcasting, reproduction on microfilms or in any other physical way, and transmission or information storage and retrieval, electronic adaptation, computer software, or by similar or dissimilar methodology now known or hereafter developed.
The use of general descriptive names, registered names, trademarks, service marks, etc. in this publication does not imply, even in the absence of a specific statement, that such names are exempt from the relevant protective laws and regulations and therefore free for general use.
The publisher, the authors, and the editors are safe to assume that the advice and information in this book are believed to be true and accurate at the date of publication. Neither the publisher nor the authors or the editors give a warranty, express or implied, with respect to the material contained herein or for any errors or omissions that may have been made. The publisher remains neutral with regard to jurisdictional claims in published maps and institutional affiliations.

Cover image © borchee / Getty Images
Cover design by Fatima Jamadar

Printed on acid-free paper

This Palgrave Macmillan imprint is published by the registered company Springer International Publishing AG part of Springer Nature.
The registered company address is: Gewerbestrasse 11, 6330 Cham, Switzerland

Acknowledgments

Editors of this volume would like to thank all contributors of this book for their willingness to bring together different empirical cases illuminating our understanding of the diversity of migrants' life trajectories in various European countries. The wide coverage of major themes such as gender, well-being, work, and family, shaping migrants' performances and outcomes in relation to parenthood, adulthood, manhood, and old age, would not have been possible without each contributor's effort to complement and harmonize others' expertise and findings. Our thanks go also to Alina Yurova, John Stegner, Katelyn Zingg, and Ben Bailey from Palgrave Macmillan for their skillful assistance.

Several chapters in this book are based on data from MIGLIFE research project aiming to unpack migrants' subjective experiences with respect to their unpatterned life courses in a context of structural uncertainty and transnational setting. Authors of these chapters, namely Ionela Vlase, Bogdan Voicu, Anca Bejenaru, Alin Croitoru, and Ana Maria Preoteasa, would like to acknowledge the financial support received from Romanian National Authority for Scientific Research and Innovation, CNCS/CCCDI—UEFISCDI, project number PN-III-P4-ID-ERC-2016-0005.

Contents

1 Introduction: Uncertain Biographies? A Focus on Migrants' Life Courses 1
Ionela Vlase and Bogdan Voicu

Part I Life Strategies and Life-Choices Depending on Social Context 13

2 Fringed Life Satisfaction? A Life-Course Perspective on the Impact of International Migration on Subjective Well-Being 15
Bogdan Voicu

3 'Walking Alongside' Polish Migrants in Ireland: Individual Life Courses in the Context of Political, Social, and Economic Change 41
Justyna Salamońska

4 'And we are still here': Life Courses and Life Conditions of Italian, Spanish and Portuguese Retirees in Switzerland 67
Claudio Bolzman and Giacomo Vagni

Part II Work and Labor Market — 91

5 Gendered Migratory Pathways: Exploring the Work Trajectories of Long-Term Romanian Migrants — 93
Alin Croitoru

6 Fragmented Careers, Gender, and Migration During the Great Recession — 117
Francesca Alice Vianello

Part III Gender and Family — 139

7 Immigration, Transition to Parenthood, and Parenting — 141
Anca Bejenaru

8 Women's Stories of Migration: Youth, Personal Agency, and Linked Lives — 171
Ana Maria Preoteasa

9 Men's Migration, Adulthood, and the Performance of Masculinities — 195
Ionela Vlase

10 Conclusion: Setting Up an Agenda for Life-Course Perspective in International Migration — 227
Bogdan Voicu and Ionela Vlase

Index — 235

Notes on Contributors

Anca Bejenaru is Associate Professor in Social Work at the Lucian Blaga University of Sibiu. Her education includes a BA in Psychology and an MA in Sociology. In 2010, she received her Ph.D. in Sociology with a thesis focusing on Romanian child adoption granted by Babeș-Bolyai University of Cluj-Napoca. Her research interests include childhood and migration, children in out-of-home care, child adoption, violence against children, young people, and women. Her publications include two books, several scholarly articles, research reports, and several chapters in books.

Claudio Bolzman holds a Ph.D. in Social and Economic Sciences from the University of Geneva. He is professor at the Geneva School of Social Work, University of Applied Sciences and Arts Western Switzerland (HES-SO), and Senior Lecturer at the Department of Sociology, University of Geneva. His main research interests are migration, life course, transnational practices, immigration policies, and social policies. He has carried out many research projects on these topics and is the author of more than 100 sociological publications.

Alin Croitoru is a lecturer at the Department of Sociology, the Lucian Blaga University of Sibiu, and a researcher at the Center for Migration Studies—CeSMig (University of Bucharest). He holds a Ph.D. in Sociology from the University of Bucharest, and during the doctoral period, he was a visiting scholar for an academic year to the Graz Schumpeter Centre (Austria). He has participated in a series of national and international research projects focused on migration topics (e.g., The Europeanisation of Everyday Life: Cross-Border Practices and Transnational Identifications among EU and Third-Country Citizens—EUCROSS; Temporary versus Permanent Migration—TEMPER; Youth mobility: maximizing opportunities for individuals, labor markets and regions in Europe—YMOBILITY; Migrant's Life Courses—MIGLIFE), and within this framework he conducted qualitative fieldwork with Romanian immigrants in Austria, Denmark, Italy, and the UK, as well as research with Romanian returnees. He has published on international migration, entrepreneurship, and economic sociology in a series of journals, including *Europe-Asia Studies, Social Change Review, Journal of Community Positive Practices, Journal of Comparative Research in Anthropology and Sociology.*

Ana Maria Preoteasa holds a Ph.D. in Sociology at University of Bucharest. She is senior researcher at the Research Institute for Quality of Life, Romanian Academy, Bucharest, and at 'Lucian Blaga' University of Sibiu, Romania. Her expertise regards the areas of social policy, minorities, employment, and migration. In recent years she has worked on projects that have used a qualitative methodology and employed the life-course perspective. Her research findings are published in books and articles in academic journals such as *Journal of Balkan and Near Eastern Studies, Social Change Review,* and *Southeast European and Black Sea Studies.*

Justyna Salamońska is an Assistant Professor at the Institute of Sociology, University of Warsaw. She leads a project about multiple migrations (financed through the SONATA BIS grant scheme offered by the National Science Centre) at the Centre of Migration Research, University of Warsaw. Justyna holds a Ph.D. in Sociology from Trinity College Dublin. She previously carried out research and taught at Trinity College Dublin, University of Chieti, and European University Institute. Her research and teaching interests include contemporary migrations in Europe, migrant labor market integration, cross-border mobilities, and quantitative and qualitative research methods.

Giacomo Vagni is a doctoral student in Sociology at Nuffield College, University of Oxford. He received his MA in Sociology at the University of Geneva. His research focuses on the link between family, time, and social inequality. His interests include social inequality, stratification, migration, and family sociology.

Francesca Alice Vianello holds a Ph.D. and is Lecturer in Sociology of Work at University of Padua (Italy). Her main areas of research and teaching are migration, gender, and labor. She is the Scientific Responsible for the Research Unit of Padova for the project financed by the European Commission "Towards shared interests between migrant and local workers project." Furthermore, she has recently concluded a research project on the economic crisis impact on migrant workers. Results from her researches have been discussed and published in Italian, English, and Spanish in several journal articles, book chapters, and edited volumes. She is one of the regional representatives for Europe (2014–2018) of the Research Committee 32 "Women in Society" of the International Sociological Association (ISA). Additionally, she is editorial staff member of the collection "Intersezioni e Asincronie" of the publishing house Guerini & Associati and of the Journal *Mondi Migranti*. More information on the web page: www.slang-unipd.it

Ionela Vlase holds a Ph.D. in Sociology (2009) at the University of Neuchatel, Switzerland, where she has served as teaching and research assistant (2004–2008). She is Senior Lecturer in Sociology at the "Lucian Blaga" University of Sibiu, Romania. Her main research interests concern life course, migration, gender, and quality of life. She is the author of articles published in academic journals like *European Societies*, *European Journal of Women's Studies*, *Ethnic and Racial Studies*, and *Journal of Ethnic and Migration Studies*. Vlase has also a vast record of participation in research projects dealing with migration, ethnicity, gender, and social stratification. She runs an ERC (European Research Council)-like project entitled "Migrants' life courses: dealing with uncertain, highly destandardized biographies in Romania," financed by CNCS/CCCDI—UEFISCDI, project number PN-III-P4-ID-ERC- 2016-0005. Most recent publications include: "Gendered Life-Course Patterns in Post-socialist Romania: An illustration from households situated in precarious prosperity," in *Journal of Balkan and Near Easter Studies* (with Ana Maria Preoteasa, 2017), and "Romanian Households Dealing with Precariousness: A life-course approach," in *European Societies* 17(4): 512–534, 2015). She is also the author of a recently published book *Le genre dans la structuration de la migration* (2016), Institutul European.

Bogdan Voicu is Professor of Sociology with Lucian Blaga University of Sibiu and first-degree research fellow with Romanian Academy, Research Institute for Quality of Life. He also holds a BA in Economic Cybernetics and Forecasting. His main interests are related to comparative sociology, but his publications cover a broader range of issues, including social change, social values, international migration, and social/political participation.

His work is published in various peer-reviewed journals, including *Social Indicators Research*, *European Sociological Review*, *Current Sociology*, *European Political Science Review*, *Journal of Ethnic and Migration Studies*, and so on. Bogdan is author or editor of several books. He is a member of various research networks and associations, including European Survey Research Association, European Values Study (Program Director for Romania), IMISCOE, Romanian Quantitative Studies Association (president), Romanian Election Studies, World Values Survey (principal investigator—Romania), Romanian Network of Migration Scholars, the research network of Higher School of Economics (Russia), and so on. He is also part of the network of correspondents of the Eurofound. Past employment includes LISER (Luxembourg Institute of Socio-Economic Research), Eastern University (Pennsylvania), Bucharest School of Political Science and Public Administration, and University of Bucharest.

List of Figures

Fig. 4.1	MCA. Map of variables. Variances of Dim. 1 (12.33%) and Dim. 2 (6.48%)	81
Fig. 4.2	MCA. Map of individuals. Variances of Dim. 1 (12.33%) and Dim. 2 (6.48%)	82
Fig. 7.1	Mechanisms for the formation and transformation of parenting practices	151
Fig. 9.1	Men's performances according to their position on the masculinity and adulthood axes	208

List of Tables

Table 2.1	Descriptive statistics for variables in the models	26
Table 2.2	Regression models of life satisfaction (11-point scale)	28
Table 4.1	Characteristics of the sample	72
Table 4.2	First and last occupations by citizenship status and nationality	73
Table 4.3	Socio-economic characteristics, social capital and life conditions by citizenship status and nationality	76
Table 5.1	A gendered view of two contrasting types of Romanian returnees' work trajectories	110

CHAPTER 1

Introduction: Uncertain Biographies? A Focus on Migrants' Life Courses

Ionela Vlase and Bogdan Voicu

The past two decades have witnessed an increasing interest in life-course perspectives, with scholars being actively involved in the development of life-course approaches and contributing to the cross-fertilization of various disciplines (Elder et al. 2003). The tendency is noticeable in natural sciences as researchers seek to observe regularities and stable patterns in the creation of molecules, atoms, and beings. Behavioral and social sciences are also exposed to an ongoing process to incorporate life sequencing into the canonical explanations of social life (Alwin 2012; Wingens et al. 2011). Human beings are often described as subjects whose life courses are made of more or less patterned sequences of life events and transitions that are shaped by institutional forces and structural constraints. The whole mix confers a certain biographical stability over a life-

I. Vlase (✉)
'Lucian Blaga' University of Sibiu, Sibiu, Romania

B. Voicu
'Lucian Blaga' University of Sibiu, Sibiu, Romania

Romanian Academy, Research Institute for Quality of Life, Bucharest, Romania

© The Author(s) 2018
I. Vlase, B. Voicu (eds.), *Gender, Family, and Adaptation of Migrants in Europe*,
https://doi.org/10.1007/978-3-319-76657-7_1

time. This book focuses on the uncertainties revealed by migrants' biographies whose life journeys are less conventional or patterned, while their family, work, and educational trajectories are simultaneously more fragmented and intermingled.

As Gardner (2002) contends, there is a more pressing need to address the meaning and shape of life course in migrants' cases. Various questions immediately arise, and the chapters in this book seek to answer them. What challenges do migrants and returnees face when trying to make sense of their life courses after years of experiences in other countries with different age norms and cultural values? How can they reconcile competing cultural expectations of both origin and destination societies regarding the timing of transitions between roles to provide a meaningful account of their life courses? It is reasonable to ask such questions because migrants, more than non-migrants, must pursue life goals in increasingly uncertain times and transnational settings. Migration is, itself, a major life event for individuals, with profound implications for the pursuit of life goals, organization of family life, and personal networks, and it can affect, to a considerable degree, their subjective well-being, the sense that migrants make of their existence, and the planning of their future life stages. The discomfort, uncertainties, and troubles that migrants, both men and women, may witness after a long period of living and working abroad, sometimes with long undocumented stays, need to be thoroughly considered by researchers and policymakers.

The book's overall objective is to produce new knowledge about migrants' and returnees' strategies in dealing with life transitions and achieving normative milestones in major life domains (e.g., education, work, and family), while at the same time properly performing their gender roles. This book puts together two streams of research that rarely ever cross paths, that is, the increasingly appealing life-course perspective and studies on international migration. In this way, we not only place the reader close to current debates in social sciences but also bring into focus one of the major themes of the contemporary globalized world's public agenda: international migration.

Individuals' life courses often contain a sense of predictability since people are expected to pass from one life stage to another, and their transitions between life stages are marked by the assignment and undertaking of social roles. The succession of social roles, their attached meaning, and their recurrence form certain pathways (George 2009; Macmillan 2005; Macmillan and Copher 2005). Pathways are social in the sense that they depend on structural constraints, including social norms and cultures, as well as on the broader structures of opportunity. As Elder and colleagues (2003: 4) put it: "Age-graded patterns […] are embedded in social institutions and history." Individual agency may intervene in this social context, but many coping strategies are actually common across various groups and individuals. Pathways become social and start to act as distinct social locations; that is, they offer a structural element, socially modeled, providing both constraints and opportunities for personal agency. Consequently, pathways act as contexts and can be studied either to understand how they are shaped by various factors or as prerequisites and/or causes for various individual or social outcomes.

"Pathway" is quite an abstract concept. One may easily understand it as a sequence of personal life events related to family. For instance, a typical familial pathway unfolds with an individual's journey through a sequence of stages, including childhood, teen years, young adulthood, getting married, having children, and becoming a grandparent. But divorce, repeated parenthood and couple formation, widowhood, and so on can elicit variations in family pathways. The order of such life milestones is not pre-set, and events can be recurrent and break from the usual patterns due to childlessness, long spells of not having a partner, or parenthood after becoming a grandparent—phenomena that are more common these days.

We already implicitly have introduced time as an intrinsic dimension of the life-course perspective. By discussing personal events and the sequencing of social roles over a lifetime, time implicitly is defined as a basic element in the approach (Allan and Jones 2003). Personal time, however, needs to be complemented by social/historical time features. Entering and exiting educational or labor markets provide supplementary specifications for personal pathways. A succession of changes in family, employment, and/or education roles can create intricate conditions usually considered, under the life-course perspective, to be essential to understanding individual traits (Levy and Bühlmann 2016). Residency adds to the story because moving from one house to another tends to reshape personal and familial pathways (Elder et al. 2003). Life courses become an essential "ingredient of the notion of a socially structured space inhabited by individual actors," thereby necessarily defining any social analysis (Levy and Bühlmann 2016: 36). In fact, by virtue of their institutionalized character, life courses are genuine social locations in which individuals are embedded. De-standardized life courses are likely to act similarly, given the social embeddedness of every single transition within them; that is, life courses provide context, as social locations, for individual traits, values, gestures, behaviors, attitudes, and choices. Nevertheless, as active agents of their biographies, individuals permanently meld with their social locations in a way that combines agency with dependency on structures of opportunity. Their previous experience, expressed as a life pathway, is such a structure, to provide opportunities as well as a history that may be reflected in future decisions and present individual values and preferences.

Migration events, particularly international migrations, also provide relevant social locations. Successive migration decisions, including moving, staying, settling down, remigrating, returning, and so on, form sequences in which changes in social roles, their meanings, and interactions with existing contexts are salient to one's life and can be seen either as outcomes or as causes of various phenomena and processes. Migration is never definitive (Engbersen et al. 2010), and it often builds as a sequence of migrations, remigrations, return migrations, irregular migrations, and spells of nonmigration. Interpretation of the movement comes through different terms that describe particular forms and motivations, including labor migration (Kogan et al. 2011), lifestyle migration (Benson and O'Reilly 2016), family reunification (Bailey and Boyle 2004), migration for care (Lutz and Palenga-Mollenbeck 2012), migration for studies (Li et al. 1996), migration of high-skilled workers (Kõu et al. 2015), and so on. It becomes obvious that a migration career—understood as a sequence of events and decisions linked to migrating, staying, returning, or migrating to other destinations—is intertwined with education, family, and work trajectories. Hence, migration trajectories cannot be adequately understood apart from major life domains that shape individuals' life outcomes. Moreover, migration can take place depending on individuals' positioning within their life courses, family situations, parental roles, economic status, and prospects for career promotions. In turn, migration also can affect the timing of family formation, transitions to parenthood, parenting practices, professional mobility, well-being, and other life events and aspects. Because of this unpredictable interaction of migration career and life trajectories, the uncertainty of one's life course could grow even larger during migration.

Life-course perspective is not a consistent theory but a unifying framework to study social roles and changes to these roles taking place within particular structural contexts, at both the meso- and macrolevels. In doing so, this framework enables linkages with individual experiences and structural contexts, while creating room for the enactment of individual agency (Mortimer and Shanahan 2003). In other words, life-course approach urges the researcher to consider personal life sequencings (Elder et al. 2003; Thomas and Znaniecki 1996). Personal biographies are judged against historical time and social structures, affecting individual life courses and conceding that individuals' lives also may deviate from "normal" life scripts, thereby contributing to the occurrence of innovations and social changes when circumstances enable the institutionalization of deviant life pathways. The chapters of this book aim to offer a fresh analysis of dilemmas and ambiguities reflected in migrants' narratives regarding their life choices and outcomes. Migration adds uncertainty to traditional pathways related to family, employment, gender, and education, with which migration careers intertwine and create new social locations. It also opens up possibilities for new ways to pursue life courses. This book explores the consequences of international migration at the individual level, from a life-course perspective. Contributors to the book address three specific fields: life drivers (decisions to migrate or to stay, post-retirement transitions, and life satisfaction as a motivator), work and labor market, and gender and family. In this way, the book covers a small part of private life, as well as a part of public space, and it delves into the more complicated realm of life choices, shaped by both external circumstances and private life.

The overall aim is to understand how migrants make sense of their life outcomes by considering the broader temporal frame and multiple geographical scales in which immigrants' lives unfold, while also taking into account changes in the web of social relationships in which migrants are embedded, and the changes in values, behaviors, and attitudes as a result of living abroad for a considerable length of time. In doing so, this volume aims to answer three basic questions: How do individual migrants, both men and women, at various life stages handle the uncertainty of migration and its attendant structural forces? What meanings do migrants assign to their unconventional life outcomes resulting from the unpatterned sequencing of their life transitions? What problems do migrants face while growing old in host countries?

For the past half century in Europe, successive waves of migrants have contributed to changes in the demographic, economic, and cultural landscapes of European countries. While much data and literature address such changes, the focus generally has been on the consequences for destination societies (de Haas and Vezzolli 2011: 2). There is still little knowledge on the effects of migration on migrants' lives, and this book fills part of that gap. Starting from the assumption that at the individual level migration is a major life event, this book documents the multiple ways that migration careers intersect and unsettle migrants' life-course trajectories, leading to unexpected life outcomes. Various aspects such as gender, family status, life stage at the time of migration, length of time spent abroad, and societal constraints in destination countries impact migrants' capabilities to plan their life transitions and take on social roles, according to gendered and age-based normative expectations. The following chapters examine the changes affecting migrants' life courses and their agency in pursuing their values and goals of self-actualization and self-identification in increasingly uncertain times, across and between places of destination and origin.

The book's contributors aim to unpack migrants' experiences coping with competing cultural expectations of both origin and destination societies regarding the occurrence of major life events (e.g., marriage, entry into the labor market, childbirth, divorce, retirement, etc.), their sequence, and the timing of transitions between roles to provide a meaningful account of their lives, which may drift away from the prevalent cultural script of a conventional life.

The themes we have selected follow a clear reasoning for today's individualized society (Beck and Beck-Gernsheim 2002; Halman 1996), with a prevalence of non-normative life patterns and a flourishing variety of lifestyles (Giddens 1990; Lash 2010) in which individuals may change preferences and positions over their lifetimes, in a liquid way (Bauman 2000), and life courses become de-standardized (Brückner and Mayer 2005). Nevertheless, the process of de-standardization is still in its initial phases and did not produce deep changes in societies, according to some authors (see Nico 2014). However, transformations are more visible for certain parts of society, particularly with respect to gender (Widmer and Ritschard 2009). In an emerging, de-standardized society, being a migrant is likely to break traditional life patterns and challenge belonging within bonding relationships. In fact, migration adds a further element of diversity, and one may consider whether this increases uncertainty to unsettling levels or helps by fortifying coping strategies.

The first part of this book focuses on intimate reasons that affect migrants' lives. Its chapters seek to unravel migrants' shifting life goals over their life courses, depending on the structure of opportunities provided by social context. We also investigate to what extent migration reflects changes in life satisfaction (seen as major outcomes) during life courses. Work trajectories, the complications that divert them, and the ensuing faltering progress affecting the whole shape of migrants' lives are scrutinized in the second part of the book. Private life, particularly in the family realm, and gender relations and identity are core structural aspects in societal organization and individual existence. This is the focus of the last part of the book, which extends efforts to incorporate life-course perspectives in understanding family, gender, and parenthood during migration and upon return.

Among the red lines connecting all chapters in the book, there is an understanding of how de-standardized, flexible life courses deal with the uncertainty derived from the mere de-normalization of life transitions. As explained, migration interrupts the typical life trajectory, disrupting family ties, postponing or anticipating personal life events such as marriage or family, and setting up a different context in social locations provided by personal biographies. With such departures from conventional life scripts, uncertainty is likely to be introduced and becomes persistent in migrants' lives. Several contributors (e.g., Croitoru, Vianello, Vlase) to the book explain how coping strategies are observed and how migrants react and adapt to make sense of their non-normative life courses.

The chapter by Bogdan Voicu addresses differences in life satisfaction depending on past transitions from one marital status to another and from childlessness to parenthood. Life satisfaction is seen as an indicator of self-fulfillment and social integration, and migrants are contrasted with Germany's native population. Panel data from the Socio-Economic Panel, covering more than two decades, allows for studying causality. Being a migrant proves to increase, at least partially, sensitivity to personal life events.

In their study on Italian, Spanish, and Portuguese retirees in Switzerland, Claudio Bolzman and Giacomo Vagni document the past life trajectories, stances, and dilemmas of migrants from Southern Europe who came to Switzerland for work during their adult lives and who are now retired. The authors focus on these retired migrants' mobility, their legal, professional, and family trajectories, and how their economic, social, family, and health situations were impacted during their transition to retirement and after retirement, including some decisions they had to take. Based on data from the Vivre-Leben-Vivere (VLV) survey, which focuses on the living conditions and health of individuals aged 65 and older currently residing in Switzerland, Bolzman and Vagni address the increasing diversity of Switzerland's elderly population and compare the living conditions and life trajectories of older migrants with those of natives.

Justyna Salamońska uses a qualitative panel study of Polish migrants in Dublin to follow life courses lived internationally. Starting with retrospective accounts from male and female Polish migrants, the author "walks alongside" research participants, seeking to shed light on their stumbling decisions to stay put, return home, or remigrate. Family and work dimensions often appear to be intertwined in participants' process of decision-making, sometimes colliding, thereby complicating efforts to plan future life stages and achieve life milestones. The chapter documents the temporal character of settlement and mobility decision-making processes. The longitudinal analysis also highlights how migrants construct and negotiate life choices, their career, and other trajectories at different life stages by considering multiple factors, indicating that these phenomena go well beyond typical labor-migration arguments describing East-to-West intra-European migration.

In the next chapter, Alin Croitoru analyzes the work trajectories of Romanian returnees who lived and worked for a long period of time in other EU countries. To understand the evolution of the work dimension in migrants' lives, the chapter is built on subjective evaluations of their work experiences before migration, during their stays abroad, and after their return. The qualitative methodology and homogenous sample allow for a gendered perspective on the relationship between international migration and individuals' work trajectories. Based on a classical sociological distinction between agency and structure, the chapter illustrates four contrasting patterns of work trajectories. Agentic models are differently oriented, depending on gender—men toward entrepreneurship and women toward furthering their education. Croitoru concludes that the traditional model is seen as more present in women's work trajectories.

Francesca Vianello's chapter focuses on the fragmented work trajectories of Moroccan and Romanian migrant workers in Italy, engendered by both the experience of migration and the experience of precarization. It explores migrants' different working conditions and trajectories based on their class, gender, family status, life stage, and ethnicity to illuminate how increasing labor insecurity is shaping the lives of migrants. Moreover, it investigates the impact of career instability on both material and socio-relational conditions, as well as the meanings that such experiences hold for migrants, particularly in relation to gender norms and migration expectations. Vianello finds that declining working opportunities have contradictory effects on gender relations: The return of women to the care and domestic sector reinforces gender stereotypes, but at the same time, the rising availability of jobs for women, even during the economic downturn, has given them more chances to continue working, demonstrating the importance of their income to their husbands and households. As for male migrants, employment precarity puts men in a dependent position in relation to their wives, forcing them to recognize that they are not the sole breadwinners anymore. This vulnerability and dependency trigger a process of reflection that drives men and women to renegotiate conventional gender roles.

Anca Bejenaru brings valuable insights into changes in the transitions to parenthood and migrants' parenting practices based on data from the MIGLIFE project, carried out in Romania with migrant returnees from different Western countries. She shows that transitioning to parenthood and parenting practices are negotiated and adjusted under the influence of both migrants' childhoods and migration contexts. Some mechanisms of parenting formation and transformation were identified by using both inductive and deductive procedures for data analyses. These methods elicited novel information on how women change during migration with respect to child-rearing and familial patterns. The empirical data suggest that self-change in the case of young migrant mothers gradually has developed through awareness of one's own qualities and internalization. These results show that understanding acculturation requires a deeper analysis of psychological mechanisms developed and activated over life courses and within particular circumstances, such as those present in international migration.

The chapter by Ana Maria Preoteasa addresses the case of Romanian migrant women, considering life stage as part of their migration decisions and as a constraint on migration trajectories. To document such embeddedness, an exploration of narratives from migrant women from Romania is provided. Factors such as education, employment, marriage, parenthood, and filial care for elderly parents are considered in connection with initial situations and migration decision(s). An intricate interconnectivity between migration and other life-course elements is revealed, in a pleading for considering a multilevel approach (individual-family-community) to study international migrations.

The final chapter, by Ionela Vlase, illustrates some patterns of adult male formation in migration and the tensions involved in the intersection of gender and age-identity dimensions within a sample of men returnees who migrated in their youth. Migration context shaped male migrants' adulthood roles and transitions, as well as their performance of masculinities. Starting from recent theoretical insights into the socially constructed nature of adulthood in the contemporary world (Panagakis 2015) and manhood (Schrock and Schwalbe 2009), the chapter reveals the ambivalences and ambiguities men migrants experience regarding adulthood and manhood as a result of their long-term migration.

The whole book draws on rich empirical material produced from various research projects, combining both qualitative and quantitative approaches, as well as cross-sectional and longitudinal analyses. They include MIGLIFE (focusing on Romanian migrants and returnees); a qualitative panel study, carried out with Polish migrants in Dublin (part of the Migrant Careers and Aspirations project, comprising six waves of interviews conducted between 2008 and 2010); a longitudinal, qualitative study based on Moroccan and Romanian workers in Northern Italy, carried out between 2010 and 2015; the Swiss VLV survey; and the German Socio-Economic Panel.

The breadth of empirical sources created a diverse enough information source to understand migration to European countries. The geographical distribution allows for observing a wide range of situations that, in turn, lead to grasping a comprehensive view of life-course changes under circumstances provided by international migration. Such diversity is useful to increase the capacity for exploring the field. A major strength of this book is derived from its methodological diversity. Both qualitative studies and quantitative surveys are considered. The book offers empirical pieces of evidence that complement each other to create a comprehensive view of the three interconnected life domains of work, family, and their gendered constitution.

Chapters overlap at times, as one cannot artificially separate life domains and trajectories that often develop jointly and intersectionally. In addition, such overlapping stresses the fluidity of the social realm and is welcome from the book's perspective as a whole. The overall aim is to show how migration shapes the ways in which these individuals navigate life events in given social contexts, providing authentic social locations in which individuals find a playground for their agency.

References

Allan, Graham, and Gilles Jones. 2003. Introduction. In *Social Relations and the Life Course. Age Generation and Social Change*, ed. Graham Allan and Gilles Jones. Basingstoke: Palgrave Macmillan.

Alwin, Duane F. 2012. Integrating Varieties of Life Course Concepts. *The Journals of Gerontology, Series B: Psychological Sciences and Social Sciences* 67 (2): 206–220.

Bailey, Adrian, and Paul Boyle. 2004. Untying and Retying Family Migration in the New Europe. *Journal of Ethnic and Migration Studies* 30 (2): 229–241.

Bauman, Zygmunt. 2000. *Liquid Modernity*. Cambridge: Polity.
Beck, Ulrick, and Elisabeth Beck-Gernsheim. 2002. *Individualisation*. London: Sage.
Benson, Michaela, and Karen O'Reilly. 2016. From Lifestyle Migration to Lifestyle in Migration: Categories, Concepts and Ways of Thinking. *Migration Studies* 4 (1): 20–37. https://doi.org/10.1093/migration/mnv015.
Brückner, Hannah, and Karl Ulrich Mayer. 2005. De-standardization of the Life Course: What it Might Mean? And if it Means Anything, Whether it Actually Took Place? *Advances in Life Course Research* 9: 27–53.
de Haas, Hein, and Simona Vezzoli. 2011. Leaving Matters. The Nature, Evolution And Effects Of Emigration Policies. *International Migration Institute*, WP 34.
Elder, Glen, Jr., Monica Kirkpatrick Johnson, and Robert Crosnoe. 2003. The Emergence and Development of Life Course Theory. In *Handbook of the Life Course*, ed. Jeylan T. Mortimer and J. Shanahan Michael. New York, Boston, Dordrecht, London, Moscow: Kluwer Academic Publishers.
Engbersen, Godfried, Erik Snel, and Jan de Booman. 2010. 'A Van Full of Poles': Liquid Migration from Central and Eastern Europe. In *A Continent Moving West. EU Enlargement and Labour Migration from Central and Eastern Europe*, ed. Richard Black, Godfried Engbersen, Marek Okólski, and Cristina Panţiru. Amsterdam: Amsterdam University Press.
Gardner, Katy. 2002. *Age, Narrative and Migration: The Life Course and Life Histories of Bengali Elders in London*. Oxford: Berg Publishers.
George, Linda K. 2009. Conceptualizing and Measuring Trajectories. In *The Craft of Life Course Research*, ed. Glen H. Elder Jr. and Janet Giele. New York and London: Guilford Press.
Giddens, Anthony. 1990. *The Consequences of Modernity*. Stanford: Stanford University Press.
Halman, Loek. 1996. Individualism in Individualized Society? *International Journal of Comparative Sociology* 37 (3): 195–214.
Kogan, Irena, Frank Kalter, Elisabeth Liebau, and Yinon Cohen. 2011. Individual Resources and Structural Constraints in Immigrants' Labour Market Integration. In *A Life-Course Perspective on Migration and Integration*, ed. Matthias Wingens, Michael Windzio, Helga de Valk, and Can Aybek. Dordrecht, Heidelberg, London, New York: Springer.
Kõu, Anu, Leo van Wissen, Jouke van Dijk, and Ajay Bailey. 2015. A Life Course Approach to High-Skilled Migration: Lived Experiences of Indians in the Netherlands. *Journal of Ethnic and Migration Studies* 41 (10): 1644–1663.
Lash, Scott. 2010. *Intensive Culture: Social Theory, Religion and Contemporary Capitalism*. Los Angeles: Sage.
Levy, René, and Felix Bühlmann. 2016. Towards a Socio-Structural Framework for Life Course Analysis. *Advances in Life Course Research* 30: 30–42.

Li, F.L.N., A.M. Findlay, A.J. Jowett, and R. Skeldon. 1996. Migrating to Learn and Learning to Migrate: A Study of the Experiences and Intentions of International Student Migrants. *Population, Space and Place* 2 (1): 51–67.

Lutz, Helma, and Ewa Palenga-Mollenbeck. 2012. Care Workers, Care Drain, and Care Chains: Reflections on Care, Migration, and Citizenship. *Social Politics* 19 (1): 15–37.

Macmillan, Ross. 2005. The Structure of the Life Course: Classic Issues and Current Controversies. *Advances in Life Course Research* 9: 3–24.

Macmillan, Ross, and Ronda Copher. 2005. Families in the Life Course: Interdependency of Roles, Role Configurations, and Pathways. *Journal of Marriage and Family* 67 (4): 858–879.

Mortimer, Jeylan T., and Michael J. Shanahan. 2003. Preface. In *Handbook of the Life Course*, ed. Jeylan T. Mortimer and Shanahan Michael. New York, Boston, Dordrecht, London, Moscow: Kluwer Academic Publishers.

Nico, Magda. 2014. Variability in the Transitions to Adulthood in Europe: A Critical Approach to de-Standardization of the Life Course. *Journal of Youth Studies* 17 (2): 166–182.

Panagakis, Christina. 2015. Reconsidering Adulthood: Relative Constructions of Adult Identity during the Transition to Adulthood. *Advances in Life Course Research* 23: 1–13.

Schrock, Douglas, and Michael Schwalbe. 2009. Men, Masculinity, and Manhood Acts. *Annual Review of Sociology* 35 (1): 277–295.

Thomas, William, and Florian Znaniecki. 1996. *The Polish Peasant in Europe and America: A Classic Work in Immigration History*. Urbana: University of Illinois Press.

Widmer, Eric, and Gilbert Ritschard. 2009. The De-Standardization of the Life Course: Are Men and Women Equal? *Advances in Life Course Research* 14 (1–2): 28–39.

Wingens, Matthias, Helga de Valk, Michael Windzio, and Can Aybek. 2011. The Sociological Life Course Approach and Research on Migration and Integration. In *A Life-Course Perspective on Migration and Integration*, ed. Matthias Wingens, Michael Windzio, Helga de Valk, and Can Aybek. Dordrecht, Heidelberg, London, New York: Springer.

PART I

Life Strategies and Life-Choices Depending on Social Context

CHAPTER 2

Fringed Life Satisfaction? A Life-Course Perspective on the Impact of International Migration on Subjective Well-Being

Bogdan Voicu

In contrast with other chapters in this book, as well as with the typical life-course perspective in migration studies, this chapter does not look at how life course is shaped, or how rites of passage are constructed in the case of migrants, but instead considers the impact of essential transitions on family and cohabitation status. Marriage, divorce, separation, widowhood, and having children are treated as givens, and the chapter considers their impact on life satisfaction. International migrants (here labeled *migrants*) are treated as *professionals* in their migration careers (Martinello and Rea 2014). They build their subjective views on life and integration depending on societal (historical) and personal events. This chapter focuses on personal events, while societal events are controlled through comparisons with natives. Therefore, one's view of one's life is isolated as the variable of interest. The main hypothesis is that migrants, given their increased vulnerability (Lewis et al. 2015), are more sensitive to shocks in everyday life.

B. Voicu (✉)
'Lucian Blaga' University of Sibiu, Sibiu, Romania

Romanian Academy, Research Institute for Quality of Life, Bucharest, Romania

© The Author(s) 2018
I. Vlase, B. Voicu (eds.), *Gender, Family, and Adaptation of Migrants in Europe*,
https://doi.org/10.1007/978-3-319-76657-7_2

In recent decades, the life-course approach became increasingly salient in all sciences to deal with the dynamics of certain processes (Alwin 2012), with social and behavioral sciences particularly prone to using such a perspective, which allows for observing intricate details and disentangling connections that otherwise would be hidden if individual traits and longitudinal variations in their levels and manifestations were ignored.

In studies of international migration, the life-course perspective is used mainly alongside the biographical method. Descriptions of one's life come together in a search for understanding, but not proving, causality. This chapter takes a different approach, one still included among typical life-course exercises, as categorized by Alwin (2012). The idea is to consider four streams of literature to show how life satisfaction is supposed to be sensitive to life events in the case of international migrants. Panel data coming from the German Socio-Economic Panel (GSOEP) are later used to test the derived hypotheses. The four streams of literature refer to subjective well-being (SWB), cultural embeddedness of life satisfaction, the uncertainty assumption, and the vulnerability of migrants. In three conceptual sections, SWB-related theoretical entries are examined first, and then I discuss uncertainty and vulnerability among migrants. All these perspectives are wrapped together when considering the need for a life-course approach. The basic assumption is that hyper-vulnerability in transnational contexts increases both fluidity and uncertainty, and, in turn, makes life satisfaction more sensitive to life events. When experiencing such events, SWB fluctuates among migrants more than non-migrants, thereby leading to a fringed trajectory.

To keep argumentation simple, only life events related to marital status are considered: marriage, couple dissolution, widowhood, and births of children. They will be labeled *personal events*.

Personal events are common in the lives of all individuals. One actually can encounter huge difficulties in the endeavor to depict human life and its dynamics outside of personal life events. Describing life cannot obliterate well-being as an intrinsic trait in the human condition. SWB recently has become indispensable in the agendas of most developed societies, and it is regularly seen as a vital goal for societal organization. Nations and international organizations such as the UN, Organization for Economic Cooperation and Development (OECD), US, and European Union include indicators of life satisfaction among their regular appraisals of development (Lu et al. 2015: 1).

Life satisfaction is not supposed to be extremely sensitive to personal events, but they are likely to bear some impact. In fact, the argument developed in the first part of the chapter follows the set-point theory and claims that life satisfaction has a certain inertia, being relatively stable during one's lifetime, given its homeostatic properties (Cummins 2000). This means it floats around a certain fixed point or evolves gradually toward a new equilibrium. However, amendments to set-point theory in recent decades are considered as well (Headey 2008; Lucas 2007). Some personal events may induce stable trends that point toward more satisfaction, such as marriage (Layard et al. 2014), or toward discontent, such as widowhood (Chipperfield and Havens 2001). For personal events such as divorce, existing proof is rather mixed (Bourassa et al. 2015). This chapter examines the extent to which being a migrant may change such effects.

The second section explains the special situation with international migrants, sometimes described as being hyper-precarious (Lewis et al. 2015; Pajnik 2016), given their limited access to social networks, less knowledge about their host societies, job mismatches, exposure to stigmatization and resentment, and so on. Vulnerability typically increases material and axiological uncertainty, leading migrants to retreat toward more traditional values (Immerzeel and Van Tubergen 2011; Inglehart and Baker 2000). However, focusing on life satisfaction is more common in less-traditional societies (Welzel and Inglehart 2010). Therefore, stress resulting from negative life events tends to harm, to a greater extent, the SWB levels of those in more vulnerable positions.

Positive events are also hypothesized to have a greater impact on migrants, given the circumstances of their transnational condition (Vertovec 2009). Stability of life satisfaction relies on its cultural embeddedness (Voicu and Vlase 2014), but migrants are exposed to at least two sets of cultural influences: one from their countries of origin and the other from their host societies. This brings fluidity to their life-satisfaction embeddedness. Fluidity becomes more salient, given the liquidity of migration, which is, by default, a less-stable equilibrium and may comprise a new spatial mobility at virtually any time (Engbergsen et al. 2010). Such preconditions increase axiological uncertainty, leaving migrants' life satisfaction more exposed to personal events—particularly negative ones.

Overall, the expected result is that life events are more important in determining migrants' SWB. Additionally, following assumptions from assimilation theory, one may expect that the effect will fade the longer migrants live in host society. To test these hypotheses, data from the

GSOEP are employed, and fixed-effects (FE) models are tested. The findings provide support for a life-course approach to migrant life satisfaction. The policy implications are considered in the discussion section.

The novelty of the approach lies in considering the hyper-vulnerability and double contextuality of migrants' lives as preconditions for their higher uncertainty. These create premises for higher sensitivity to negative changes in life satisfaction depending on personal events and lower sensitivity when positive effects are expected. While personal events may occur quite often, the smooth transitions in life satisfaction transform into fringed variations. Such a process challenges the canonical view of life satisfaction and proves the utility of a life-course approach in migration studies, complementing the usual social theory that explains life as such but not necessarily related to or determined by migration.

Life Satisfaction and Stability: Beyond the Set-Point Theory

Individuals grow up within contexts in which they learn what to expect out of life, how to form aspirations, and how to deal with fulfillment or failure to fulfill aspirations. Over time, they are exposed to consistent norms that guide formation and changes in levels of life satisfaction. Such norms influence societies broadly and explain long-term stability in societal levels of life satisfaction, leading to the Easterlin paradox, which contends that average life satisfaction and happiness change very little over time, regardless of variations in material wealth (Easterlin 2015). In fact, Easterlin's original work asserted almost complete stability, and this was once the canonical view of life satisfaction, but this assumption has been challenged in recent decades (Veenhoven and Vergunst 2014). Life satisfaction in certain nations is said to be sensitive to fluctuations in economic conditions, including growth.

At the individual level, various hypotheses also contend that there is contentment stability over time. The salient set-point theory (Cummins et al. 2014) imagines SWB as being linked to personality. Given the genetic determination on personality, life satisfaction and related measures should be stable as well. Empirical proof has contradicted the idea of stability, instead proposing a softer set point that is exposed to changes, despite its long-term stability for a large part of the population (e.g., Fujita and Diener 2005). The assumption of a very stable set point also was subject to conceptual challenges coming from various directions and empirically tested and confirmed. Life events were the main triggers of change to be considered for several decades (Headey and Wearing 1989), but other individual traits, such as life goals (Headey 2008), also were considered and proved to be related to at least fluctuations in life satisfaction, or even longer-term effects.

Contextual determinants also were addressed, consisting of, among others, impacts from the quality of society (Abbott et al. 2016), policy mix (Karabchuk 2016), and claims of life satisfaction as cultural constructs, shaped by social norms of being more or less satisfied (Voicu and Vlase 2014). The latter view is consistent with life-satisfaction dependency on exposure to social norms, particularly the prevalence of agentic strategies (Welzel and Inglehart 2010). The argument also has been developed by Abbott et al. (2016) in their claim that shifts in societal norms toward individualization and personal agency explain changes in life satisfaction in China. Dependency of life satisfaction on society-wide norms also was demonstrated in experimental settings (Tam et al. 2012), very-small-scale cross-cultural quantitative explorations of differences in SWB meanings (Lu and Gilmour 2006), and meta-analysis (Uichida et al. 2004). Such embeddedness leads to life satisfaction behaving like social values, internalized by individuals, and later manifested through behaviors and attitudes. Consequently, one may consider the early socialization assumption and institutionalization hypothesis from the sociology of values (Arts 2011), describing the embeddedness of individuals in the contexts of social norms during childhood and adulthood. Therefore, one's life satisfaction reflects both the context during early childhood and the context to which one is currently exposed (Voicu and Vlase 2014). In the case of migrants, this implies a fluid determinacy from the cultures of life satisfaction in origin countries and from the host countries' cultures. Such a view also is consistent with the life-course approach to life satisfaction (Layard et al. 2014), which claims that life satisfaction during adulthood reflects the conditions and events that one experiences over a lifetime.

Such debates over changing life satisfaction are rather complementary to the set-point theory (Fujita and Diener 2005). The set point around which one's SWB fluctuates displays a long-term stability, but also may change under specific conditions. Stability implies that the changes are rather smooth, and fringes within life-long trajectories are unlikely to be detected.

An impressive body of literature has been developed on changes in life satisfaction due to life events. Existing studies report a positive impact from *marriage* (Layard et al. 2014; Næss et al. 2015; Zimmermann and Easterlin 2006), but marriage boosts life satisfaction only under certain conditions. For instance, large differences between partners reduce the marital premium in SWB (Stutzer and Frey 2006), while appraisals of happy marriages increase the bonus in SWB levels (Carr et al. 2014). The effect is also time dependent in the sense that it declines over time—peaking when the couple get married. The basic mechanism through which marriage is a "doorway to happiness" (Lucas 2008) resides in its promise to provide comfort, stability, security, companionship, social control, economic benefits, social status, and so on. If fulfilling such promises leads to a better appraisal of the marriage, as shown by Carr et al. (2014), it will maintain higher life satisfaction. *Having children* has been shown to increase SWB levels (Clark et al. 2008; Frijters et al. 2011; Mikucka 2016; Pollmann-Schult 2014), at least around the time the children are born (Hansen 2012). Explanations include feelings of fulfillment of life goals, emotional rewards, and/or anticipatory expectations for extending the social network directly (through the children) or indirectly (through the offspring's social network). One may interpret all these explanations as ways to secure personal development. Parenthood also comes with material, psychological, and lifestyle costs that actually threaten life satisfaction (Hansen 2012). Such costs also may be considered harmful to material security and a way to increase vulnerability.

Widowhood (Anusic et al. 2014; Chipperfield and Havens 2001), *dissolution of cohabitation* (Ambrey and Fleming 2014; Blekesaune 2008), and *divorce or separation* (Ambrey and Fleming 2014; Næss et al. 2015) trigger negative impacts. All these processes involve departures from existing reality and loosening or breaking bonds that once shaped one's life. However, their impact is not always negative. For instance, depending on the quality of the dissolved partnership, divorce may or may not be harmful (Bourassa et al. 2015). Appraisals of the quality of marriage boost or decrease the impact of such a dissolution on one's life satisfaction (Carr et al. 2014). This results in an implicit argument about the feelings of security that one experiences within the couple.

Uncertainty, Transnational Contexts, and Hyper-vulnerability

Common lay beliefs and academic proof indicate marriages and cohabitations as societal setups applied to individual-level relations can create safe environments for partners. Participating in a successful partnership creates a secure place where uncertainty is more bearable, and predictability of everyday life is a given. Such an environment is essential in shaping one's life outlook and attitudes.

Turning toward more traditional values when confronted with stressors is one way to deal with uncertainty, with religion being one example. One's faith provides comfort, fosters feelings of control, reshapes significance, and fortifies social solidarity and identity (Pargament et al. 2005). Overall, religiousness reestablishes security, at both societal and individual levels. Security threats experienced during one's formative years, at both societal and individual levels, push individuals toward more religious values (Norris and Inglehart 2004). In such cases, religion acts as a reassurance, a way to cope with insecurity, and such insecurity may be expressed during adulthood as well (Immerzeel and Van Tubergen 2011). As a traditional value, religious belief is just one example of societal turning toward premodern stances when confronted with insecurity, as explained by Inglehart and Baker (2000).

Security can be seen from both material and axiological perspectives (Voicu 2001). Material security has been conceived as important in predicting individual actions, particularly consumer behaviors. One's expenses depend on one's past, current, and projected incomes (Modigliani 1944); that is, one decides on current actions depending on past experiences and anticipated views on one's material security. Axiological uncertainty is easier to accept and deal with under conditions of material security. If facing economic difficulties, one is less able to deal with diversity in values and behaviors expressed by others, which become stressful (Voicu 2001). Retreat toward more traditional positioning is likely to occur, including intolerance to diversity (Inglehart and Baker 2000). A propensity toward lower life satisfaction is also expected. Economic insecurity, particularly when repeated, triggers psychological distress with negative consequences for mental health and SWB (Watson and Osberg 2017). Case studies show optimism is raised from agency, even under conditions of precarious prosperity (Vlase 2015). However, agency is related to other existing resources (e.g., education) and a positive outlook on the capacity to convert such capital into well-being. Conversely, precariousness is reflected in the lack of exit strategies and leads to resilience of bad moods.

From this point of view, it is useful to consider to what extent migrant conditions are related to uncertainty. Migration may be conceived of as a career (Martinello and Rea 2014), marked by a state of liquidity (Engbersen et al. 2010). Migrants already have experienced at least one geographic movement, from one country to another, so it is easier for them to conceive of their current state as temporary, as a stage on the "professional" migration ladder. This is easier to imagine for high-skilled workers, particularly expats, but it is conceivable for low-skilled workers as well. Furthermore, recent economic recessions have increased the potential for remigration and return migration. The temporal nature of migration adds to transformations in institutions such as family, fluidity, and unpredictability of migration flows, including circularity. Dissolution or lack of meaning of national borders, particularly in Europe, allows for recurrent migration, conducive to migration spells combined with temporary return periods living in home countries.

Liquidity boosts the transnational context. More and more migrants, over the past couple of decades, have been placed in a dual contextuality (Voicu and Vlase 2014), manifested through their transnational condition (Vertovec 2009). Cheap and instant communication over mobile phones and the Internet, consumption of media from home countries via satellite dishes and online sources, globalization of distribution chains for local products, and low-cost carriers have made the world much less confined to local and national boundaries. Exposed to influences from two cultures, migrants are likely to belong to a state of at least slightly higher axiological uncertainty. In other words, they experience exposure and find ways to comply to social norms that may or may not clash with each other culturally.

From the perspective of economic certainty, migrants are confronted with a hyper-precarious condition involving job mismatches, usually due to downgrading their own qualifications (Galgóczi and Leschke 2016), becoming trapped in restrictive labor relations (Strauss and McGrath 2017), and lacking support from social networks and families, which were disrupted as a consequence for migration itself. Vulnerability is increased by political uncertainty as well, especially for undocumented migrants (Bloch et al. 2015). Precarity is extended by restricted or prohibited access to social protections (Pajnik 2016). Not necessarily just for migrants, precarious work is often a means to cope with precarious prosperity

(Preoteasa et al. 2016), reflecting a broader condition of vulnerability. In fact, the whole setup of migrant life is hyper-vulnerable. The condition goes beyond employment and welfare coverage, and extends to lower dependability of existing networks, insufficient knowledge about the host society, and threatening of discrimination, although in Europe, the situation can be eased, depending on EU citizenship (Urzi and Williams 2017).

Life Course and Fluidity

Depending on the controls they have used, some scholars found no difference in SWB levels between international migrants and natives (de Vroome and Hooghe 2014), while others found more satisfaction among natives (Bartram 2011; Safi 2010). Few studies found differences between groups of migrants, depending on origin (Magee and Umamahesvar 2011; Van Praag et al. 2010; Voicu and Vlase 2014). However, the life satisfaction of migrants per se is of marginal importance to this chapter. The focus is on the impact of personal events, and the life-course approach is key from this perspective.

The life-course perspective is quite popular in migration studies. Despite their skepticism on the popularity of the approach, Wingens et al. (2011) provide quite an impressive list of examples. However, confusion over the perspective persists, particularly due to a variety of meanings in which life-related concepts are used (Alwin 2012). Moreover, the typical life-course approach refers to describing life course in itself. However, using life course as a way to study theoretical assumptions is more productive (Wingens et al. 2011: 5), and this is the path that this chapter follows. Given this approach, individual agency is implicit in constructing life paths. The task of the researcher is to observe the common effects of various personal events, regardless of other individual traits and following the principle of linked lives. Individual pathways are viewed as dependent on the structure of opportunities provided by society, which include social norms and also consist of cultural construction of SWB meanings.

With respect to SWB, the literature lacks explicit life-course approaches to migrant-life satisfaction and a comparison to natives missing from research as well. However, the idea of liquid life paths in migration, referring particularly to the family and including "fluid and uncertain futures and histories" (Girart and Bailey 2010: 397), resonates with the argument for uncertainty and insecurity being the basis for a deeper impact from personal events on SWB. De-standardization of the life course in the general population is expected to involve changes in residential mobility, including international mobility, and to transform the meaning of *migration* over the life course (Findlay et al. 2015).

Given such fluidity, the comparison between migrants and natives over the life course is the primary endeavor when considering the impact of life events on SWB.

Hypotheses

Facing both axiological uncertainty and being more exposed to material insecurities compared with natives, migrants are in a situation in which life satisfaction is likely to be less stable, as they are more exposed to influence from life events, which can further decrease levels of perceived security. Personal events are likely to influence one's feelings of security, and I expect that they do it in a way that should be more important for migrants. Starting a relationship or a family increases levels, or at least the promise, of security and certainty. Its marginal utility should be higher for an individual who experiences a more precarious context. Moreover, it also means a change in one's condition, which adds to existing fluidity. Experienced uncertainty may exceed acceptable levels, so the marital bonus to life satisfaction should be lower for migrants. Having a child elicits more certainty concerning personal fulfillment, at least based on widespread, traditional societal norms. It may also increase exposure to hazards due to associated costs. However, costs are less likely to be visible immediately after birth (Pollmann-Schult 2014). Couple dissolution through any means (separation, divorce, etc.) is likely to be more harmful when vulnerability is higher and safety nets, such as stable social networks and close kinships, are no longer available.

The main hypothesis (H1) considers an increased negative impact from personal events on life satisfaction in the case of migrants: Divorce, separation, and widowhood should be (more) harmful in the case of migrants. Additionally, marriage is expected to have a less positive impact, while parenthood should have a more positive impact.

The complex (H1) hypothesis relies on mechanisms explained by the uncertainty assumption and hyper-vulnerability expectations. However, one may expect that discontinuity in social networks, lack of knowledge of the host nation, uncertainty from liquid migration, and so on, diminish over time during migration spells. A learning process is in place, leading to typical adaptation disputed by life-satisfaction scholars. Therefore, as a subsequent hypothesis, one expects (H2) more recent migrants to exhibit higher sensitivity to personal events on life satisfaction. Such time-related effects were demonstrated by Angelini et al. (2015), who found a stronger impact from cultural assimilation on migrants' life satisfaction in Germany if they lived there for more than ten years. However, other studies (Voicu and Vlase 2014) found no impact on life satisfaction from time spent in the host society.

Several moderating variables are expected to intervene. Existing literature found differences between men and women with respect to the resented effects on life satisfaction from widowhood and divorce (Næss et al. 2015), and from having a child (Baranowska and Matysiak 2011; Myrskylä and Margolis 2014; Rizzi and Mikucka 2014). The impact of parenthood has been shown to depend on relationships with others, particularly relatives (Mikucka and Rizzi 2016). In fact, relationships are the kind of capital that reduce uncertainty (Voicu 2010), and existing kinship networks are more frequently accessed during stressful events (see Mikucka and Rizzi 2016: 946 for a review). Other kinds of capital may be important as well, particularly education, with its ability to help deal with stress, proven in the case of migrants in Europe during the economic crisis in the 2000s (Voicu and Vlase 2014). In sum, additional hypotheses assume moderating effects from (H3) gender, (H4) social networks, and (H5) education.

Data

To study changes along the life course, panel data are the most appropriate. The GSOEP provides probably the source of such data that covers the longest period and include a large sample of foreign-born residents. Data collection started in 1984, with annual representative waves of repeated interviews. Considering all cases with information on migration backgrounds and life satisfaction, there are 60,916 individuals (14,094 migrants) who have been interviewed 555,864 times between 1984 and 2014 (samples A-M1). In the case of panel data, one recommends using all cases that have a probability of experiencing a treatment (Brüderl and Ludwig 2014). The treatments in our case are changes in marital status and having children; therefore, all cases are included in the analysis (see Table 2.1).

Table 2.1 Descriptive statistics for variables in the models

Variable	Mean	Std. Dev.	Min	Max	N	N(id)	Events[c]
Overall life satisfaction	7.06	1.82	0	10	557,832	76,202	
–Born abroad	0.13	0.33	0	1	754,417	100,964	
Years since arriving in Germany	19.2	10.9	0	65	89,925	14,143	
–*Married*	0.62	0.49	0	1	563,380	77,723	306,328
–*Divorced*	0.07	0.25	0	1	563,380	77,723	32,978
–*Separated*	0.02	0.14	0	1	563,380	77,723	8536
–*Widowed*	0.06	0.24	0	1	563,380	77,723	31,023
–*No. of children in the household*	1.03	1.21	0	11	772,667	109,342	65,340
No. of members in the household	3.24	1.47	1	17	772,667	109,342	
Age	37.06	21.92	0	104	769,910	108,133	
Number of years of education	11.74	2.66	7	18	541,615	73,129	
Employed	0.56	0.50	0	1	597,256	83,835	
No. of health problems (out of 17)[a]	0.15	0.50	0	10	772,667	109,342	
Condition of house (0 = dilapidated; 3 = in good condition)	2.62	0.57	0	3	768,716	109,160	
Size of housing unit in Sq M	103.92	45.32	6	938	771,930	109,275	
Social time with friends[b]	3.16	0.86	1	4	228,879	59,611	
Perform volunteer work[b]	1.51	0.95	1	4	227,852	59,524	
Attends church or other religious events[b]	1.74	0.96	1	4	184,919	53,672	
Participates in sports[b]	2.12	1.28	1	4	227,767	59,553	
Household income (logarithmic)	10.28	0.65	0	15	760,793	108,607	

[a]Ever had a stroke, blood pressure/circulation problems, diabetes, cancer, psychiatric problems, arthritis, angina or other heart conditions, asthma, or breathing difficulty, or the need for help to perform various types of daily physical activities

[b]Never/Seldom/Monthly/Weekly

[c]Changes to marital status or in number of children from previous year

Respondents were asked annually, "How satisfied are you with your life, all things considered?" Answers ranged from 0 = "completely dissatisfied" to 10 = "completely satisfied." Along with marital status and having children, data include information on basic demographics and life conditions, to be used as confounders (Table 2.1).

Method

Several other studies (including Stutzer and Frey 2006; Lucas et al. 2003; Luhmann and Eid 2009; Myrskylä and Margolis 2014; Zimmermann and Easterlin 2006) used prior versions of GSOEP data to analyze changes in life satisfaction, including controlling for or focusing on changes in marital status. They tested for the presence of the effect immediately after a change, as well as in relation to the time period after the personal event. Immediate significant effects from marriage and having children (positive), and widowhood and separation (negative) were observed, along with a less-conclusive impact from divorce. Although this chapter does not examine the adaptivity-reactivity model, I use the above results as a basis from which to start; that is, I do not discuss in detail the impact of personal events on life satisfaction, but I focus on what being a migrant adds to understanding changes in life satisfaction following personal events.

FE models with robust standard errors are employed. The Hausman test indicates differences between FE and RE (random effects) coefficients; thus, the FE models are reported in the chapter. They are compared with ordinary least squares (OLS) estimates to assess the importance of unobserved factors. For sensitivity analysis, the dependent variable is considered first as being continuous, and all models are repeated later as conditional (fixed effects) logistical regressions. In this last scenario, a life satisfaction above 7 becomes the dependent variable.

To test the first hypothesis, the interactions between being a migrant and (changes to) marital status and having children are considered. For the second hypothesis, the analysis is run on a subsample of migrants, and interactions within a year of their arrival in Germany are considered. H3–H5 require three-way interactions, adding to the first set of models the interactions with gender, spending time with friends, and education, respectively.

Findings

Table 2.2 shows the estimates that are relevant to the hypotheses. The first two columns reproduce the basic FE model, which does not include any three-way interaction effects. The number of cases decreases sharply after adding controls for social life and income (model m1c), which led to running models for H2–H5 using m1a as a starting point. The third column shows the estimates from the OLS regression. The overall FE versus OLS differences are not large (models m1c compared with ols1c). For the

Table 2.2 Regression models of life satisfaction (11-point scale)

	(H1)-FE			(H1)-OLS	(H2)-FE		(H3)-FE		(H4)-FE		(H5)-FE	
	m1a	m1c		ols1c	m2		m3a		m4a		m5c	
Married	0.16***	0.12***		0.05***	0.33***		0.15***		−0.15†		0.01	
Married # born abroad (# years since arriving in Germany—for m2)	−0.17**	−0.10		−0.04***	−0.013*		−0.16*		−0.12		−0.48*	
Divorced	0.06†	0.09†		0.01	−0.49**		0.03		−0.41**		−0.01	
Divorced # born abroad (# years in Germany—for m2)	−0.45***	−0.43**		−0.09***	0.006		−0.46**		−0.55		−1.20***	
Separated	−0.25***	−0.29***		−0.01	−0.40**		−0.33***		−0.67***		−0.57**	
Separated # born abroad (# years in Germany—for m2)	−0.13	0.04		−0.05***	0.004		−0.01		−0.13		0.39	
Widowed	−0.10*	−0.11†		Reference	−0.57*		−0.14†		−0.62***		−0.35**	
Widowed # born abroad (# years in Germany—for m2)	−0.50***	−0.43*		−0.10***	0.002		−0.37†		−0.52		−0.29	
No. of children in the HH	0.01*	0.09***		0.04***	0.01		0.03**		0.15***		0.13***	
No. of children HH # born abroad (# years in Germany—for m2)	0.03†	0.01		0.00	0.000		0.02		−0.08		0.06	
No. of members in the HH	−0.03***	−0.11***		−0.05***	−0.03*		−0.03***		−0.03***		−0.11***	
Woman				0.01***			n.s.					
<Marital status / children> # born abroad # woman												
Number of years of education	−0.00	−0.00		0.00***	−0.00		−0.00		0.00		−0.00	
<Marital status / children> # born abroad # education									n.s.			
Social time with friends		0.13***		0.05***							0.00	
Born abroad # social time with friends											−0.09†	
Married # born abroad # social time with friends											0.11†	

FRINGED LIFE SATISFACTION? A LIFE-COURSE PERSPECTIVE... 29

	(1)	(2)	(3)	(4)	(5)	(6)	(7)
Divorced # born abroad # social time with friends							0.23*
Separated # born abroad # social time with friends							−0.12
Widowed # born abroad # social time with friends							−0.06
Born abroad # no. children in the HH # social time with friends							−0.01
Constant	8.31***	4.82***	−0.86***	7.19***	8.31***	8.35***	4.95***
Age, age sq., education, employment, health, housing conditions	Yes	Yes	Yes	Yes	Yes	Yes	Yes
Ln (income)		Yes	Yes				Yes
Spends time with friends, volunteers, attends church, participates in sports		Yes	Yes				Yes
Year dummies	Yes	Yes	Yes	Yes	Yes	Yes	Yes
Observations	519,557	167,023	167,023	77,595	519,557	519,557	167,023
Adjusted R-squared (within)	0.032	0.040	0.086	0.039	0.032	0.032	0.041

†$p < 0.10$, *$p < 0.05$, **$p < 0.01$, ***$p < 0.001$

variables of primary interest, they refer mainly to the size of the effects. Although small, the differences suggest that the FE model captures unobserved confounders that OLS does not account for. Consequently, in the remaining of this chapter, I discuss only FE results.

The first hypothesis is tested by the three models mentioned in the previous paragraph. The effects of changes in marital status for the general population are the ones reported in the existing studies. Marriages increase SWB, as do additional children in the household. Separation and widowhood are harmful, while divorce has a slightly positive effect.

Being a migrant adds to these impacts. The interaction of terms indicates a clear additional negative impact from experiencing divorce and widowhood. In both cases, the size of the effect equals roughly the 20th part of the life-satisfaction scale, which also means a fourth of the standard deviation of life satisfaction in the sample. The effects are more than ten times larger than the one being employed, experiencing 2.5 health problems (out of 17), and can be compensated by an increase with one-seventh on the logged-income scale. Such effects are relatively powerful, as both contrasts to the variations of life satisfaction within the sample and with the impact from other variables.

In the case of marriage, the expected impact is noticeable in model m1a, in which the interaction term cancels out the positive marriage impact recorded for the general population. However, the effect disappears when controlling for other confounders in model m1c, in which the number of cases also severely drops out due to lack of registration of respective information in all the GSOEP waves. Nevertheless, even in the models in which one controls for these confounders, the size of the (insignificant) effect resembles the (significant) impact of marriage on the general population. One can conclude that the positive impact of marriage on life satisfaction might be diluted for migrants, but no solid proof can be provided in this respect.

In the case of separation, the effect is insignificant, and the sign fluctuates depending on which variables are considered as confounders. However, mere separation may be seen as a transitory phase in couple dissolutions in which the chances of returning to the previous situation are unclear.

In the case of parenthood, the expected, slight increase in the positive impact on migrants is shown in m1a but becomes insignificant when controlling for other confounders (m1c).

Therefore, the first hypothesis is partially confirmed. An additional negative impact is reported for divorce and widowhood, a possible positive effect is observed for parenthood, and a negative effect is reported for entering into a new marriage, with no effect seen from separation. The second hypothesis assumed a moderating effect over time for migrants in Germany. Such an impact was observed only with marriage. In all other cases, the estimated parameters were very small and far from significant. For marriage, the impact is the opposite of the one expected under assimilationist assumptions: The more years one spends in the host society, the lower the marital premium on life satisfaction. However, the effect is not very big. It takes 30 years of living in Germany to cancel out the marital bonus. The effect is interpretable under the uncertainty assumption: Marrying soon after migration provides confirmation of a successful migration and a promise of stability in the new setup. With increasing security, marriage soon after migration boosts life satisfaction more than marrying a long time after the move. One concludes that H2 is confirmed only on the positive effect of marriage.

The third and fourth hypotheses are rejected. Gender and education proved to have no moderating role on the impact of marital status on life satisfaction. All estimated three-way interactions in models m3a and m4a are quite small and insignificant (given space constraints, they were not reported in Table 2.2).

Spending time with friends changed the impact of marital status, as H5 assumed. The results from model m5c are reported in the last column in Table 2.2. Not included in the table was that the two-way effects are insignificant. For marriage, unless frequent interaction with friends is reported, the impact on life satisfaction is likely to be negative. But more frequent interactions with friends—which are signs of embeddedness in more extended social networks—diminish the negative effect. Active social life also fades the negative influence of divorce. All other three-way interactions that included time spent with friends are insignificant.

Model m5 was repeated in three different scenarios, instead considering time spent with friends, time spent volunteering, and participating in sports and religious activities, respectively. Sports and religious activities elicited no significant impact, but volunteering boosts the positive effect of parenthood. The effect is significant at $p = 0.01$. Volunteering, however, changes the impact of parenthood and separation. A one-point change on the scale of spending time in volunteer activities adds 0.04 in additional life satisfaction for migrants who experience an increase in the number of children in the household. With the two-way effects (<born abroad>#<kids>, respectively <volunteering>#<kids>) being insignificant, a full change on the scale of voluntary work, that is, three points—from no volunteering to weekly volunteering—is like the initial impact of parenthood (0.12, significant at $p < 0.001$).

The impact of volunteering on the migrant-separated joint effect is negative (-0.35) and significant at $p < 0.10$ ($p = 0.053$). All two-way interactions are also significant: Separated#volunteer is 0.08 ($p = 0.068$) and separated#migrant is 0.49 ($p = 0.050$), as is the direct effect of recent separation (-0.41, $p < 0.001$). Overall, the surprising effect is that, for migrants, volunteering leads to a more harmful effect in the case of separation. The effect is opposite in the case of native Germans, for which the total effect for non-volunteers is -0.41, while for volunteers, it is -0.34. For migrants, separated volunteers suffer a decrease of -0.29 in the year after separation, while the corresponding point estimate for non-separated volunteers is 0.08. Even if the 95% confidence intervals overlap, the difference remains significant, at 90%. Comparisons with peer volunteers may be part of the explanation, but this should be tested.

Summing up, if considering all significant interactions that involve social network, time with friends reduces the negative impact of divorce and the positive impact of marriage, while volunteering boosts the impact of parenthood and makes separation more harmful.

Discussion, Limitations, and Conclusion

This chapter adds knowledge to the debate on effects from personal events on life satisfaction. With an increasing amount of panel data available, literature on the topic has flourished in recent years (Ambrey and Fleming 2014; Clark et al. 2008; Frijters et al. 2011; etc.). The life-course approach is logically followed, given the availability of data to study so many cases and so many transitions, from one nation to another.

This chapter brought migrants into focus and considered their hyper-vulnerable liquid condition to explain higher sensitivity to personal events. The results are apparently mixed. In the case of marriage, migrants are less likely to feel an immediate change in levels of life satisfaction in the next year after the event, except when they marry soon after migrating or if they experience more frequent interactions with friends. In the case of widowhood and divorce, being a migrant accentuates negative consequences on life satisfaction. Increased sociability, however, acts as a painkiller in cases of divorce. Also on the bright side, the immediate increase in life satisfaction that follows an additional child in the household is slightly boosted for migrants in general, particularly for those migrants who perform volunteer work. The findings on separation are confusing, with the effect being negative for those who do volunteer work.

The exploration of the uncertainty assumption provides a consistent explanation of the mechanisms underlying such processes. Given their transnational living conditions, which increase exposure to uncertainty as contended earlier, migrants' SWB changes more often in the case of negative events. Confronted with an even further increase in insecurity, they adapt by diminishing their levels of life satisfaction. An earlier marriage and their social networks provide protection and decrease sensitivity to negative life events. Having a child is another path to success in terms of boosting immigrant life satisfaction. This makes migrant life less smooth than for non-migrants. Changes are steeper in the case of widowhood, parenthood, and divorce, and lead to more fringed trajectory in life satisfaction. One may further ask whether past *fringeness* in life satisfaction does not propagate into the future, affecting the stability of SWB even further.

However, the findings do not pose a challenge to set-point theory because long-term adaptation was not considered. As in most of the previous studies, this chapter considered only short-term reactions. As shown by others in the case of the general population, longer-term effects are to be expected, at least for some personal events, including having children (Myrskylä and Margolis 2014), getting married, or becoming a couple (Anusic et al. 2014). As far as for other life events, such as divorce, time may actually reverse the initial effect (Clark et al. 2008). Also, pre-event levels of life satisfaction may matter beyond the impact of changes in marital status (Zimmermann and Easterlin 2006). The number of older children also may be important (Mikucka 2016). Having migrant parents and the migrant status of the spouse can be considered from the perspective of changing uncertainties. To keep the argument simpler and fit the limited available space, this chapter avoided going further into these directions. It remains a task for future researchers to inspect the stability of the differential effect for migrants and non-migrants over time.

A dynamic approach that also encompasses time dependency on the effects is closer to the life-course perspective as well. The findings in this chapter contribute to setting up the agenda in the field and stressing the necessity of such an approach. The results emphasize particular behaviors of migrants when confronted with personal events. All sociological laws apply in their cases, but increased vulnerability is likely to lead to more uncertainty, and to changes in sensibility to transformations in marital status and parenthood. One may go even further and look to other important life events, such as employment and unemployment spells, job changes, graduating to new levels of education, and so on. Repeated events already were tested for the general population (Luhmann and Eid 2009; Mikucka 2016) and need exploration in the case of migrants as well.

The beginning of the chapter eluded direct references to migration. Au contraire, an argument on life satisfaction, uncertainty, and personal life events was developed and only ultimately applied to the hyper-vulnerability of migrants. Migration became a simple setup in which social theory was tested. Such perspectives go beyond the relative isolation of migration studies, which are sometimes tempted to see the process as unique. In fact, international migration proves to be nothing more than a facet of everyday life, a sort of façade that social and behavioral scientists can use to better explain social processes. Given its peculiarity as a total social phenomenon, international migration poses the ultimate challenge for developing a life-course approach in social sciences. This chapter can be viewed as proof that the life-course approach is productive and can be used beyond isolated case studies. Even if confined to the German context from which data were collected, the results are likely to be replicable with other datasets as well, if given an explanation that is not country-specific. Generalized conclusions were stressed, and they can prove valid both for larger populations and on a more abstract level of conceptualization.

In conclusion, one needs to review the contributions of these findings in relation to the conceptual streams on which the hypotheses were built. It is obvious that the vulnerability assumption for migrants, the uncertainty hypothesis, the set-point theory, and the embeddedness of life satisfaction in contextual traits should be considered together in explaining personal feelings of satisfaction. Migrants prove to be more sensitive to disruptive personal life events and less sensitive to marriage (coupling), leading to refinements in the specifications of consequences from the vulnerability assumption and from the uncertainty assumption. Cumulative effects from risk factors seem more important, while events traditionally considered positive are not necessarily alleviating vulnerability. From the perspective of the SWB literature, life satisfaction proves to be embedded in the social locations provided by life trajectories. Such observations challenge the string set-point assumption and soften it, urging for inclusion of a more comprehensive view over the contextual determinism of life satisfaction.

The findings also elicit an important lesson for policymakers and welfare providers. By being more sensitive to personal events, migrants are likely to experience smaller fluctuations when such events occur. In the case of negative impacts, alleviating decreases in SWB levels should be of particular interest for policymakers and practitioners. Life satisfaction is a sign of integration—the capacity to blend into the host society and contribute to the well-being and development of both the host country and, through various forms of material and social remittances, to the country of origin. Therefore, one should consider a preventive approach from social workers and social setups in the case of widowhood or other negative life events, targeted toward immigrants and, correspondingly, emigrants. Programs to increase awareness and support from existing social networks that migrants are part of, both in their host countries and in their origin countries, easily can be designed as preemptive means to provide comfort to those in need. Such flexible approaches to individual needs are part of the postmodern welfare-provision mix, and it has the capacity to consider life course as an essential variable in societal care for individuals without interfering with one's life other than through already existing societal web of relationships that encapsulates individuals.

REFERENCES

Abbott, P., C. Wallace, K. Lin, and C. Haerpfer. 2016. The Quality of Society and Life Satisfaction in China. *Social Indicators Research* 127 (2): 653–670.

Alwin, D.F. 2012. Integrating Varieties of Life Course Concepts. *The Journals of Gerontology, Series B: Psychological Sciences and Social Sciences* 67 (2): 206–220.

Ambrey, C.L., and C.M. Fleming. 2014. Life Satisfaction in Australia: Evidence from Ten Years of the HILDA Survey. *Social Indicators Research* 115 (2): 691–714.

Angelini, V., L. Casi, and L. Corazzini. 2015. Life Satisfaction of Immigrants: Does Cultural Assimilation Matter? *Journal of Population Economics* 28 (3): 817–844.

Anusic, I., S.C. Yap, and R.E. Lucas. 2014. Testing Set-point Theory in a Swiss National Sample: Reaction and Adaptation to Major Life Events. *Social Indicators Research* 119 (3): 1265–1288.

Arts, W. 2011. Explaining European Value patterns: Problems and Solutions. *Studia Universitatis Babes-Bolyai, Sociology* 56 (1): 7–31.

Baranowska, A., and A. Matysiak. 2011. Does Parenthood Increase Happiness? Evidence for Poland. *Vienna Yearbook of Population Research* 9: 307–325.

Bartram, D. 2011. Economic Migration and Happiness: Comparing Immigrants' and Natives' Happiness Gains From Income. *Social Indicators Research* 103: 57–76.

Blekesaune, M. 2008. Partnership Transitions and Mental Distress: Investigating Temporal Order. *Journal of Marriage and Family* 70 (4): 879–890.

Bloch, A., L. Kumarappan, and S. McKay. 2015. The Working Lives of Undocumented Migrants: Social Capital, Individual Agency and Mobility. In *Vulnerability, Exploitation and Migrants: Insecure Work in a Globalised Economy*, ed. L. Waite, G. Craig, H. Lewis, and K. Skrivankova, 187–199. Basingstoke: Palgrave.

Bourassa, K.J., D.A. Sbarra, and M.A. Whisman. 2015. Women in Very Low Quality Marriages Gain Life Satisfaction Following Divorce. *Journal of Family Psychology* 29 (3): 490.

Brüderl, J., and V. Ludwig. 2014. Fixed-Effects Panel Regression. In *The SAGE Handbook of Regression Analysis and Causal Inference*, ed. H. Best and C. Wolf, 327–358. Sage.

Carr, D., V.A. Freedman, J.C. Cornman, and N. Schwarz. 2014. Happy Marriage, Happy Life? Marital Quality and Subjective Well-being in Later Life. *Journal of Marriage and Family* 76 (5): 930–948.

Chipperfield, J.G., and B. Havens. 2001. Gender Differences in the Relationship Between Marital Status Transitions and Life Satisfaction in Later Life. *The Journals of Gerontology Series B: Psychological Sciences and Social Sciences* 56 (3): P176–P186.

Clark, A.E., E. Diener, Y. Georgellis, and R.E. Lucas. 2008. Lags and Leads in Life Satisfaction: A Test of the Baseline Hypothesis. *Economic Journal* 118 (529): F222–F243.

Cummins, R.A. 2000. Objective and Subjective Quality of Life: An Interactive Model. *Social Indicators Research* 52 (1): 55–72.

Cummins, R.A., N. Li, M. Wooden, and M. Stokes. 2014. A Demonstration of Set-points for Subjective Wellbeing. *Journal of Happiness Studies* 15 (1): 183–206.

de Vroome, T., and M. Hooghe. 2014. Life Satisfaction Among Ethnic Minorities in the Netherlands: Immigration Experience or Adverse Living Conditions? *Journal of Happiness Studies* 15 (6): 1389–1406.

Easterlin, R.A. 2015. Happiness and Economic Growth—The Evidence. In *Global Handbook of Quality of Life: Exploration of Well-being of Nations and Continents*, ed. W. Glatzer, L. Camfield, V. Møller, and M. Rojas, 283–299. New York: Springer.

Engbersen, G., E. Snel, and J. de Boom. 2010. 'A Van Full of Poles': Liquid Migration from Central and Eastern Europe. In *A Continent Moving West. EU Enlargement and Labour Migration from Central and Eastern Europe*, ed. R. Black, G. Engbersen, M. Okólski, and C. Pantiru, 115–141. Amsterdam: IMISCOE.

Findlay, A., D. McCollum, R. Coulter, and V. Gayle. 2015. New Mobilities Across the Life Course: A Framework for Analysing Demographically Linked Drivers of Migration. *Population, Space and Place* 21 (4): 390–402.

Frijters, P., D.W. Johnston, and M.A. Shields. 2011. Life Satisfaction Dynamics with Quarterly Life Event Data. *The Scandinavian Journal of Economics* 113 (1): 190–211.

Fujita, F., and E. Diener. 2005. Life Satisfaction Set Point. *Journal of Personality and Social Psychology* 88 (1): 158–164.

Galgóczi, B., and J. Leschke. 2016. *EU Labour Migration in Troubled Times: Skills Mismatch, Return and Policy Responses.* Routledge.

Giralt, R.M., and A.J. Bailey. 2010. Transnational Familyhood and the Liquid Life Paths of South Americans in the UK. *Global Networks* 10 (3): 383–400.

Hansen, T. 2012. Parenthood and Happiness: A Review of Folk Theories Versus Empirical Evidence. *Social Indicators Research* 108 (1): 29–64.

Headey, B. 2008. Life Goals Matter to Happiness: A Revision of Set-point Theory. *Social Indicators Research* 86 (2): 213–231.

Headey, B., and A. Wearing. 1989. Personality, Life Events, and Subjective Well-Being: Toward a Dynamic Equilibrium Model. *Journal of Personality and Social Psychology* 57 (4): 731.

Immerzeel, T., and F. Van Tubergen. 2011. Religion as Reassurance? Testing the Insecurity Theory in 26 European Countries. *European Sociological Review* 29 (2): 359–372.

Inglehart, R., and W.E. Baker. 2000. Modernization, Cultural Change, and the Persistence of Traditional Values. *American Sociological Review* 65 (1): 19–51.

Karabchuk, T. 2016. The Subjective Well-being of Women in Europe: Children, Work and Employment Protection Legislation. *Mind & Society* 15 (2): 219–245.

Layard, R., A.E. Clark, F. Cornaglia, N. Powdthavee, and J. Vernoit. 2014. What Predicts a Successful Life? A Life-course Model of Well-Being. *The Economic Journal* 124 (580): F720–F738.

Lewis, H., P. Dwyer, S. Hodkinson, and L. Waite. 2015. Hyper-precarious Lives: Migrants, Work and Forced Labour in the Global North. *Progress in Human Geography* 39 (5): 580–600.

Lu, L., and R. Gilmour. 2006. Individual-Oriented and Socially Oriented Cultural Conceptions of Subjective Well-being: Conceptual Analysis and Scale Development. *Asian Journal of Social Psychology* 9 (1): 36–49.

Lu, C., G. Schellenberg, F. Hou, and J. F. Helliwell. 2015. How's Life in the City?: Life Satisfaction Across Census Metropolitan Areas and Economic Regions in Canada. Statistics Canada. *Economic Insights*, no. 46.

Lucas, R.E. 2007. Adaptation and the Set-point Model of Subjective Well-being: Does Happiness Change After Major Life Events? *Current Directions in Psychological Science* 16 (2): 75–79.

———. 2008. Personality and Subjective Well-being. In *The Science of Subjective Well-Being*, ed. M. Eid and R.J. Larsen, 171–194. New York: The Guilford Press.

Lucas, R.E., A.E. Clark, Y. Georgellis, and E. Diener. 2003. Reexamining Adaptation and the Set Point Model of Happiness: Reactions to Changes in Marital Status. *Journal of Personality and Social Psychology* 84 (3): 527.

Luhmann, M., and M. Eid. 2009. Does it Really Feel the Same? Changes in Life Satisfaction Following Repeated Life Events. *Journal of Personality and Social Psychology* 97 (2): 363.

Magee, W., and J. Umamahesvar. 2011. Immigrant Group Differences in Job Satisfaction. *Race Social Problems* 3 (4): 252–265.

Martinello, M., and A. Rea. 2014. The Concept of Migratory Careers: Elements for New Theoretical Perspective of Contemporary Human Mobility. *Current Sociology* 62 (7): 1079–1096.

Mikucka, M. 2016. How Does Parenthood Affect Life Satisfaction in Russia? *Advances in Life Course Research* 30: 16–29.

Mikucka, M., and E. Rizzi. 2016. Does it Take a Village to Raise a Child?: The Buffering Effect of Relationships with Relatives for Parental Life Satisfaction. *Demographic Research* 34: 943–994.

Modigliani, F. 1944. Liquidity. Preference and the Theory of Interest and Money. *Econometrica* 12 (1): 45–88.

Myrskylä, M., and R. Margolis. 2014. Happiness: Before and After the Kids. *Demography* 51 (5): 1843–1866.

Næss, S., M. Blekesaune, and N. Jakobsson. 2015. Marital Transitions and Life Satisfaction: Evidence from Longitudinal Data from Norway. *Acta Sociologica* 58 (1): 63–78.

Norris, P., and R. Inglehart. 2004. *Sacred and Secular: Religion and Politics Worldwide*. New York: Cambridge University Press.

Pajnik, M. 2016. 'Wasted precariat': Migrant Work in European Societies. *Progress in Development Studies* 16 (2): 159–172.

Pargament, K.I., G.G. Ano, and A.B. Wachholtz. 2005. The Religious Dimension of Coping. In *Handbook of the Psychology of Religion and Spirituality*, ed. R.F. Paloutzian and C.L. Park, 479–495. New York: Guilford Publications.

Pollmann-Schult, M. 2014. Parenthood and Life Satisfaction: Why Don't Children Make People Happy? *Journal of Marriage and Family* 76 (2): 319–336.

Preoteasa, A.M.D., R. Sieber, M. Budowski, and C. Suter. 2016. Household Role in Coping with Precarious Work. Evidence from Qualitative Research in Urban Romania and Switzerland. *Social Change Review* 14 (2): 177–201.

Rizzi, E., and Mikucka, M. 2014. The Happiness–Parenthood Link in a Context of Limited State Support: The Case of Switzerland. *FORS Working Paper Series*, Paper 2015-3. Lausanne: FORS.

Safi, M. 2010. Immigrants' Life Satisfaction in Europe: Between Assimilation and Discrimination. *European Sociological Review* 26 (2): 159–176.

Strauss, K., and S. McGrath. 2017. Temporary Migration, Precarious Employment and Unfree Labour Relations: Exploring the 'Continuum of Exploitation' in Canada's Temporary Foreign Worker Program. *Geoforum* 78: 199–208.

Stutzer, A., and B.S. Frey. 2006. Does Marriage Make People Happy, or Do Happy People Get Married? *The Journal of Socio-Economics* 35 (2): 326–347.

Tam, K.P., H.P.B. Lau, and D. Jiang. 2012. Culture and Subjective Well-Being: A Dynamic Constructivist View. *Journal of Cross-Cultural Psychology* 43 (1): 23–31.

Uichida, Y., V. Norasakkunkit, and S. Kitayama. 2004. Cultural Constructions of Happiness: Theory and Empirical Evidence. *Journal of Happiness Studies* 5(3): 223–239.

Urzi, D., and C. Williams. 2017. Beyond Post-national Citizenship: An Evaluation of the Experiences of Tunisian and Romanian Migrants Working in the Agricultural Sector in Sicily. *Citizenship Studies* 21 (1): 136–150.

Van Praag, B., D. Romanov, and A. Ferrer-i-Carbonell. 2010. Happiness and Financial Satisfaction in Israel: Effects of Religiosity, Ethnicity, and War. *Journal of Economic Psychology* 31: 1008–1020.

Veenhoven, R., and F. Vergunst. 2014. The Easterlin Illusion: Economic Growth Does go with Greater Happiness. *International Journal of Happiness and Development* 1 (4): 311–343.

Vertovec, S. 2009. *Transnationalism*. London and New York: Routledge.

Vlase, I. 2015. Romanian Households Dealing with Precariousness: A Life-course Approach. *European Societies* 17 (4): 513–534.

Voicu, B. 2001. Pseudomodern Romania. *Sociologie românească* 1 (4): 35–69.

———. 2010. *Social Capital in Romania at the Beginning of the Millenium: Traveler in the Land of Those Without a Friend*. Lumen: Iași.

Voicu, B., and I. Vlase. 2014. High-Skilled Immigrants in Times of Crisis. A Cross-European Analysis. *International Journal of Intercultural Relations* 42: 25–37.

Watson, B., and L. Osberg. 2017. Healing and/or Breaking? The Mental Health Implications of Repeated Economic Insecurity. *Social Science & Medicine* 188: 119–127.

Welzel, C., and R. Inglehart. 2010. Agency, Values, and Well-being: A Human Development Model. *Social Indicators Research* 97 (1): 43–63.

Wingens, M., H. Valk, M. Windzio, and C. Aybek. 2011. The Sociological Life Course Approach and Research on Migration and Integration. In *A Life-course Perspective on Migration and Integration*, 1–26. In Wingens, M., M. Windzio, H.D. Valk, and C. Aybek. (2012). *A Life-course Perspective on Migration and Integration*. Springer.

Zimmermann, A.C., and R.A. Easterlin. 2006. Happily Ever After? Cohabitation, Marriage, Divorce, and Happiness in Germany. *Population and Development Review* 32 (3): 511–528.

CHAPTER 3

'Walking Alongside' Polish Migrants in Ireland: Individual Life Courses in the Context of Political, Social, and Economic Change

Justyna Salamońska

This chapter focuses on Polish migration to Ireland post-2004, an example of new mobilities in Europe (Favell 2008a; Krings et al. 2013). Polish migrations post-2004 developed in the context of the accession to the European Union (EU) in 2004 and following the opening of the labor market to nationals of EU new member states (NMS) by Ireland (along with the UK and Sweden). Ireland at the time was experiencing an economic boom, which only a few years later shifted into deep economic recession. The trajectories of Polish migrants, who increasingly took Ireland as their destination, were shaped by these new institutional arrangements in Europe and changing business cycles. Movers who engaged in mobility at the time were also different from earlier waves of migrants (Kaczmarczyk 2008), being younger and with more educational resources, leading perhaps to more individualized migration paths.

J. Salamońska (✉)
University of Warsaw, Warsaw, Poland

This chapter documents the new migration waves, analyzing them from a life-course perspective. The story of the post-2004 Polish migrants in Ireland is one which describes how Europe for many Europeans has become a space of new opportunities for living and working. Exercising the right to intra-European mobility has become a taken-for-granted part of the life course of many young Poles. Yet we still know relatively little about the intersection of life course and migration.

The originality of the analysis presented here lies in linking two sets of literature so far rarely brought together. Since the case at hand is Central and Eastern European (CEE) migration, largely seen through the lenses of labor migration, one frame of reference is studies on migrant labor market integration (see, for instance, Barrett and Kelly 2012, for Ireland; the classic studies by Chiswick et al. 2005a, b, for Australia). The work element has been crucial for cohorts of NMS migrants moving within the EU since 2004. Migrant mobility is often taken up early in the life course (Hall and Williams 2002). In fact, there are numerous studies on youth mobilities, for work, for studies, or simply for lifestyle opportunities (e.g. Boyle 2006; Conradson and Latham 2005a, b; Kennedy 2010; King et al. 2016; Ní Laoire 2000; Scott 2006). I refer to these in the following empirical analysis, as recent movements from the CEE countries seem to have much in common. Combining themes of employment and lifestyle when studying young CEE migrants offers a more comprehensive understanding of how migration trajectories from Poland to Ireland developed.

What is more, we can hardly understand how people construct their life trajectories across their life course if we carry out research at one point of time only. From a methodological point of view, therefore, the novelty and strength of this study lie in analyzing the life courses diachronically. Using qualitative longitudinal research, which has already established itself internationally, this chapter pushes forward our understanding of migrant life courses. A longitudinal approach within qualitative research has been applied to studying various phenomena within community studies, education research, organizational studies, life history, and child development (Thomson and McLeod 2015). Its particular advantage is the focus on temporality embedded in social processes. A qualitative longitudinal approach has particular potential for studying temporality in the migration field, since '[s]tories—of where one has come from, and where one plans to go—seem particularly important for migrants' (Gardner 2002: 29). Gardner explains that stories describe the movement, but also how the stories themselves are told is subject to change.

This was precisely what lay behind the qualitative panel study (QPS) of Polish migrants in Dublin run by the Migrant Careers and Aspirations project at Trinity College Dublin. Between 2008 and 2010, the QPS followed a sample of 22 migrants (males and females, in their 20s and 30s, mostly university educated) in time and space (if the participants decided to move in the meantime; for details of the QPS methodology, see Krings et al. 2013). Following Thomson (2007), this chapter privileges individual cases. It focuses on the longitudinal element of the collected data set, presenting and analyzing diachronically the two migrant stories of Oskar and Anita as they narrated them. The two migrants are a male and a female graduate who arrived in Ireland in their mid-20s, at the height of the boom and at the beginning of the recession, respectively. The 'conversation' of the two cases is constructed by intertwining the participants' narratives in the text. The chapter includes comparisons to other QPS participants in order to position the two accounts in the collected QPS data set. It follows an analysis that 'walks alongside' (Neale and Irwin n.d.) participants in their lives at each successive wave of interviews. The structure of the chapter is organized around the 'conversation' of two biographies set in chronological order of six waves of interviews. This strategy follows the lives of the migrants as they develop in Ireland (as the two migrants continued to be based in Ireland during the QPS). Even if these are two cases of migrant stayers, they illustrate clearly that settlement cannot be taken for granted. Rather, it is an ongoing calculation.

'Walking alongside' migrants portrays a dynamic account of the life course lived across time and space. In particular, it sheds light on the temporal character of migration decisions, which are made and renegotiated as time passes. Many Polish migrants made the decision to leave Poland around the time of Polish accession to the EU. However, with economic recession and changing individual circumstances, the decision to settle or to move onward or backward was negotiated again, individually or as a couple. One fascinating feature of these accounts is that they cannot be reduced to labor mobility, as some migration literature would suggest. Their stories allow us to learn about many aspects of labor mobility, which can be motivated by career rather than financial considerations, or where financial gains are immediately translated into personal development projects. This reading of youth East-to-West migrations is an important contribution to migration research, adding new layers of understanding into what lies behind moving from Eastern to Western Europe. Let us then begin our walk with Oskar and Anita in order to understand how their stories evolved, as these stories are at the core of migration processes as they happen in contemporary Europe.

Wave 1: Oskar Looking Back

When we first met Oskar in 2008, he was 31 and had been resident in Ireland for six years. Oskar had received his engineering degree in Poland. At the time, Ireland was not his first international destination. His first migration experiences had been during his university years, when he worked abroad during vacations. He assessed his first migration to Germany positively in financial terms, and as an opportunity to travel (see also other research on young people on the move: Conradson and Latham 2005b; Boyle 2006; Trevena 2010). Oskar reported that:

> Well, there were good earnings back then, but when you compare them to the earnings today, then... it isn't that much, but compared to the Polish earnings... They were good. ... I managed to see Germany... to live in Germany for about three months... altogether... To travel as well.

Importantly, previous work experience abroad provided him with a new frame of reference not only in comparison to his employment experiences in Poland but also in relation to a different regulatory environment pre- and post-EU accession migration. He contrasted the experience of an intra-European migrant with that of the insecurity and uncertainty of an illegal worker, which in literature is referred to as 'privileged, internal EU-nationals or non-privileged, third-country nationals' (Currie 2007: 87):

> I remember the stress on the German border when we were crossing it, when we were going there with the laborers... I was a student, I had this student card that would have always helped me if anything had happened... And it was an illegal job, completely different... Different... world. The one from before the EU.

After graduating in the early 2000s, Oskar worked in jobs within his profession, across different sectors and workplaces, including construction sites and architectural offices in Poland. Interestingly, he attributed his experiences to luck when speaking about a positive work environment and development opportunities in Poland. His positive experience was exceptional among the QPS participants in terms of working conditions in Poland:

I was lucky because I worked in nice companies in Poland, in small ones, and the only big one that I worked for was very decent, it was a well-known company ... So I didn't drop all of that because something was wrong with the job, but because the market simply collapsed and we had less and less work to do, it was more and more difficult to get some reasonable money... And besides that, the opportunity came up, so I packed my stuff and left.

Oskar's postgraduation trajectory in the Polish labor market changed with an opportunity that came up when he found out about vacancies advertised by Irish employers. He migrated in the early 2000s, before the Irish labor market opened up to EU NMS nationals, at a time when the Irish economy was still booming. Unlike his experience of work in Germany, the move to Ireland was undertaken with the prospect of legal work.

Upon arrival in Ireland, Oskar shared an apartment in a small town outside of Dublin with two other Polish workers. He accepted lower-skilled employment than what he had left in Poland. Oskar understood taking a job as a machine operator in a factory as a temporary fix, enabling him to enter the Irish labor market. While working there, he actively searched for a skilled job in his profession. Once he received such an offer, entry into professional work in Ireland constituted 'a downgrading *within* that profession' (as described earlier by Currie 2007: 99, with reference to Polish migrants in the UK; emphasis in original), since Oskar started with technician duties, as opposed to an engineering job. From then on, his career progressed fast, as after six months, he was promoted to project work in his firm. Consequently, he reached a similar occupational position to the one he had left in Poland. His next promotion included moving to another department, where Oskar was working when he was first interviewed in spring 2008. After a series of promotions, he was in charge of small projects and also responsible for contacts with clients.

Transferability of engineering skills across national boundaries is enhanced by fewer language barriers, due to the project-based character of the work, the relevance of technical software, and little contact with individual clients (Le Bianic and Svensson 2008). However, while the literature on immigrant economic integration points to transferability of skills and self-motivation of migrants as principal determinants of advancement in the labor market of the destination (e.g. Chiswick et al. 2005a, b), Oskar's case illustrates how the individual work trajectory is intertwined with the economic context of a gold-rush labor market (Wickham et al. 2009). In fact, a sense of a 'crazy market' permeated Oskar's account. For him, coming to Ireland had clearly meant 'stepping onto the escalator' and progressing up the career ladder. When describing his career advancement, Oskar estimated that the company had grown three- or fourfold since he had been employed there. As the company grew, the number of top positions available also increased, and he was among those who took the opportunity that presented:

> *Because the higher you get, the tighter it gets, right? And there are less of those kinds of positions… the construction industry was developing so fast, and we got our careers … Because within a normal market all of those stages would take three or four times longer. … So from that point of view it is maybe slightly too fast, but on the other hand, of course, I am happy and I would probably want more.*

In spring 2008, Oskar was well aware that the situation of the market had changed with the start of the recession and with it his career prospects. In this new economic context, he claimed that his decision on whether to stay or to move on was taken on 'professional-career-materialistic-ambition' levels. Oskar's strategy for the future was cautiously flexible. Clearly, deciding to stay or leaving was an ongoing assessment in which career considerations were of key importance:

> *I keep thinking about going back to Poland. … I keep thinking 'what if'… 'what's going to happen if I stay', 'what's going to happen if I leave' … I am afraid that if I stay here, and it's all slowing down a bit in here at the moment, that I will be doing what I'm doing at the moment, but on a smaller scale as all of the huge projects will be finished one day… And I will stop developing, I will hit the glass ceiling and in the meantime I will miss some opportunities that are maybe there in Poland.*

It was also clear that when Oskar had first moved from Poland to Ireland, he had been single and with no career or family commitments. The mobility decision was easier to make at that stage. Now, however, he was in a stable relationship with an Irish woman. He lived with her and her child in a rented apartment, and he described how his home was in Ireland now. While during the interview he expounded upon career opportunities available to him elsewhere, one issue that he did not elaborate on in detail was how he would negotiate his mobility plans with his family. Moving within an Anglophone context would perhaps be the least problematic from the point of view of his English-speaking partner. However, the move would be more difficult because of her school-aged child.

From being a fresh graduate, with little professional experience and a low-skilled job, within six years, Oskar had become what Favell (2008b) calls a 'Eurostar' with even higher aspirations. At the time of the first interview, there was a sense of his career suddenly slowing down. Opportunities were identified elsewhere, and it seemed that Poland in turn might have become an emerging 'escalator' for professionals working in the construction sector. On the other hand, because of his family situation, Oskar seemed more rooted in Ireland than he would admit. The opening interview teased out the temporal and spatial calculations Oskar made in relation to his future trajectory, and also implied a sense of change coming up.

Wave 1: Anita Looking Back

While Oskar during his first interview was describing the end to his fast-track career in what used to be a 'crazy' market, Anita had only just arrived in Ireland. She was 25 years old. When migrating to Ireland, she had left her hometown, but she had been an internal migrant when she moved to Northern Poland to study. She obtained a political sciences degree from a public university. During her studies, she worked part-time, which was instrumental for other goals, like traveling. During a summer break in 2005, Anita had come to Ireland, where she worked as a cleaner. At the time, she and her friends were focusing on saving up what they had earned so that they could use the money back in Poland. In 2008, she compared the two situations:

> *I was cleaning offices, similar offices I'm working in at the moment. I was working in [company name], and sometimes I think about what the people beside me or in such a big… what do they think … And it makes me laugh a little bit as well, that, yes, some time ago I was cleaning such offices, and now I've managed to get a job in such an office. For me it's a kind of achievement.*

In Poland, before moving to Ireland, Anita was employed in an administrative position in her hometown. She reported dissatisfaction with her work experience, with no employment contract, low earnings, and continuous delays with payments. She was unsatisfied with the working culture of the place too. This mirrored more generally the picture of discontent with working in the Polish labor market reported by other QPS participants.

Anita's story must be read in a broader context than that of labor migration only. Many accounts of migration are taken up as 'self-realization' or 'self-fashioning' projects (see, e.g. Conradson and Latham 2005b; Kennedy 2010; King 2002). Indeed, in Anita's understanding, leaving for Ireland was intended as a path to financial independence, an opportunity to move from her parental home to live on her own, and a step toward adulthood. Her rationale for moving abroad was a multilayered one (see also Ní Laoire 2000 with reference to Irish emigrants), with the migration decision encompassing simultaneously a way of escaping from the local area, gaining financial independence and growing up:

> So when I graduated I had the feeling that even if I earned, the money I got was not enough even to strike out on my own. … I wanted to be financially independent, to support myself, and not to stay with my mum.

In addition, being young and single made the decision to move easier and left the time aspect open. Eade et al. (2007), researching Polish migrants in the UK, coined the term 'intentional unpredictability' to describe migrants' open strategy for their migratory future. In fact, for Anita, this 'intentional unpredictability' was a choice deeply rooted in the stage of the life cycle that she was in:

> I came here with a blank slate … when I came…I had no commitments in Poland: … I didn't leave any boyfriend in Poland, nothing like that. So I came here and I can stay here for as long as I want to. I don't know what I will do.

Some migration narratives document how migrants 'are continually ambivalent about where they want to be and how they want to live' (Gardner 2002: 87). Anita explained that her initial plan was to stay there short term and accumulate financial resources as well as acquiring English language competences. She wished to enroll for a postgraduate course in Poland that would lead her to a diplomatic career. At the time of the first interview, however, she was no longer sure about her future plans:

> Anita: When I came here, I didn't dream that I would get such a job [white-collar job]. And I didn't want to stay here for five years at all, and now I don't rule that out, so I say…

Interviewer: And in what place would you like to be in five years?

Anita: I've always been attracted by Italy, so I think... [talks about the opportunities in Mediterranean countries] So I really don't know what I will do in five years' time. I will see.

Like Oskar, upon arrival, Anita accepted a low-skilled job, in a delicatessen in her case, and searched for more skilled employment in the meantime. Importantly, on her reentry to the Irish labor market, Anita already possessed location-specific information, which is crucial to economic success in the destination. She used some of her networks at the recruitment agency in order to secure temporary administrative work in a bank. An employment agency often shifts costs and risks of employment onto workers (Forde 2001). This also happened to Anita, but she downplayed these concerns, perceiving temping as a path to permanent employment with the bank, even if she did not link her future career to this area. Perhaps quite paradoxically, she believed that the quality of her job compared favorably with opportunities for graduate employment in Poland. Like Oskar, she linked her future to the structure of opportunities:

I'm the kind of person that changes her plans once every three months on average. So I don't know, because everything depends on what I will come across in my life: which people I will meet, what the opportunities will be, because they emerge from time to time, so there is a question of making use of them, choosing something. So if I have some other opportunity, if something comes up, some other company ... and so on, I'm not saying no...... So here I have an opportunity to live the way I want to live.

In Anita's story, immediately upon arrival, there was a subjective sense of success, which came from securing white-collar employment. She highlighted how the move was open-ended, also because she was single when leaving Poland. Clearly, a sense of freedom permeated her account. She was full of the enthusiasm that comes with a fresh start in a new place. On the other hand, Ireland was not a gold-rush destination any more, and her future projects upon arrival were many and rather vague, and consequently perhaps too difficult to achieve.

Wave 2: Oskar in Summer 2008

The second interview with Oskar took place in late August 2008. The meeting started with a quick update on his situation:

> *Not much has changed. I am fed up with work a little bit because it's Friday. And there is a lot of pressure so... Lately I have been doing more thinking about whether it might be time to change job. ... I will not find anything better here in the whole of Ireland.... And in order to change something and jump another step further I would probably need to move. ... To Poland or... somewhere else in the world. And it is kind of a bigger decision.*

During the second meeting, the story of the slowing down of the market permeated Oskar's account. Snippets of the conversation referred to how the slowdown affected his work.

Considering his next career move, he resembled some of the transnational elites described by Beaverstock (2005), for whom career progress was dependent on and accelerated by geographical mobility. For them, new destinations bring about new responsibilities and opportunities, and experience from some destinations is of more value than others.

One opportunity that he saw for himself in this situation was his company expanding into the Polish market to compete for projects there. He believed that under these circumstances, being Polish, speaking Polish, and having a degree from Poland would for him finally be 'an advantage and not an unnecessary characteristic'. Through networks in Poland, he had information about labor market opportunities over there. Moving on from Ireland would also be a plausible option if:

> *a technically amazing thing appeared. So something that you can actually see on postcards ... Some kind of a story that you do once in your lifetime. And that is raising your status from the very beginning and you become one of the hundred or thousand people in the world who have done something like that.*

Here, Oskar was describing what literature refers to as the 'new social spiralism' (Favell 2008b). Geographical mobility, still quite a rare experience among Europeans, was something that he perceived as a means of achieving occupational and social upgrading, and consequently as a means of distinction (see also Scott 2006, describing British middle-class migrants in Paris). At the same time, taking the decision to move on or to return was not as easy as when he had first decided to migrate to Ireland. When asked directly if he would return to Poland, he commented that it was a difficult question for him to answer. Career ambitions may have been driving him away from Ireland, but his private life kept him rooted in the country. The calculation had ceased to be a low-cost one, and there was much more at stake than there had been when he was still a fresh graduate in Poland just a few years earlier.

Wave 2: Anita in Summer 2008

In contrast to Oskar's account, Anita did not yet mention the crisis that hit Ireland in the summer of 2008. Perhaps one sign of a recession was that her request to be employed directly by the bank she worked for (rather than by the agency) had been rejected, leaving her in a precarious employment situation.

Similarly to Oskar, Anita declared that she would not return to Poland yet, even if she was offered work with similar financial conditions. This was contrary to her initial plans. Place played a role (see also Boyle 2006, describing the pull of Dublin; Scott 2006, focusing on the pull of Paris), as she enjoyed living in Dublin, the atmosphere of the city, its cosmopolitan nature expressed in contact with people from different parts of the world:

> *This place suits me, Dublin's climate, people… [with climate] I don't mean rain, but the fact that you meet so many different people in here, different nationalities, different cultures, and that's what keeps me with this city as well.*

A sense of personal autonomy, which she lacked back in Poland, also played a role (similarly to migrants studied by Kennedy 2010). Poland, instead, was becoming a location for a holiday rather than a permanent destination: 'I can go to Poland for a holiday, but then leave' was how she put it. She underlined how she was young and hungry to see the world, but mobility also had emotional costs, being far away from family and friends. Importantly, she mentioned that she would be able to find a job within a month or two if she were to lose her current one. In a deepening recession in Ireland, she was about to prove this.

Wave 3: Oskar in Winter 2008–2009

In March 2009, Oskar described the situation in the construction sector in Ireland as a 'complete disaster'. Between the last quarter of 2008 and the last quarter of 2009, almost four out of every ten jobs were shed (Central Statistical Office 2010). Job losses had also taken place in Oskar's company, and there was an expectation of further layoffs. The atmosphere at work was worsening.

As the topic of this wave of interviews was the social connections of Polish migrants, Oskar described how he lived with his Irish partner and her child. He reported how he had little free time beyond work and family and spent it mostly around other Poles in Dublin. He travelled to Poland often to visit his family, usually on his own. However, he would mostly spend Christmas in Ireland. He and his partner would also travel around Europe for short breaks.

While during the previous interview Oskar had declared that working in Poland would be more attractive to him if comparable pay conditions were offered, when an actual job offer came from an Irish company office in Poland he declined it. He explained that accepting the job would have meant that he would be based in Poland and only delegated to Ireland on occasions. Instead, he chose to stay in Ireland.

Wave 3: Anita in Winter 2008–2009

Anita was made redundant in October 2008. She said that her department's operations had been moved to another branch of the transnational company that owned the bank as a result of a cost-cutting strategy. She was what Pijpers (2010) called a 'migrant flexiworker' and was not entitled to any redundancy payments or notice.

Redundancy came as a critical event. She did not apply for social welfare benefits as she was not eligible. She had not accumulated enough social insurance contributions to qualify for jobseeker's benefits in Ireland. What is more, she could not avail of the family networks that are normally utilized by young unemployed people, but these were substituted by friendship networks, not compromising her independence from her family. Anita had moved out of the flat shared with international flatmates so that she could save up rent money and stay in Ireland longer. She had moved back in with the Polish people with whom she had first stayed when she arrived to Dublin in 2008. She described how she missed the atmosphere of international flair (her best friend, and at the time of interview ex-boyfriend, was Italian), sharing ethnic food during international dinners with flatmates, or communicating in a foreign language at home. She could rely on the help of Polish ties, but in terms of lifestyle (she explained these in terms of age and education differences), she was not entirely happy with this new co-habitation arrangement. What is more, the immediate weakness of friendship ties lay in the provision of only temporary help.

Anita considered returning to Poland to be only a last-resort option. Her main rationale when making the decision about staying or returning was that of financial, and consequently personal, independence. She still travelled to Poland in search of what she called 'emotional support' after redundancy. Staying in Ireland meant that she could continue with a path of exploration like other young people moving internationally described by Conradson and Latham (2005a, b):

> *[I decided that] I will stay in Ireland. I didn't want to return to Poland very much. Now I see it in a slightly different way, because I have… [I see] Poland as a place where I can return … for a short period, so to earn in order to go somewhere else … However, my first idea was obviously that I would stay here.*

She had received no response to her applications, for both skilled and unskilled jobs. Her situation was not unlike that of other professionals, migrants, and Irish alike, who had joined the queue for new, possibly low-skilled employment. She felt that she could not take advantage of friendship resources any longer. Her timeline for finding new employment was a return ticket she had bought but did not intend to use unless she did not find a new job:

> *Anita:* Basically I have my ticket bought for 5th of February…
> *Interviewer:* Is it a one-way ticket?
> *Anita:* Yes, this is a one-way ticket. I hope I won't use it, to be quite frank.

Still in January, Anita had three interviews for administrative jobs. Coincidentally, the meeting with the researcher took place just hours after one of her job interviews. Just minutes after Anita reported having bought a return ticket, the recorder was stopped as she received a phone call from the company with which she had had the job interview earlier that day. She was informed that she had been accepted for the position. 'That means that I stay here,' she commented immediately, even if this meant a substantial downgrade on the pay scale.

Anita's long job search illustrated growing unemployment levels in Ireland, especially among migrants from EU NMS. NMS females were affected less than the NMS males, who were particularly vulnerable to job losses compared to natives, controlling for age and education (Barrett and Kelly 2012). One of the explanations for the higher risk of unemployment was the initial poor labor market performance of NMS migrants in terms of earnings and occupational positions. Anita's prolonged period of unemployment stood in contrast to how just five months before she had expressed her certainty that it would take her a month or two to find a new job. It was clear that in Anita's case, having work was necessary to continue her migration project, but the importance of living in Ireland went well beyond a job.

Wave 4: Oskar in Summer 2009

In summer 2009, Oskar reported pay cuts and further dismissals in his company, which, as in Anita's case, reflected a worsening economic situation in the country's economy. The grim prospects for winning new tenders in Ireland made more redundancies likely in the company. In addition, Oskar reported that his employer was increasingly involved in searching for contracts in the Polish market. Oskar was attempting to make use of this new context:

> I knew that here it's a disaster and it was necessary to show some initiative and to make use of the situation. Because so far the fact that you spoke Polish and that you were doing something back in Poland and that you graduated from a Polish university was not… any advantage. However, now it's starting to be useful. And you have to make use of it.

Perhaps better than anyone else, he understood how his fast-track career depended on mobilizing resources in the right context. Poland, as opposed to Ireland, was becoming a potential escalator to further career progress. He read this new situation also as an opportunity to network in Poland and get up to date with the Polish market. He had considered returning to Poland. Similarly, Arabic countries were perceived as another destination that offered professional opportunities for engineers with experience working on large projects in a transnational company environment. Asked about his plans to change his job, Oskar applied the same 'intentional unpredictability' strategy mentioned earlier. Aydemir and Robinson (2008) point to an emerging migration system in which onwards and return migration are becoming commonly considered options. Oskar's and Anita's accounts are an example of this. The calculations Oskar made concerning further mobility were also dependent on quality of life in the potential destination (similarly to the migrant accounts reported by Boyle 2006; Bozkurt 2006). The costs of moving, even within the Anglosphere, would involve starting from scratch, obtaining the recognition of qualifications, getting to know the regulatory context, and so on. This is why onward mobility would only be attractive in terms of higher quality of life or excellent professional opportunities. It seemed that the booming Irish economy, the Celtic Tiger escalator, had made him hungry for big projects:

I think that the next step would be bigger, different. I would have to do something different. For example to make use of the opportunity that in Poland something is starting to change and that some new companies are trying to get in there.

The job had given Oskar a sense of stabilization in Ireland: he was able to lead a comfortable life there. He could afford to rent a flat and own a car. He could also afford to be mobile: visiting his family and friends back in Poland, but also visiting Ireland and travelling to other places in Europe and beyond with his partner and child. His weekends were mostly work-free, and apart from home duties, he spent them going out with his partner or on his own, reading, watching TV, and surfing the Internet. Generally, his standard of living in Ireland had become higher than the one before migration, and he seemed to enjoy the lifestyle he had.

The Celtic Tiger made a comfortable life possible, but it had its career costs as well. Oskar recognized that he increasingly felt burned out and that he would need to change his job in the near future. The interview was filled with an anticipation of change. He also mentioned that he was planning to leave the flat he shared with his partner; however, he did not wish to elaborate further on his private life. Dublin in Oskar's narrative was becoming a stepping-stone toward a better job or better life somewhere else.

Wave 4: Anita in Spring 2009

In spring 2009, Anita described her new job, which involved a similar back-office routine administrative duties as her employment in the bank. She worked in a very international circle, where low-skilled white-collar jobs were performed by overeducated young people:

> *Really, when you came at first it is OK, but after a month everybody says: 'God, that's terribly boring, we can't stand it anymore, anyway we're looking for a completely different job now'. But there is nothing [jobs]. Because in reality if somebody has higher ambitions, then... I mean the job is OK for a year or so, but in the longer term, if you don't change it, then it's a disaster really.*

Even if she was aware that her education had nothing to do with the nature of her job, she compared her returns to tertiary-level education in Ireland favorably to those in Poland:

> *In Poland my degree meant that I could get 700 zlotys [less than 200 euros] ... and anyway ... I was exploited there. Yes, many people over there have higher education and it's not a trump card... Over here the value of the education and even value of work experience in the bank is much higher, in my opinion, than in Poland.*

Negotiation of staying or moving was an ongoing process, and the job situation affected the reasoning. If the Polish families researched by White (2009) assessed their time in the UK in terms of their rent agreements, Anita rather assessed her stay in terms of the length of her job contract. Asked if she would have returned to Poland if her contract had not been prolonged, she said she would have. The risk that job hunting in a recession labor market implied seemed too high. Although initially unhappy about the new job, at the time of the interview, the situation at work had improved and Anita was again starting to think about staying in Ireland. Staying was a clear lifestyle and self-realization choice: she had plans to enroll in an evening course, to sign up for salsa classes, and to join the gym. Dublin had also become a gateway to further mobility, as with low-cost airlines she was able to explore European destinations on short holidays, just like the other young migrants described by Conradson and Latham (2005a). Being a low-paid worker in Ireland, she was able to afford these by working overtime and therefore increasing her spending capacities. She claimed that she would not be able to afford a similar lifestyle in Poland.

Anita was clear about her work-life aspirations, but over a year after relocating to Ireland, she had not taken any action in this direction. She was aware of being stuck in routine administrative work, but perhaps this perception of continuous or permanent temporariness made it bearable:

> I change my mind every three weeks. And I call my mum, saying: 'Mum, I'm coming back.'—'OK, honey, your room is waiting for you, you needn't be unhappy there, if you're unhappy in your job, then come back.' But then suddenly it all starts to get better and I say, 'Well, mum, maybe not yet, I'm not coming back. I'm coming back in three months, that's for sure.' But then I started to think if I shouldn't [stay for] five months… So nobody takes what I say seriously.

Anita did not really refer to her work life as a 'career' in the sense in which Oskar did. Her pathway in Dublin consisted of temporary employment spells with no major responsibilities, no family commitments, and no roots. While she had moved back to the flat that she shared with international circle of friends, there was a sense of isolation in her words. She was describing how her circle of friends to a large extent consisted of other young migrants, many of whom had either completed their international adventure and returned to settled life back home or moved on to other destinations.

In this sense, Anita's trajectory perhaps involved a paradox. She had initially perceived the move abroad as leading to independence and adulthood. In effect, however, migration had provided her with financial independence that allowed a holiday from traditional life commitments. One interpretation is that Anita's international move could have been an option of escaping the traditional trajectory of a settled life, important especially for women who migrate (reported also by Favell 2008b, with regard to some of the female Eurostars). Whether this was the case or not, surely Anita's migration does not resemble one single pattern outlined in the migration literature.

WAVE 5: OSKAR IN WINTER 2009–2010

In winter 2009–2010, Oskar changed his job. His company had reported high losses and its future was uncertain. Regardless of the recession, his knowledge of the Polish market and Polish language were in high demand. Oskar himself decided to move to the contracting area of construction in order to gain the experience on building sites required for a full engineering license from the Polish Chamber of Engineers. In the meantime, his qualifications were only partially recognized in Poland, which meant that he would not be able to work on a construction site in Poland. His time in Ireland was prolonged by the period of work experience needed to receive full recognition of his engineering work in Poland.

Oskar was hired in a project manager position. His pay remained at a similar level. His main duties were related to tenders in Poland, as his new employer planned to set up their business in Poland. He was successful in obtaining the job as he emphasized his Polishness and being mobile. He claimed that he would be able to travel between Poland and Ireland if that was required by the job.

The turning point in Oskar's career coincided with changes in his personal life, as his relationship ended after a few years. This indicated that the ties that had kept him in Ireland loosened. Moving on became an individualized choice again rather than a family matter. This ability to be mobile that he had emphasized during the job interview with his new employer stemmed precisely from his being single.

His accommodation situation in Dublin reflected uncertainty about his future. He only mentioned the changes in his personal life in passing, explicitly stating that he did not want to dwell on them. This seemed to be too fresh and emotional an issue to discuss. When he broke up with his partner, he had moved out from the apartment he had shared with her and moved to a new place with his friends. He said that this was because he was not sure where his next workplace would be. He claimed that he had some of his belongings packed, as that would make it easier to move them swiftly to Poland if need be, just like the 'Eurostars' described by Favell, who were 'ready to move in five minutes, with all you can carry, if you feel the *heat* around the corner' (2008b: 110, emphasis in original).

WAVE 5: ANITA IN AUTUMN 2009

In September 2009, Anita said that she had been issued with another fixed-term contract until the end of the year. She described a worsening atmosphere in the company, as there was fear among employees that redundancies were to come.

Her flat situation was changing again. She had moved out of the flat located in a disadvantaged area of Dublin because she no longer felt safe there. Otherwise, she enjoyed living in Dublin and being able to travel from there. She described recent trips to Florence and Paris with her flatmate. She was also planning a trip to Malta to meet a friend who was getting married to a Maltese. One downside of the new apartment was the lack of an Internet connection, making her feel 'as if I vanished into thin air'. She called her family in Poland though, especially as her grandmother had become ill.

As her contract would expire in the following months, Anita was searching for new jobs in the meantime. She described this as 'a disaster', as there were no vacancies of interest to her. She claimed that even if her manager had assured her not to worry about her job, perhaps redundancy from the previous job in the bank had had a scarring effect, as she preferred to remain cautious and keep looking for other opportunities.

WAVE 6: OSKAR IN SPRING 2010

Oskar still worked in Ireland, but his aim was to return to Poland in order to lead a big project either with his company or with one of its competitors. He claimed that Poland was where he would probably be in five years' time. He had an apartment in Kraków, which he had bought as a form of investment, but also 'a kind of spot that would maybe pull me back to Poland, because I was afraid that I would stay out in the world forever'. As with other Polish migrants interviewed by White (2009: 81, emphasis in original), property in Poland constituted a 'place to return', suggesting that 'there will be a *time* to return'.

Oskar did not wish to elaborate much on the changes in his private life, which had taken place at about the same time as his job change. He explained how he did not negotiate better conditions with his employer as his focus was not on that. He mentioned that he had left the flat he had shared with his friends to move back in with his ex-partner. With this, he also noticed that the extent of his 'being mobile' changed as his private life kept him tied to Ireland.

Oskar's trajectory at the end of the QPS was left in a kind of limbo. On the one hand, there was his professional life, in which he was clearly working toward moving to Poland. On the other hand, changes in his personal situation had started to hold him in Dublin.

WAVE 6: ANITA IN 2010

Anita was issued with a new job contract at the beginning of 2010, but despite the fact that she and other employees had been promised open-ended contracts and pay rises, this did not happen. She was also unsuccessful in her search for new employment.

At the time, Anita talked about her new partner, who was from Asia and was planning to return there, having finished building a house back home. At the time of the interview, Anita did not know what she would do then. She also felt her relationship with a man from Asia would not be accepted in Poland. Anita declared that she could not imagine going back to Poland and working there. She assessed her experience in Ireland in relation to multiple aspects: she had learned to be independent, how to maintain relationships, and how to manage money. The economic aspect of her stay was not that important after all:

> *I'm not a person who came here in order to save up for a house for instance. … Probably I don't bear the grudge towards Poland that I did when I was leaving: that the country was hopeless, that it didn't give me any opportunities and so on. But well, I learnt something over there, … which helped me to move here. Now that I came back after a year … basically I couldn't find my way around, not at all. … And when I come back here, then I come back home.*

When asked about her perspective for the next five years, she declared that she did not know where she would be. She had no plan. She did mention, half-seriously, half-jokingly, that apparently houses in Asia were cheap. She declared that she had further international destinations in her mind, such as Italy, which she had mentioned at the first meeting. She was still thinking about working in third-sector organizations in an international context. However, two years after the start of the QPS, she had not done anything toward going there.

Conclusions

We leave Oskar and Anita in spring 2010. One can think of the QPS as like a drama series, with spring 2010 the season's finale, a cliffhanger. Oskar's and Anita's stories were cut not only in the depths of the Irish recession but also at transition points in individual biographies. Oskar had to negotiate international professional mobility around his family life. There was an anticipation of a major change in his trajectory which was not realized. Anita had to negotiate her future life and work trajectory once she became involved with her Asian partner. The two stories of Oskar and Anita from the QPS sample were juxtaposed in a way that allows for a conversation in multiple dimensions. The context for both is similar: young people facing an unsatisfactory labor market in Poland, the EU accession, and a sense of opportunities in Ireland. Differences were visible in terms of the aspirations and resources which the participants possessed.

One of the advantages of looking at Oskar and Anita was that of analyzing two contrasting temporalities of migration. While both had arrived in Ireland in their mid-20s, the socioeconomic situation in the country was very different. Oskar had arrived in boom-time Ireland, and at the time of the interview, he was already well on track in his professional career in the country. For Anita, the migration coincided with a global recession, which had an impact on her precarious situation on the Irish labor market. The two cases also represent how career trajectories are shaped by different degrees of skills transferability in the gendered domains of the labor market. Oskar's story describes how an international move may accelerate professional development for a male engineer in the highly international construction sector. Anita's case portrays perhaps more the common case of females working 'in the middle' of the labor market, with routine white-collar employment. Human-capital theories may explain migrant labor market performance using large data sets, but it is in the accounts presented earlier that we can observe the texture of migrant lives in work and beyond.

The QPS repeated interview strategy revealed how life and work careers were constantly constructed and reconstructed against changes in perceived opportunities. Life-course events feature strongly in the two accounts of negotiating geographical mobility. Many international movements take place at the extremes of the life course (Hall and Williams 2002), as younger age cohorts taste mobility before they have family and career commitments, and older cohorts move once these commitments are gone. Migration, then, is not a one-off decision but a process embedded in changing temporal frames. 'Walking alongside' Oskar's and Anita's lives documents these shifts, uncertainties, and anxieties every time when settlement and mobility are discussed.

The two trajectories from Poland to Dublin described in the chapter highlight many of the issues set out in the literature on intra-European East-to-West movement and studies of mobilities of young people. The stories of Oskar and Anita are not very dissimilar to the accounts of Western European movers documented by Favell (2008b), Scott (2006), or Boyle (2006). Perhaps in the case of CEE movers, employment opportunities in the destination country remain a more necessary condition to facilitate the movement. However, labor alone is not sufficient to understand this kind of mobility. Oskar's focus on career is different from a simple account of labor migration which explains mobility with wage differentials. Anita's move to Ireland cannot be understood without thinking about sets of motivations specific to young migrants who want to try a new life outside of their parents' nest. With the passing of time, however, migrating may take on different meanings. The 'walking alongside' metaphor encapsulates tracking this movement in time and space.

Perhaps one weakness of the diachronic investigation presented in this chapter is that systematic thematic analysis remains a challenge. However, highlighting the flow and change is crucial in order to understand life courses lived internationally, rather than simply focusing on the consequences of mobility and business cycles at a specific point of time. Taking a comparative strategy across a bigger number of cases bears the cost of breaking individual stories into smaller chunks and does not allow individual trajectories to be represented across time in their full richness. This said, a thematic approach to the QPS data has also been taken, and is presented elsewhere (see e.g. Krings et al. 2013; Wickham et al. 2009).

Where we leave Oskar and Anita is a very specific moment for intra-European migrations. Both migrants are part of a new generation of East-to-West movers who tried living abroad and learned its ups and downs on the way. While the QPS tracked only a small chunk of the young Poles' lives, it managed to highlight how mobility is negotiated and renegotiated as the personal situation and broader socioeconomic context change. Further research should seek to explore the question that this chapter leaves open: What are the medium- and long-term consequences of geographical mobility and recession on Oskar's and Anita's life courses and the life courses of millions of other Europeans who took on a similar journey? A tentative continuation of the QPS in a few years' time may bring new answers.

Acknowledgments This chapter builds on the PhD research carried out at Trinity College Dublin under the valuable supervision of Professor James Wickham. I acknowledge generous funding from the Migrant Careers and Aspirations project and the Irish Research Council for the Humanities and Social Sciences. I also thank the editors, Ionela Vlase and Bogdan Voicu, for their thoughtful feedback on this chapter.

References

Aydemir, Abdurrahman, and Chris Robinson. 2008. Global Labour Markets, Return, and Onward Migration. *Canadian Journal of Economics/Revue canadienne d'Economique* 41 (4): 1285–1311.

Barrett, Alan, and Elish Kelly. 2012. The Impact of Ireland's Recession on the Labour Market Outcomes of its Immigrants. *European Journal of Population/ Revue européenne de Démographie* 28 (1): 91–111.

Beaverstock, Jonathan V. 2005. Transnational Elites in the City: British Highly-Skilled Inter-Company Transferees in New York City's Financial District. *Journal of Ethnic and Migration Studies* 31 (2): 245–268.

Boyle, Mark. 2006. Culture in the Rise of Tiger Economies: Scottish Expatriates in Dublin and the 'Creative Class' Thesis. *International Journal of Urban and Regional Research* 30 (2): 403–426.

Bozkurt, Ödül. 2006. Wired for Work: High-Skilled Employment and Global Mobility in Mobile Telecommunications Multinationals. In *The Human Face of Global Mobility. International Highly Skilled Migration in Europe, North America and the Asia-Pacific*, ed. Michael Peter Smith and Adrian Favell. New Brunswick: Transaction Press.

Central Statistics Office. 2010. Quarterly National Household Survey. Quarter 4 2009. Accessed March, 14, 2011. http://www.cso.ie/en/media/csoie/releasespublications/documents/labourmarket/2009/qnhs_q42009.pdf

Chiswick, Barry R., Yew Liang Lee, and Paul W. Miller. 2005a. Immigrant Earnings: A Longitudinal Analysis. *Review of Income and Wealth* 51 (4): 485–503.

———. 2005b. A Longitudinal Analysis of Immigrant Occupational Mobility: A Test of the Immigrant Assimilation Hypothesis. *International Migration Review* 39 (2): 332–353.

Conradson, David, and Alan Latham. 2005a. Transnational Urbanism: Attending to Everyday Practices and Mobilities. *Journal of Ethnic and Migration Studies* 31 (2): 227–233.

———. 2005b. Friendship, Networks and Transnationality in a World City: Antipodean Transmigrants in LONDON. *Journal of Ethnic and Migration Studies* 31 (2): 287–305.

Currie, Samantha. 2007. De-Skilled and Devalued: The Labour Market Experience of Polish Migrants in the UK Following EU Enlargement. *International Journal of Comparative Labour Law Industrial Relations* 23 (1): 83–116.

Eade, John, Stephen Drinkwater, and Michal Garapich. 2007. Class and Ethnicity: Polish Migrant Workers in London. *Research Report for the RES-000-22-1294 ESRC Project*. Accessed July 8, 2017. https://www.surrey.ac.uk/cronem/files/POLISH_FINAL_RESEARCH_REPORT_WEB.pdf

Favell, Adrian. 2008a. The New Face of East-West Migration in Europe. *Journal of Ethnic and Migration Studies* 34 (5): 701–716.

———. 2008b. *Eurostars and Eurocities: Free Movement and Mobility in an Integrating Europe.* Oxford: Blackwell.

Forde, Chris. 2001. Temporary Arrangements: The Activities of Employment Agencies in the UK. *Work, Employment & Society* 15 (3): 631–644.

Gardner, Katy. 2002. *Age, Narrative and Migration: The Life Course and Life Histories of Bengali Elders in London.* Oxford: Berg Publishers.

Hall, C. Michael, and Allan M. Williams. 2002. Tourism, Migration, Circulation and Mobility: The Contingencies of Time and Space. In *Tourism and Migration. New Relationships between Production and Consumption*, ed. C. Michael Hall and Allan M. Williams. Dordrecht: Kluwer Academic Publishers.

Kaczmarczyk, Paweł. 2008. Migracje z Polski przed i po 1 maja 2004 roku' Migrations from Poland before and after 1 May 2004. Paper presented to Congress of Polish Scientific Societies Abroad, Kraków.

Kennedy, Paul. 2010. Mobility, Flexible Lifestyles and Cosmopolitanism: EU Postgraduates in Manchester. *Journal of Ethnic and Migration Studies* 36 (3): 465–482.

King, Russell. 2002. Towards a New Map of European Migration. *International Journal of Population Geography* 8 (2): 89–106.

King, Russell, Aija Lulle, Laura Moroșanu, and Allan Williams. 2016. International Youth Mobility and Life Transitions in Europe: Questions, Definitions, Typologies and Theoretical Approaches. *Working Paper No. 86.* University of Sussex, Sussex Centre for Migration Research.

Krings, Torben, Elaine Moriarty, James Wickham, Alicja Bobek, and Justyna Salamońska. 2013. *New mobilities in Europe. Polish Migration to Ireland post-2004.* Manchester: Manchester University Press.

Le Bianic, Thomas, and Lennart G. Svensson. 2008. European Regulation of Professional Education. A study of Documents Focussing on Architects and Psychologists in the EU. *European Societies* 10 (4): 567–595.

Neale, Bren, and Sarah Irwin. n.d. The Young Lives Study: Researching Time and Processes of Change. Accessed October 3, 2011. http://www.google.com/url?sa=t&rct=j&q=&esrc=s&source=web&cd=1&cts=1331295984478&ved=0CCYQFjAA&url=http%3A%2F%2Fwww.ccsr.ac.uk%2Fmethods%2Ffestival%2Fprogramme%2Fwor%2Fneale.ppt&ei=7fZZT4qhI4bO8QPPkaDUDg&usg=AFQjCNHEnQYbigJJdj2hl8--G35zgwRwcw

Ní Laoire, Caitríona. 2000. Conceptualising Irish Rural Youth Migration: A Biographical Approach. *International Journal of Population Geography* 6: 229–243.

Pijpers, Roos. 2010. International Employment Agencies and Migrant Flexiwork in an Enlarged European Union. *Journal of Ethnic and Migration Studies* 36 (7): 1–19.

Scott, Sam. 2006. The Social Morphology of Skilled Migration: The Case of the British Middle Class in Paris. *Journal of Ethnic and Migration Studies* 32 (7): 1105–1129.

Thomson, Rachel. 2007. The Qualitative Longitudinal Case History: Practical, Methodological and Ethical Reflections. *Social Policy and Society* 6 (4): 571–582.

Thomson, Rachel, and Julie McLeod. 2015. New Frontiers in Qualitative Longitudinal Research: An Agenda for Research. *International Journal of Social Research Methodology* 18 (3): 243–250.

Trevena, Paulina. 2010. Degradacja? Koncepcje socjologiczne, percepcja społeczna, a postrzeganie własnego położenia przez wykształconych migrantów pracujących za granicą poniżej kwalifikacji. In *Drogi i rozdroża. Migracje Polaków w Unii Europejskiej po 1 maja 2004 roku*, ed. Halina Grzymała-Moszczyńska, Anna Kwiatkowska, and Joanna Roszak. Kraków: Nomos.

White, Anne. 2009. Family Migration from Small-Town Poland: A Livelihood Strategy Approach. In *Polish Migration to the UK in the New European Union: After 2004*, ed. Kathy Burrell. Aldershot: Ashgate.

Wickham, James, Elaine Moriarty, Alicja Bobek, and Justyna Salamońka. 2009. Working in the Gold Rush: Polish Migrants' Careers and the Irish Hospitality Sector. In *Work Matters: Critical Reflections on Contemporary Work*, ed. Sharon Bolton and Maeve Houlihan. Basingstoke: Palgrave Macmillan.

CHAPTER 4

'And we are still here': Life Courses and Life Conditions of Italian, Spanish and Portuguese Retirees in Switzerland

Claudio Bolzman and Giacomo Vagni

INTRODUCTION

In this chapter, we analyse the past trajectories and situations of migrants from Southern Europe who came to work in Switzerland during their adult life and who now are retired. We focus on past migratory, citizenship status and professional trajectories. We analyse how they influence the

---

This chapter is the result of research executed within the framework of the National Competence Centre in Research LIVES and the SINERGIA Project CRSII1-129922, which are financed by the Swiss National Science Foundation. The authors are grateful to the Swiss National Science Foundation for its support.

C. Bolzman (✉)
School of Social Work, University of Applied Sciences Western Switzerland (HES-SO), Geneva, Switzerland

G. Vagni
Nuffield College, University of Oxford, Oxford, UK

© The Author(s) 2018
I. Vlase, B. Voicu (eds.), *Gender, Family, and Adaptation of Migrants in Europe*,
https://doi.org/10.1007/978-3-319-76657-7_4

economic, social and health situations of migrants during the transition to retirement and after retirement. We compare their trajectories and situations with those of the Swiss-born population of the same ages. We are particularly interested in the concept of path dependency (Di Prete and Eirich 2006; O'Rand 2009). According to this concept, a position in the social space is defined by its structure of opportunities and constraints that leads or not to a further step in the life course that engenders new opportunities or new constraints and so on. The successive steps lead to a process of cumulative advantages or disadvantages across the life course. Data collection of information referring to such past successive steps can be mobilized in order to analyse the path dependency that structures the life course (Bolzman et al. 2017) from the starting position and status of being immigrant workers to the end of the professional life and the situation after retirement.

We explore the main question: To which extent foreign-born people, recruited to work in subordinate jobs, are likely to experience cumulative disadvantages/advantages in the socio-economic and health areas with respect to 'national' workers? We take as example the case of Switzerland, a country which has experienced a very significant immigration, especially from Southern Europe since the 1950s (Piguet 2004). Nowadays, the Swiss society experiences both a general aging of the population, on the one hand, and the aging of the immigrant population, on the other hand (Wanner 2012).

Indeed, when one looks at the statistics on the resident population in Switzerland, it can be seen that by the end of 2013, 1,432,000 persons out of a total of 8,139,000 were aged 65 and over. They represent 17.6% of the total resident population (OFS 2014). As for the population of foreign nationalities of the same age classes, it is 151,000, or 7.8% of the foreign resident population. By way of comparison, this proportion was 4.8% in 1980 (OFS 2010).

The demographic aging represents a considerable challenge for European societies (Eurostat 2012). This challenge seems to have been met rather satisfactorily, at least until the crisis of 2008. Indeed, various studies published in Switzerland and elsewhere in Europe have shown an improvement in the living conditions of new cohorts reaching the age of retirement. Some scholars view this general trend as an indicator of the democratization of old age. Thus, in the case of Switzerland, Lalive d'Epinay and colleagues, who conducted two reference surveys in French-speaking Switzerland in 1979 and 1994, write that 'the condition of the elderly has changed profoundly. At the same age, they are now healthier and benefit from the material conditions of existence that have been strengthened. They manifest a feeling of well-being superior to that of the generation of 1979' (Lalive d'Epinay et al. 2000: 377). The authors add that the family life of the elderly has become richer, that they are more active and willing to take advantage of the possibilities offered and that they have become more autonomous. In the authors' words, there was a 'general upturn' (Lalive d'Epinay et al. 2000: 378). At the same time, however, they recognize that important needs persist, particularly for people of very advanced age, particularly in terms of health, assistance to the economically weak, support for people living at home and for the isolated.

It should be noted, however, that these results concerning the improvement of the living conditions of the elderly are not, for financial and linguistic reasons, based on samples sufficiently large or representative of the population to include former migrant workers who also are more numerous nowadays to reach the age of retirement. These people, mostly from Southern European countries (Spain, Italy, Portugal) and the East (former Yugoslavia, Turkey), represent a significant proportion of the workers in Switzerland. Thus, studies on aging in Switzerland do not reflect the situation of a large part of the elderly population from the most modest social backgrounds, who have stayed in Switzerland after retirement (Bolzman et al. 2006).[1] In order to overcome this absence of data, this chapter examines whether the general trend towards the democratization of old age also applies to older immigrants, which would mean a limitation of cumulative disadvantages between adult life and old age.

State of the Art

Research on the relationship between age and migration has highlighted a number of factors suggesting that more attention should be paid in the aging studies to former migrant workers and, more generally, to elderly immigrants. One of these factors is that, contrary to popular belief, migration is not a parenthesis that is ultimately followed by a return to the country of origin. In fact, most migrants remain after retirement in the society in which they have spent their adult lives (Attias Donfut 2006; Bolzman et al. 2006, 2016). As Sayad points out, 'there is no immigration, even the one whose purpose has been to work and exclusively work ... which does not turn into family immigration, that is to say, in settlement immigration'[2] (Sayad 1991: 19). The other option is to travel back and forth between the two countries, staying part of the year in the country of work (often the country of official residence) and the other part in the country of origin (Serra-Santana 2000; Schaeffer 2001; Bolzman 2013).

European research has also highlighted the more precarious living conditions of these older immigrants compared with those of older nationals. This situation manifests itself in several ways:

- A high rate of early departures from the labour market for health reasons (disabling accidents or illness) or long-term unemployment (Dorange 1998; Bolzman et al. 1999).
- A financially precarious situation, the average income of immigrants being lower than that of elderly nationals (Alidra et al. 2003; Patel 2003; de Almeida 2011); in this context, women are particularly disadvantaged (Fibbi et al. 2001).
- Poor health, due to the painful nature of the jobs held (Ba et al. 2009; Samaoli 2011). Bollini and Siem (1995) call this phenomenon the 'exhausted migrant effect': while these people were often recruited by the host country precisely because they were in good health and therefore particularly fit for work, at the age of retirement, they are weakened by years of hard work.

In this chapter, we explore to which extent these results can also be observed in Switzerland when the situation of older immigrants is compared with that of the non-immigrant population in a systematic way. In Switzerland, it is very difficult to obtain Swiss nationality, which remains a very long process (12 years of uninterrupted stay) and also socially selective and expensive (Studer et al. 2013). The majority of Spaniards, Italians and Portuguese did not get it. It is thus interesting to explore whether people who became Swiss experienced better socio-economic and health conditions than other immigrants of the same generation. Indeed, access to citizenship also implies access to equal rights and greater recognition (Schnapper and Bachelier 2000), which may have an influence on other dimensions of life course. The comparative dimension is thus central to the chapter. We have proceeded to a retrospective design of life-course data collection in which the past biographies of individuals are collected at one moment in time (Scott and Alwin 1998; Ruspini 2002), in this case after the retirement age.

Sampling

This chapter is based on data from the Vivre-Leben-Vivere (VLV) survey, which focuses on the living conditions and health of individuals aged 65 and above currently resident in Switzerland. In order to address the increasing diversity of Switzerland's elderly population, VLV has developed a sub-project that questions these living conditions and the life trajectories of older migrants compared to the national population. The CIGEV (University of Geneva) carried out the VLV study in 2012 in five cantons in Switzerland. A total of 3,600 randomly selected individuals aged over 65 constituted the main sample, stratified by age and gender. An oversample of older migrants was conducted in Geneva (natives of Italy, Spain and Portugal aged between 65 and 79 years) and Basel (natives in the same age group from Italy only). This choice of groups and sites was determined by the distribution of these populations relative to the national population and other ethnic minority groups. The data were collected by means of Computer Assisted Personal Interviews. Local interviewers, who received extensive training, conducted the interviews, usually at the home of the respondent. A flyer and a short letter presenting the survey and announcing a phone call were sent individually to each respondent. The original questionnaire in French was translated into Portuguese, Spanish, Italian and German. Bilingual interviewers were also recruited (Ludwig et al. 2011).

The final sub-sample used for this chapter included 930 respondents. Five citizenship status categories were retained for the analysis: 489 Swiss (53%), 91 Naturalized (10%), 49 Naturalized from Southern Europe (5%), 242 Italians and Spanish (26%) and 59 Portuguese (6%). 'Naturalization' refers to the process of acquiring the Swiss nationality. The main difference between the Swiss and the Naturalized is that individuals in the latter group were not born as Swiss citizens. We differentiated between naturalized citizens from Southern Europe (mainly Italy, Spain and Portugal) and other naturalized citizens in order to have a more fine-grained comparison between migrants and Swiss citizens. The other group of naturalized citizens mainly comes from Continental and Northern Europe. We split the migrant groups in two: Spanish/Italians and Portuguese. This partition will help us understand better the logic at play between integration and social inequalities. These two populations of migrants also differ in their period of immigration (Bolzman et al. 2004). Other migrants were excluded from the analysis because their origin was too heterogeneous and the sample extremely small.

The characteristics of the sample are presented in Table 4.1.

Table 4.1 Characteristics of the sample

	Swiss	Naturalized	Naturalized South	Italians/ Spaniards	Portuguese	Total
Canton						
Geneva	42.54	52.75	69.39	59.92	98.31	493
Basel	57.46	47.25	30.61	40.08	1.69	437
Gender						
Women	49.69	63.74	53.06	46.69	50.85	470
Men	50.31	36.26	46.94	53.31	49.15	460
Age groups						
65–69	35.38	23.08	36.73	32.64	50.85	321
70–74	32.11	37.36	36.73	35.95	32.20	315
75–79	32.52	39.56	26.53	31.40	16.95	294
Total	100%	100%	100%	100%	100%	100%
	489	91	49	242	59	930

Note: Authors' calculation of VLV. $N = 930$

The higher proportion of young retirees among Portuguese reflects their more recent arrival in Switzerland (from the 1980s onward) compared with the Spanish and Italians, already present in the 1960s and 1970s.

Results

Socio-professional Trajectories: The Hierarchy of Arrivals and Nationalities

Table 4.2 shows the types of jobs carried out at the beginning and end of the career by the different national groups. We used a five occupational social class schema: Class I 'unskilled', Class II 'manual skilled', Class III 'non-manual skilled', Class IV 'intermediate' and Class V 'salariat'. Because we are looking at jobs performed from 1950s until about the end of the 1990s, the distinction manual/non-manual as well as skilled/non-skilled is very relevant for these older cohorts. Class I "unskilled" includes all unskilled low pay jobs, as well as a small proportion of individuals out of the labour market. Class IV 'intermediate' is a rather heterogeneous category including standard intermediate occupations, as well as small employers and independent workers and lower supervisory and technical occupations (Erikson et al. 2005). The Class V 'salariat' groups all the top

Table 4.2 First and last occupations by citizenship status and nationality

	Swiss	Naturalized	Naturalized South	Italians/ Spaniards	Portuguese
I unskilled	10.63	10.99	20.41	55.79	62.71
II manual skilled	18.00	12.09	28.57	27.69	15.25
III non-manual skilled	43.56	32.97	24.49	7.85	5.08
IV intermediate	25.15	41.76	22.45	7.85	15.25
V salariat	2.66	2.2	4.08	0.83	1.69
Total	100%	100%	100%	100%	100%
I unskilled	13.5	9.89	8.16	38.43	52.54
II manual skilled	5.93	7.69	34.69	35.12	25.42
III non-manual skilled	30.06	19.78	22.45	9.5	3.39
IV intermediate	38.45	46.15	26.53	14.46	18.64
V salariat	12.07	16.48	8.16	2.48	0
Total	100%	100%	100%	100%	100%
N	489	91	49	242	59
%	53%	10%	5%	26%	6%

Note: Authors' calculation of VLV. N = 930. Results presented in percentage

occupations, such as higher managerial and professional occupations, lower managerial and professional occupations and liberal professions.

The gradient in the social distribution of citizenship status and nationalities is very clear, with on the one hand the Swiss and Naturalized starting their career in the highest occupations and ending in the highest occupations, and on the other hand the Spanish/Italians and Portuguese migrants starting and ending their career in the lowest occupations. The Naturalized Swiss citizens from Southern Europe have an intermediate position between the two extremes.

Fifty-five percent of Italians and Spaniards began their professional career as unskilled manual workers, 27% in skilled manual occupations and about 8% in skilled non-manual occupations. About 8% of these Italian/Spanish immigrants began their career in intermediate professions, and virtually none started in a top occupation (*salariat*). Sixty-two percent of Portuguese immigrants started their career in an unskilled profession, 15% in a manual skilled profession and 5% in non-manual skilled occupations. Fifteen percent started in an intermediate profession and about 2% in a *salariat* occupation.

In comparison, only 10% of Swiss started their career in an unskilled occupation, 18% in a manual skilled job, 43% in a non-manual skilled job, 25% in an intermediate occupation and about 3% in a *salariat* occupation. The Naturalized group distribution of first occupations is very close to the distribution of the Swiss group.

About 20% of naturalized citizens from Southern Europe started their career in an unskilled profession, 28% in a manual profession, 25% in a non-manual skilled profession and about 4% in a *salariat* profession. The occupational distribution for this group is both very different from the Swiss group, the Naturalized group and the migrant groups.

The occupational mobility between the first and the last job varies according to the citizenship status of the respondents. Interestingly, the Portuguese who started their career in top occupations will eventually experience a downward mobility. For Spanish/Italians, about 31% who started with an unskilled job will stay in an unskilled job, while 13% will move up to a manual skilled job and 5.4% in a non-manual skilled job.

Portuguese, on top of starting in the lowest occupations, experience very little upward mobility. About 50.8% Portuguese starting in an unskilled occupation will end up in an unskilled occupation. Ten percent will move up to a manual skilled occupation.

Regarding Naturalized Swiss citizens from Southern Europe, only 4% of unskilled workers will stay in an unskilled position, 6% will move up to a manual skilled position and 8% to a non-manual skilled position. About 12% starting in a non-manual occupation will stay in similar occupations and 16% starting in an intermediate position will stay in such positions.

With respect to absolute occupational mobility rate, even though most groups do not experience either upward mobility or downward mobility, in other words will stay *immobile*, Portuguese nationals are the group of people experiencing the least absolute social mobility, with about 81.4% of individuals starting and ending up in similar occupations (conversely 18.6% experience mobility). The rate of absolute mobility is more similar, around 40%, for all the other groups, even though the starting point is different for each group.

We can observe that Swiss nationals, on top of starting with better jobs than immigrants, also experience the most upward mobility (33.9% of Swiss experience upward mobility). Nine percent of Swiss nationals experience downward mobility, 7.7% of Naturalized, 12.2% of Naturalized from Southern Europe, 9.1% of Spanish/Italians and 5% of Portuguese (for this group, this small proportion reflects a ceiling effect).

About 12% of Swiss end up in top occupations, compared to only 3% of Italians/Spanish and almost no Portuguese. The Naturalized group has actually the highest rate of finishing their career in a top position (16%). About 8% of the naturalized from Southern Europe group end up in a top position.

Immigrants from the South were recruited for low skill, low-skill jobs for which neither a high level of training nor language skills were required (Piguet 2004). Only a small fraction of them were able to pursue more skilled jobs for which more diplomas and language skills were required. The difference in level of education might help explain the differences between the naturalized group from Southern Europe and the migrant groups.

We explore in the next section the differences in individual characteristics of these different populations.

This first section clearly shows a very unequal distribution of professional trajectories between 'Swiss' and 'foreigners' in a segmented labour market (Piore 1979). However, there is a hierarchy between immigrants from the South, depending on the duration of their presence in Swiss society. Thus, the Spaniards and Italians benefited from a higher upward mobility than the Portuguese did during their professional career.

Cultural Capital and Economic Capital

One explanatory factor for various types of professional trajectories is the unequal distribution of cultural capital (education, language skills), social and economic capital (Bourdieu 1979a). Table 4.3 shows the distribution of these capitals among the respondents.

About 65% of Spanish and Italian nationals, 78% of Portuguese and 39% of Naturalized citizens from Southern Countries only obtained a primary school degree, whereas no more than 9% of Swiss and 6% of Naturalized citizens have stopped school at this level.

About 17% of Swiss nationals and more than 30% of Naturalized citizens have reached higher education, compared to 3% of Italian/Spanish and 3% of Portuguese. The Naturalized citizens from Southern Countries have a similar level of higher education than Swiss nationals (around 16%).

One may claim that such inequalities are actually due to return migration: immigrants with higher education, for some reasons, decided to return; therefore, the resulting structure of the retired immigrants still living in Switzerland is biased towards low education and low skills. However, former research shows that this bias is highly unlikely to occur. Actually, social profiles of candidates to return or returnees do not differ

Table 4.3 Socio-economic characteristics, social capital and life conditions by citizenship status and nationality

	Swiss	Naturalized	Naturalized South	Italians/ Spaniards	Portuguese
Socio-economic capital					
Education					
Primary	9.48	6.82	39.58	64.58	78.85
Secondary	32.16	40.91	22.92	7.92	13.46
Vocational	40.62	19.32	20.83	23.75	3.85
Higher education	17.73	32.95	16.67	3.75	3.85
Language skills					
Difficulties speaking French or German	0.61	2.2	2.04	19.42	25.42
Speak French or German	99.39	97.8	97.96	80.58	74.58
Make ends meet					
Difficult	10.81	13.64	19.15	31.09	52.54
Easy	89.19	86.36	80.85	68.91	47.46
Wealth/patrimony					
Nothing	10.02	13.19	12.24	21.49	42.37
Less than 60,000 frs	10.22	17.58	12.24	13.22	37.29
Between 60,000 and 150,000 frs	15.34	15.38	10.2	11.98	13.56
Between 150,000 and 1 million	34.15	19.78	26.53	23.14	1.69
More 1 million	15.95	9.89	8.16	2.89	1.69
No answer	14.31	24.18	30.61	27.27	3.39
Number of rooms in apartment					
1–2 rooms	10.49	11.11	12.5	26.36	28.81
3 rooms	27.98	26.67	25	35.98	30.51
4 rooms	28.81	31.11	25	25.1	28.81
5 rooms or more	32.72	31.11	37.5	12.55	11.86
Social capital					
Social isolation					
Often feel isolated	5.38	13.19	12.5	14.64	20.69
Rarely feel isolated	37.06	46.15	35.42	27.62	41.38
Never feel isolated	57.56	40.66	52.08	57.74	37.93
Receiving or visiting family					
At least once a year	96.01	94.38	100	95.26	83.05
Never	3.99	5.62	0	4.74	16.95
Phone calls with family					
At least once a year	97.5	96.59	97.96	97.85	91.53
Never	2.5	3.41	2.04	2.15	8.47

(*continued*)

Table 4.3 (continued)

	Swiss	Naturalized	Naturalized South	Italians/ Spaniards	Portuguese
Receiving or visiting friends					
At least once a year	95.24	95.51	97.96	89.36	74.58
Never	4.76	4.49	2.04	10.64	25.42
Phone calls with family					
At least once a year	97.29	98.88	95.92	94.85	82.76
Never	2.71	1.12	4.08	5.15	17.24
Health and well-being					
Depression					
Not depressed	83.64	69.23	71.43	65.7	72.88
Feel depressed	13.29	25.27	22.45	30.58	20.34
Feel very depressed	3.07	5.49	6.12	3.72	6.78
Self-reported health					
Poor health	5.38	12.09	10.2	13.81	22.03
Satisfactory health	27.95	30.77	32.65	43.51	47.46
Good health	50.52	41.76	48.98	33.05	23.73
Very good health	16.15	15.38	8.16	9.62	6.78
Last job physically demanding					
No	74.27	75	55.1	42.44	43.86
Yes	25.73	25	44.9	57.56	56.14
Satisfied with your life?					
Agree	73.62	58.24	71.43	54.13	54.24
Disagree	26.38	41.76	28.57	45.87	45.76
N	489	91	49	242	59
% =	53%	10%	5%	26%	6%

Note: Authors' calculation of VLV. N = 930. Results presented in percentage

significantly from stayers. The most important variables explaining return are social attachment to the country of residence and to the country of origin (Bolzman et al. 2006; see also Constant and Massey 2003, for the German case). On the other hand, there are some important social differences between the immobile retired immigrants living in Switzerland and those who have also their main residence in Switzerland but are moving regularly to their home country. These have a better socio-economic situation than the first (Bolzman et al. 2016).

Inequality is also present in the mastery of local languages: about 19% of Italian/Spanish speakers and about 1 in 4 Portuguese speakers do not speak the language of the canton where they reside, whereas among Swiss natives and both Naturalized groups, the lack of linguistic local knowledge is virtually non-existent.

Inequalities in cultural capital and occupational trajectories are also expressed at the level of the various indicators concerning the socio-economic situation of the respondents. The question regarding the difficulty of 'making ends meet' with the income available shows that about one third of Spaniards/Italians and half of Portuguese are in a difficult financial situation, whereas 1 in 10 Swiss nationals and about 13% Naturalized citizens have problems covering their expenses. The Naturalized citizens from Southern Europe held an intermediate position, with about 20% of individuals indicating being in difficult financial situation.

Regarding the wealth of the respondents, we find that foreigners from Southern Europe did not compensate for their low income by accumulated assets during their working years in Switzerland. In fact, 4 out of 10 Portuguese say they have no or almost no patrimony, which is the case for about 21% of Spaniards and Italians and about 1 in 10 Swiss nationals. At the other extreme, there are about 15% millionaires among native Swiss, and only 2% to 5% among Spaniards, Italians and Portuguese. Interestingly, both Naturalized groups did not accumulate as much wealth as Swiss natives.[3]

Finally, about 26–28% of Spaniards, Italians and Portuguese live in apartments with only one or two rooms, while the proportion is around 11% for Swiss citizens and the Naturalized groups. We refer to apartments because this is the type of housing that predominates in urban cantons such as Geneva and Basel. At the other extreme, about one-third of older people of Swiss nationality lives in a five-room apartment, which is the case for just over one in ten Spanish, Italian and Portuguese.

Thus, the material conditions of life are unequally distributed according to the respondents' current nationality and citizenship status. Despite the years spent in Switzerland, a significant proportion of older immigrants from southern Europe experience a precarious material situation, which is less common among respondents of Swiss nationality, either by birth or by acquisition.

Social Capital

Another important dimension of inequality between Swiss citizens and migrants is social capital. We focus here mostly on family social capital and other access to personal networks. Regarding interactions with family members, we find that about 16% of Portuguese never either visit or receive visits from family members, compared to about 4% for Swiss citizens and Italian/Spanish migrants. Regarding receiving phone calls from family members, we estimate that about 8% of Portuguese never receive any phone calls, compared to about 2–3% for all other groups.

Regarding visiting or receiving friends at home, we find that about 25% of Portuguese never interact with friends, compared to 10% of Italian/Spanish migrants and only 5% of Swiss citizens. About 18% of Portuguese never receive any phone calls from friends, 5% of Italians never receive any calls and only 2% of Swiss never receive phone calls from friends.

Portuguese are therefore much more likely to be socially isolated compared to Swiss citizens and to Italian/Spanish migrants to a certain extent. This is reflected by a question asking directly about social isolation. About 57% of Swiss report never feeling isolated, compared to 37% of Portuguese. Twenty percent of Portuguese report that they often feel isolated compared to 15% of Italians and only 6% of Swiss. It is worth noting that regarding social isolation, the two Naturalized groups are more similar to the migrant groups than to the Swiss nationals. About 13% of Naturalized individuals often feel isolated.

Health and Well-Being

We explored health status with a self-reported question: 'Please evaluate your current state of health', with possible answers ranging from 'very poor' to 'very good'. The self-reported health status used in this chapter was strongly correlated with other health questions such as body pain, number of hospitalizations, autonomy of movements, diseases and psychological distress.

Asked to assess their health, 22% of Portuguese and 13% of Spanish/Italians consider themselves in poor health compared to 6% of Swiss citizens. Regarding their health status, the Naturalized citizens from Southern Europe are much closer to the health status of the Spanish/Italians than the Swiss. The Naturalized group however seem more heterogeneous regarding their health status (see Table 4.3).

In terms of mental health (Wang et al. 1975; Cavalli et al. 2013), we find that Spanish/Italians and Portuguese are more likely to report experiencing depression compared to Swiss nationals. Surprisingly, the two Naturalized groups have high depression rates, very close to the Portuguese rate of depression (around 6%).

We consider the question whether the last job before retirement was physically hard and demanding. About 56–57% of Portuguese and Spanish/Italians describe their last job as physically hard. About 44% of

Naturalized citizens from Southern countries also describe their last job as physically hard. Only 25% of Swiss and Naturalized refer to their last job as physically demanding.

Finally, regarding the subjective assessment of personal life, 73% of Swiss consider themselves satisfied with their life. The Naturalized citizens from Southern countries also have high life satisfaction (around 71%). However, only about 54% of Naturalized citizens, 54% of Spanish/Italians and Portuguese consider their life as satisfactory.

Multiple Correspondence Analysis

In order to understand the structure of inequalities in a more synthetic manner, we used a multiple correspondence analysis (MCA)[4] with some of the main variables discussed earlier (Le Roux et al. 2008). The MCA technique enables a visualization of the position of individuals in the social space (Bourdieu 1979b) (see Figs. 4.1 and 4.2).

As seen in Fig. 4.1, a U-shape is clearly distinguishable, indicating a strong structure of inequality in the data. On the right, we find the Portuguese group next to the following characteristics: *difficulties speaking French or German, primary education, difficulties making ends meet, poor health, feeling isolated and very depressed* as well as *unskilled occupations, living in small apartments* and *having no or almost no wealth*. On the opposite side of the figure, we find the Naturalized and the Swiss with *good health, secondary or higher education, in either salariat or intermediate professions, rarely feeling isolated, easily making ends meet, living in four (or more)-bedroom apartments with significant accumulated wealth*. In between the Portuguese group and the Swiss, we find the Spanish/Italians in *manual skilled occupations, with satisfactory health, living in three-room apartments*.

The map of individuals (Fig. 4.2) shows that individuals are more or less concentrated in one area of the map. We can see that not all Swiss are millionaires, highly educated and living in five-bedroom apartments. The Swiss are distributed along the upper and lower left quadrant of the map. We find very few Swiss on the right-hand side of the map, where the most vulnerable and deprived individuals are located. The MCA seems to indicate that the Naturalized group have a higher social position than the Swiss citizens. The Naturalized citizen from Southern countries are more scattered between the migrant groups and the Swiss.

We can see a few Spanish/Italians in the upper left quadrant, showing that some individuals in these groups have managed to reach the same

Fig. 4.1 MCA. Map of variables. Variances of Dim. 1 (12.33%) and Dim. 2 (6.48%)

quality of life as the Naturalized and the Swiss citizens. Portuguese are most heavily concentrated in the upper right quadrant of the figure and the Spanish/Italians in the lower right quadrant, with some overlap in the lower left quadrant. The map of individuals shows clearly the social stratification between elderly migrants and Swiss citizens. Portuguese are clearly the most deprived group.

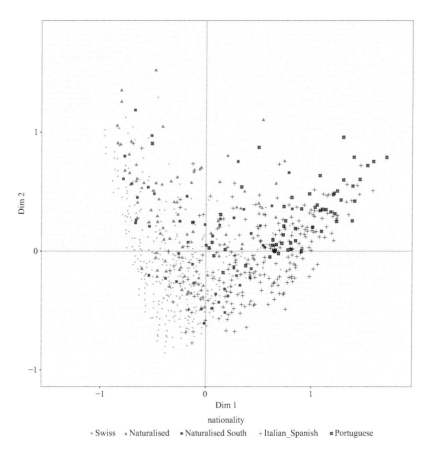

Fig. 4.2 MCA. Map of individuals. Variances of Dim. 1 (12.33%) and Dim. 2 (6.48%)

Conclusions

In this chapter, we explored whether older migrants suffer from cumulative disadvantages compared with the Swiss-born older population. The possibility to systematically compare different types of populations according to both migratory variables, national origins and the acquisition or not of the Swiss nationality allows a more precise and nuanced portrait of the problem.

Analysing occupational trajectories as well as the socio-economic and health situation of the elderly leads to the observation that life course has a significant influence on the living conditions in old age. Inequalities experienced during the adult life cumulate and crystallize during this new stage of life. Indeed, inequalities in resources (educational, economic, social, cultural, etc.) at the beginning of the working life can add up throughout the subsequent life course according to the structure of opportunities (immigration policies, employment, training, etc.) of societies and the logics of mobilizing the resources by individuals.

In the case of Switzerland, it can be observed that, as far as living conditions are concerned, there is not a single figure of immigrant old age but a *plurality of old ages*. Three factors seem to play an important role in the trajectories and situations observed: a differentiated recruitment policy based on the national origins of the workforce (preference for low-skilled workers from Southern Europe, preference for high-level educated workers from Central and Northern Europe), length of stay in the country and the possibilities of access to the Swiss nationality. Thus, naturalized persons, mostly from Northern Europe, have professional trajectories and economic situations that are as good as, or even better than, the ones of Swiss-born retirees. Naturalized people from Southern Europe, who are often long-term residents, have experienced upward mobility and socio-economic situations which tend to be similar to those of the Swiss-born. Spaniards and Italians who also reside in Switzerland for a long time but who have not become Swiss nationals have experienced some improvement in their socio-professional status between the beginning of their careers and the end of their working life; however, their living conditions after retirement are more modest than those of Swiss-born and naturalized. Lastly, the most recent arrivals, *the Portuguese*, have had the least upward mobility in their professional careers and the highest proportion of socio-economic precariousness. The selectivity of access to nationality and the dynamics of legitimation of the 'oldest' ones are in line with the classic work of Elias and Scotson (1994) on the difficulty of outsiders to overcome the barriers fixed by the 'established'.

This complex and shifting relationship between 'We' and 'Them' can be seen in the watermarked reading of indicators of health status. In this respect, the 'distance' between Swiss-born and immigrants is more important than in socio-economic terms. Even if the Swiss by naturalization are better off overall than the immigrants who have remained foreigners, they pay more than the native Swiss for their efforts to make a socially valued place in the society of residence. For instance, the percentage of 'depressive' among them is almost as high as that of Southern immigrants who remained foreigners, as well as their general health also being more similar to Southern immigrants than to Swiss nationals.

The chapter has mainly focused on the lives trajectories and situations of former guest-workers arrived to Switzerland after the Second World War from Southern Europe compared to those of the Swiss natives from the same ages. Other researches in Switzerland show that the occupational and social trajectories of immigrants from the states of former Yugoslavia (Bolzman and Poncioni-Derrigo 2012; Shabani 2014) and from Turkey (Haab et al. 2010) resemble those of Portuguese. Retired immigrants from these nationalities arrived in Switzerland in the same period of time as the Portuguese but later than Italians and Spaniards (Piguet 2004). The difference with the Portuguese is that in these migrations there is a component of former guest-workers and a component of former refugees, with a greater heterogeneity of the trajectories during the adult life and also after retirement.

If we compare our results with the situations in some other European countries, we also observe similar circumstances for other former immigrant workers who are now retired. This is the case of Italians and Portuguese in Luxembourg. Zahlen (2015), for instance, finds, as in Switzerland, a segmentation of the labour market according to the national origins of immigrants, with the Italians and especially the Portuguese at the bottom of the social scale, which has consequences in terms of socio-economic and health inequalities at the time of retirement. In Germany, Baykara-Krumme et al. (2012) show the wide variety of situations of older immigrants in an aging society. Again, former guest-workers from Italy and Turkey are in worse conditions than other categories of older immigrants or older Germans. Different comparative studies show that in the Netherlands, in the United Kingdom or in France former guest-workers are doing less well than the national retirees in terms of socio-economic situation or health condition (Patel 2003; Ruspini 2009). More systematic comparisons are needed in order to understand these general trends.

Our case study as well as other studies in Europe highlight the influence of the concept of path dependency (Di Prete and Eirich 2006; O'Rand 2009) as an explanatory factor of individual trajectories. Many former guest-workers started their adult lives in their new immigration countries in very low social positions that defined a restricted structure of opportunities for them. Their chances to reduce inequalities with respect to the native population were limited. The majority of them experienced a process of cumulative disadvantages across their active life that had consequences also after retirement. In spite of these structural inequalities, a small proportion of immigrants mobilized their resources in order to move to better social positions (naturalization, upward occupational mobility) and they have reduced the initial socio-economic inequalities with respect to the native population of the same ages. Nevertheless, they have paid these efforts in terms of some deterioration of their health condition when compared to the native population. Moreover, the possibility of upward social mobility seemed to be more important for guest-workers arrived during the 'glorious thirties' than for those arrived in more recent years. For them, there is still room for agency, but the structure of constraints seems to predominate over the structure of opportunities.

In the introductory section of our chapter we wondered about the possibility of generalizing the research results about the better living conditions of the elderly population in Switzerland. However, we have shown that there is no empirical ground for generalization: the socio-economic and health status of former guest-workers is generally less satisfactory than that of the Swiss-born population. In fact, life conditions of immigrant retirees are marked by their hard and laborious trajectories during active life.

From a methodological point of view, in order to better understand the implications of aging in our societies, it is very important to systematically include immigrants in surveys about the older population. In spite of all the difficulties to attain more vulnerable populations (Oris et al. 2016), an effort is needed to produce more accurate descriptions of the living conditions of all older people. Moreover, these surveys need to take into account longitudinal data, and particularly migration trajectories to inform public policies so that they can consider the diversity of situations and needs.

From a social policy perspective, if we want to mitigate the inequalities observed between elderly populations, it is important to intervene upstream preventively. A life-course approach could be useful to social service providers and policymakers in order to foster the conditions of a better retirement life for former blue-collar workers in general and former guest-workers in particular.

Notes

1. For this reason, our chapter is called 'And we are still here'. Many immigrants who intended to return to their home country decided finally to stay in the host country after retirement.
2. Authors' translation from French.
3. Please consider the important non-response rate to this question.
4. All the statistical analyses were conducted using R (2016). The MCA was conducted using the library FactoMineR (Le et al. 2008).

References

Alidra, Nadia, Abdellatif Chaouite, and Tasse Abye. 2003. France. In *Minority Elderly Care in Europe: Country Profiles*, ed. Naina Patel. Leeds and London: PRIAE.

Attias-Donfut, Claudine. 2006. *L'enracinement. Enquête sur le vieillissement des immigrés en France*. Paris: Armand Collin.

Ba, Abdul, Mohamed Bousnane, and Fatima Skanari. 2009. *Le vieillissement dans l'immigration: l'oubli d'une génération silencieuse*. Paris: L'Harmattan.

Baykara-Krumme, Helen Motel-Klingebiel Andreas and Schimany Peter, eds. 2012. *Viele Welten des Alterns: Ältere igranten im alternden Deutschland* [Many Worlds of Aging: Elderly Migrants in an Aging Germany]. Wiesbaden: VS Verlag für Sozialwissenschaften.

Bollini, Paola, and Herald Siem. 1995. No Real Progress towards Equity: Health of Migrants and Ethnic Minorities on the Eve of the Year 2000. *Social Science and Medicine* 41 (6): 819–829.

Bolzman, Claudio. 2013. Ageing Immigrants and the Question of Return: New Answers to an Old Dilemma? In *Return Migration in Later Life*, ed. John Percival. Bristol and Chicago: Policy Press.

Bolzman, Claudio, Laura Bernardi, and Jean-Marie LeGoff, eds. 2017. *Situating Children of Migrants across Borders and Origins. A Methodological Overview*. Dordrecht, Netherlands: Springer Open. https://doi.org/10.1007/978-94-024-1141-6.

Bolzman, Claudio, Rosita Fibbi, and Marie Vial. 1999. Les Italiens et les Espagnols proches de la retraite en Suisse: situation et projets d'avenir. *Gérontologie et Société* 91: 137–151.

———. 2006. What to do after Retirement? Elderly Migrants and the Question of Return. *Journal of Ethnic and Migrations Studies* 32 (8): 1359–1375.

Bolzman, Claudio, Laure Kaeser, and Etienne Christe. 2016. Transnational Mobilities as a Way of Life Among Older Migrants from Southern Europe. *Population, Space and Place* 23: 5. http://onlinelibrary.wiley.com/doi/10.1002/psp.2016/epdf.

Bolzman, Claudio, and Raffaella Poncioni-Derrigo. 2012. Elderly Immigrants in Switzerland: Exploring Their Social and Health Situation. *Scientific Annals of the Alexandre Ion Cuza University* 5 (1): 175–190.

Bolzman, Claudio, Raffaella Poncioni-Derrigo, Marie Vial, and Rosita Fibbi. 2004. Older Labour Migrants' Wellbeing in Europe: The Case of Switzerland. *Ageing and Society* 24 (3): 411–429.

Bourdieu, Pierre. 1979a. Les trois états du capital culturel. *Actes de la recherche en sciences sociales* 30 (1): 3–6.

———. 1979b. *La distinction. Critique sociale du jugement.* Paris: Les Editions de Minuit.

Cavalli, Stefano, Delphine Fagot, Michel Oris, and Aude Tholomier. 2013. Construction des indices de fragilité et dépendance. *Notes VLV*, no. 2, Genève.

Constant, Amelie, and Douglas S. Massey. 2003. Self-Selection, Earnings, and Out-Migration: A Longitudinal Study of Immigrants to Germany. *Journal of Population Economics* 16: 631–653.

De Almeida, Aníbal. 2011. Les Portugais en France à l'heure de la retraite: cinquante ans après leur arrivée en France, les Portugais parviennent à l'âge de la retraite. *Gérontologie et société* 139: 161–178.

DiPrete, Thomas A., and Gregory M. Eirich. 2006. Cumulative Advantage as a Mechanism for Inequality : A Review of Theoretical and Empirical Developments. *Annual Review of Sociology* 32: 271–297.

Dorange, Martine. 1998. La sortie d'activité des travailleurs migrants. *Ecarts d'identité* 87: 56–58.

Elias, Norbert, and John L. Scotson. 1994. *The Established and the Outsiders. A Sociological Enquiry into Community Problems.* 2nd Rev. ed. London: Sage Publications.

Erikson, Robert, John Goldthorpe, Michelle Jackson, Meir Yaish, and Dan R. Cox. 2005. On Class Differentials in Educational Attainment. *Proceedings of the National Academy of Sciences of the United States of America* 102 (27): 9730–9733.

Eurostat. 2012. *Structure et vieillissement de la population.* Bruxelles: Commission européenne.

Fibbi, Rosita, Claudio Bolzman, and Marie Vial. 2001. A l'écoute des femmes immigrées: témoignages et mémoire. *Revue Européenne des Migrations Internationales* 17 (1): 127–150.

Haab, Katharina, Claudio Bolzman, Andrea Kugler, and Özcan Ylmaz. 2010. *Diaspora et communautés de migrants de Turquie en Suisse.* Berne: Office fédéral des migrations.

Lalive d'Epinay, Christian, Jean-François Bickel, Carole Maystre, and Nathalie Vollenwyder. 2000. *Vieillesses au fil du temps. 1979–1994: Une révolution tranquille.* Lausanne: Réalités sociales.

Le, Sebastien, Julie Josse, and Francois Husson. 2008. FactoMineR: An R Package for Multivariate Analysis. *Journal of Statistical Software* 25 (1): 1–18.

Le Roux, Brigitte, Henry Rouanet, Mike Savage, and Alan Warde. 2008. Class and Cultural Division in the UK. *Sociology* 42 (6): 1049–1071.

Ludwig, Catherine, Stefano Cavalli, and Michel Oris. 2011. Aging in Switzerland: Progress and Inequalities. Paper distributed at the *10th European Sociological Association Conference*, Geneva, Switzerland.

O'Rand, Angela M. 2009. Cumulative Processes in the Life Course. In *The Craft of Life Course Research*, ed. Glen H. Elder and Janet Z. Giele. New York: Guilford Press.

Office fédéral de la statistique. 2010. *Statistiques des étrangers en Suisse*. Neuchâtel: OFS.

———. 2014. *Statistiques des étrangers en Suisse*. Neuchâtel: OFS.

Oris, Michel, Caroline Roberts, Domique Joye, and Michèle Ernst Stähli, eds. 2016. *Surveying Human Vulnerabilities across the Life Course*. Amsterdam: Springer.

Patel, Naina, ed. 2003. *Minority Elderly Care in Europe: Country Profiles*. Leeds and London: PRIAE.

Piguet, Etienne. 2004. *L'immigration en Suisse. Cinquante ans d'entre ouverture*. Lausanne: Presses polytechniques et universitaires romandes.

Piore, Michael J. 1979. *Birds of Passage. Migration Labour in Industrial Societies*. Cambridge: Cambridge University Press.

R Core Team. 2016. *R: A Language and Environment for statistical COMPUTING*. Vienna, Austria: R Foundation for Statistical Computing. https://www.R-project.org.

Ruspini, Elisabeta. 2002. *Introduction to Longitudinal Research*. London: Routledge.

Ruspini, Paolo. 2009. *Elderly Migrants in Europe: An Overview of Trends, Policies and Practices*. Research Report. Strasbourg: European Committee on Migration of the Council of Europe (CDMG).

Samaoli, Omar. 2011. Vieillesse des immigrés: quelques interrogations d'actualité. *Gérontologie et société* 139: 67–75.

Sayad, Abdelmalek. 1991. *L'immigration ou les paradoxes de l'altérité*. Bruxelles: De Boeck.

Schaeffer, Fanny. 2001. Mythe du retour et réalité de l'entre-deux. La retraite en France, ou au Maroc? *Revue Européenne des Migrations Internationales* 17 (1): 165–176.

Schnapper, Dominique, and Christian Bachelier. 2000. *Qu'est-ce que la citoyenneté?* Paris: Gallimard/Folio.

Scott, Jacqueline, and Duane Alwin. 1998. Retrospective Versus Prospective Measurement of Life Histories in Longitudinal Research. In *Methods of Life Course Research. Qualitative and Quantitative Approaches*, ed. Janet Z. Giele and Glen H. Elder. Thousand Oaks, London, New Dehli: Sage Publications.

Serra-Santana, Ema. 2000. L'éternel retour ou l'impossible retour. *Migrations société* 12 (68): 77–84.

Shabani, Kujtim. 2014. *Ältere Albaner in der Schweiz*. Lausanne: ISEAL.

Studer, Brigitte, Gerald Arlettaz, and Regula Argast. 2013. *Le droit d'être suisse. Acquisition, perte et retrait de la nationalité de 1848 à nos jours*. Lausanne: Antipodes.

Wang, Richard I., Sharon R. Treul, and Luca Alverno. 1975. A Brief Self-Assessing Depression Scale. *The Journal of Clinical Pharmacology* 15: 163–167.

Wanner, Philippe. Dir. 2012. La démographie des étrangers en Suisse. Zürich: Seismo.

Zahlen, Paul. 2015. Elderly Migrants in Luxembourg. Diversity and Inequality. In *Ageing in contexts of migration*, ed. Ute Karl and Sandra Torres. London and New York: Routledge.

PART II

Work and Labor Market

CHAPTER 5

Gendered Migratory Pathways: Exploring the Work Trajectories of Long-Term Romanian Migrants

Alin Croitoru

INTRODUCTION

In the past three decades, migration has shaped not only Romania's demographics but also the life experiences, biographical trajectories, and professional careers of the individuals who were engaged in this process. This chapter is built on subjective evaluations of Romanian migrants' work experiences, and we are interested in following their work trajectories using a life-course perspective. Challenging the optimistic perspective that the migration experience positively affects migrants' work life, we look at the evolution of individuals' work life during three periods of time: before migration, during migration, and upon return. This longitudinal approach allows us to draw a detailed image of the main turning points from migrants' work trajectories. Moreover, it provides us with the necessary framework to analyze how individuals' agency takes shape within the structural opportunities and constraints affecting Romanian returnees.

A. Croitoru (✉)
'Lucian Blaga' University of Sibiu, Sibiu, Romania

© The Author(s) 2018
I. Vlase, B. Voicu (eds.), *Gender, Family, and Adaptation of Migrants in Europe*, https://doi.org/10.1007/978-3-319-76657-7_5

Existing literature demonstrates that the labor market is highly gendered (Duncan and Pfau-Effinger 2002; Perrons 2007; Bettio and Verashchagina 2009—for the EU labor market; Charles 2011). In this context, we expect the work trajectories of men and women to be different and strengthen their level of agency through international migration in a specific way.

Before migration, our subjects explored labor opportunities at home, and many were unsatisfied with their life circumstances. They decided to emigrate mainly for work reasons, and in some cases, this was a family decision, not an individual one. The migration experience includes several transitions, including youth to adulthood, unemployment to (in)formal employment, unmarried to married, and so on. Within our sample, women's agency upon return is generally oriented toward new investments in accumulating human capital (higher education or specialized job training), while men are more oriented toward entrepreneurship. These forms of agency are framed by various structural determinants tied to origin and destination settings, while being differently evaluated upon return. Our empirical findings suggest that, as compared to men, women's work trajectories are more sensitive to a series of additional attributes, including marital status and the timing of their transition to motherhood. In addition to migrants' own perceptions, objective circumstances involving local economic contexts, national economic policies, and global economic crises are all constitutive parts of the framework in which migrants' work trajectories can be understood.

This chapter is crafted on the following structure. First, the study details some of the main theoretical and conceptual tools employed in our research. Second, the chapter lays out the contextual background of Romanian migration by offering essential details on national setting, as well as methodological aspects. Third, it provides a detailed, gendered analysis of several typical work trajectories of Romanian returnees who lack tertiary education. The final part summarizes the main findings and proposes an analytical typology based on central features of each work trajectory.

Theoretical Framework

Migrants are one of the most vulnerable groups on the labor market. They are often subjected to tumultuous economic integration marked by participation in segmented labor markets, leading to job insecurity, lower wages, informal employment, and so on (Anderson 2010; Schierup et al.

2015; Shelley 2007). If we factor in a lack of higher education (a common trait among those studied in our analysis), the insecurity of migrants' work trajectories becomes much more problematic (Borjas 1999). This lack of education capital leads to limited agency expected in this category of migrants, forming this study's subject matter. In this context, one expects these migrants' work trajectories to be a complex mix of regular employment, unemployment, and informal jobs (Vianello and Saccheto 2016).

Furthermore, any analysis of individuals' work trajectories must pay careful attention to general tendencies in the labor market. For example, contemporary tendencies toward "de-industrialization" and "flexibilization" provide more room for individuals' agency within the labor-market context (Qureshi 2012; Vianello and Saccheto 2016).

Drawing on existing literature on informal economic practices (C. C. Williams 2009b) and informal employment (M. Evans et al. 2006; C. C. Williams 2009a), our analysis focuses on migrants' self-reported impact from informal employment (in destination countries) on their work trajectories, work-family life, and life outcomes. In examining the work trajectories of Romanian migrants, we must consider that the transition from informal employment to formal employment is not necessarily a definitive one. Romania's entry into the EU in 2007 favorably affected numerous work trajectories of Romanian migrants already in EU destinations at that time (between 2007 and 2014, all EU countries gradually removed labor-market barriers). Since 2008, the recent economic crisis pushed some migrants from formal employment to unemployment or back to informal employment. Vianello and Saccheto's (2016) study on Moroccan and Romanian migrants' work trajectories in Italy reveals that working informally can be the result of both structural constraints and individuals' agency. Several typical employment niches for immigrants are often tied to shadow economies [e.g., immigrant women employed in the domestic sector in Italy (Scrinzi 2008) or in Germany (Lutz 2008); migrant men employed in construction (Anghel 2008)], and our analytical framework takes this aspect into consideration.

The migration experience enables returnees to more easily embrace an entrepreneurial work status (Dustmann and Kirchkamp 2002). Against this backdrop, we are interested in how these types of work trajectories emerge, as well as the specific roles played by the migration experience. Individual characteristics and structural determinants are both important in analyzing entrepreneurial activities (Thornton 1999; C. C. Williams 2009b). Formal and informal learning mechanisms are embedded into the migration experience (A. Williams and Baláž 2005). Some of this knowledge is explicit and could be measured [e.g., "language capital" (Dustmann 1999)], while other parts are linked to "tacit skills and key competences" (K. Evans 2002) or "tacit knowledge" (A. Williams 2007). Along with this accumulation of human capital, there are also other important factors for understanding returnees' higher propensity toward entrepreneurship, such as economic capital accumulated abroad, higher tolerance for risks, and transnational ties that help some of them develop transnational businesses.

Social networks are important during different periods of migrants' lives (Gurak and Caces 1992; Ryan 2011), and it is largely accepted that migration networks played an essential role in the development of Romanian migration (Constantinescu 2004; Anghel 2008; Sandu 2010; Şerban and Voicu B 2010). Following on this, we can note that migrants rely on informal networks (with a focus on acquaintances) mainly for pragmatic reasons, while relationships with relatives and friends frequently include a "mutual supportiveness which is taken for granted" (Malyutina 2015). This sociality dimension is related to our subjects' work trajectories, as many of them use informal networks to find jobs abroad (before emigration and during migration) and for re(integration) into the local labor market upon return.

Romanian migration developed as a predominantly temporary phenomenon (Sandu 2006; Tudor 2017) in which people migrated to accumulate economic resources for specific aims (e.g., improving living conditions, buying a car, starting a business, etc.) but generally aimed to return. Migration could affect domestic arrangements significantly. On the one hand, if only one partner is abroad, at the household level, some tasks must be performed by the partner who remains at home. This can negatively affect the partner at home, who is usually considered to be a beneficiary of remittances (Hennebry 2014) mainly because the partner who earns more money (abroad) usually strengthened their position at the household level (and it is usually the male who finds himself in this situation). On the other hand, a series of qualitative studies focusing on Romanians' return migration from Italy revealed that gender plays an important role in understanding economic and social remittances, as well as labor opportunities in the return context (Vlase 2013a, b).

Even if the contemporary Romanian migration population is rather heterogenous, Romanian migrants often can be commonly found working in several typical, low-skilled jobs. For example, in the Italian context, Vianello (2016) pointed out that men usually seek employment in construction, agriculture, and industrial sectors, while women are often employed in the domestic service and care sector. Her study also detailed how transnational care arrangements link destination to origin and represent an important factor in analyzing return motivations. The specific settings of destination contexts are important for understanding the work trajectories of women involved in "the global care chain." The comparative analysis conducted by F. Williams (2012: 372) in the UK, Sweden, and Spain found that "micro experiences of migrant-care worker employment are connected to institutional, cultural, and political factors at the national and supranational levels." Various strategical choices can be related to migrants' agency in a given context, and Ruhs and Anderson (2010) found empirical evidence indicating that "semi-compliance" practices offer room for agency for both migrants and employers. Migrants who are legally residents, but work without having the right to work, and their employers are, in fact, strategic actors who manage (il)legality to obtain more economic benefits from this employment (Ruhs and Anderson 2010: 207).

The migration-related experiences shared in the interviews reveal that gender is a key differential in structuring migrants' work trajectories. A series of comparative studies pointed out that within the European framework coexist different gender cultures (Pfau-Effinger 1998; Duncan and Pfau-Effinger 2002) and gender regimes (Sundström 2003), and these constitute the specific basis for better understanding the relationship between women's participation in the labor market and their share of domestic work. M. Voicu (2004) analyzed different European models of women's participation in paid work and domestic work and pointed out that Romania, similar to other Eastern European countries, is characterized by a high level of women participation in the labor market even if the bulk of domestic chores still remains women's duty. In a similar fashion, Mureşan and Hărăguş (2015) emphasized how the traditional Romanian model of family puts more emphasis on the role played by women within the family context, as they are the main family members responsible for child care and most domestic tasks. From this perspective, to better understand women's work trajectories, we have to consider several additional events in their life paths (e.g., marriage and childbirth) and other roles assumed within the family context (e.g., unbalanced gender distribution of domestic tasks, child upbringing, caring for other family members). In addition, we must emphasize that this chapter looks only at work trajectories of men and women with non-tertiary education, a factor that strongly influences their labor opportunities before migration, during migration, and upon return

(Diaconu 2014: 106). In brief, the national gender regime put pressure on women to build professional careers linked to paid employment, but simultaneously, there is a diffuse set of expectations about performing domestic tasks and providing care for other family members in need. All these aspects build a fertile ground for researching individual work trajectories of return migrants using a gendered perspective.

Methodology

To explore changes in work arrangements with a life-course perspective, this chapter is based on life story interviews conducted with long-term Romanian migrants who lived for at least five years in another EU country. Out of a total of 40 interviews collected within the MIGLIFE project, we selected only those individuals who had not graduated from a tertiary level of education and who returned to Romania. This methodological decision was taken to ensure a more homogenous sample in which a gender analysis could be better conducted. The final sample included 19 people (13 men and 6 women) between 27 and 49 years old (active in the labor market). As we pointed out, in Romania, the labor market offers disproportionate opportunities depending on rural or urban residency, and our sample is balanced in this respect.

The interview guide was designed using life-history logic that seeks to capture life experiences from childhood to interviewees' present life stage, as well as their life plans and satisfaction levels with their lives overall. The interviews were transcribed verbatim, and all aspects considered relevant for analyzing work trajectories were coded using specialized software (NVivo 11). Grounded in this analytical endeavor, we developed a typology that is explained later in the chapter. Bridging relevant literature with our findings, we developed a series of theoretical work-trajectory models, each underpinned by several cases deemed relevant for achieving a better understanding of the various factors that affect returnees' work trajectories.

All interviewees grew up in Romania and emigrated in early adulthood, lived for a long period abroad (although the aforementioned minimum period is five years, the average period for the interviewees is over 12 years), and had moved back to Romania when the interviews were conducted. This analytical distinction between three different periods is more complicated in cases when periods of circularity between origin and destinations are noted in some stories. This is one of the reasons why we decided to offer extra details on some types of work trajectories and not extract only small illustrative pieces from interviews. The qualitative analysis is presented in a way that aims to take advantage of the full richness of life stories told in the interviews. Osella and Osella (2006: 569) argued for the usefulness of unpacking qualitative data to a deeper degree "rather than chopping them into tiny ethno-bites." In a similar fashion, Qureshi (2012) used a strongly narrative approach that provides a thick description of migrant life stories, emphasizing their health problems and how they affected their working lives in London.

Analysis and Findings

The analytical part of the chapter follows returnees' work trajectories, paying special attention to the gender dimension, as well as to the distinction between periods of time spent in the origin country and abroad. Building on comprehensive case studies, our approach tries to go beyond reductive analyses, which are usually used for illustrating migrants' work experiences. To accomplish this, each subsection introduces typical cases of work trajectories that are further compared at the end of the chapter.

Women's Work Trajectories

In analyzing the work status of women before migration, it becomes clear that before migrating, none of them had a satisfying job situation in terms of earnings, stability, and prospects for a professional career, creating a strong incentive to migrate. From this perspective, working abroad holds promise for better work prospects. In this context, a difference can be drawn between women who were single when they emigrated and independently decided to leave for work reasons and those who were in stable relationships and for whom migration could be viewed as a *joint venture*. In the latter case, partners decided to emigrate together immediately after marriage or with a clear plan for a future wedding, but it is difficult to determine definitively whether the decision to emigrate was softly imposed by one of the partners.

The Agentic Model
This model is built on the idea that individual women are characterized by a high degree of autonomy in making the decision to emigrate, in taking and keeping jobs during their migration periods, and in adjusting upon

their return. This type of agency is defined as an individual's decision to overcome structural constraints, with little dependency on others (mainly partners). To illustrate how agency could manifest in the specific case of less-educated women with migration experience, we explore Anna's work trajectory as a migrant who eventually returned home. At the time of the interview, she was 31 years old.

Before migration, Anna grew up in a small industrial town that was strongly affected by the transition from communism to capitalism, which led to local industrial facilities closing down. This left her with no job prospects locally. In high school, Anna learned that some of her classmates were better off financially because their mothers worked abroad in elderly care.

> *In my hometown, there were many women abroad (...) I had some school colleagues and their mothers earned money and helped them. They had mobile phones, and at that time, the mobile phones were new things. They had sweets, they had nicer clothes, and I wished (for) all these things.*

Her decision to migrate and work in elderly care in Germany was made after trying to establish a career in Romania. She was unable to attend a university because she did not obtain a study grant, and after that, she decided to become a cook through a program for unemployed people. Anna obtained the certificate and worked for a few months as a cook, but she quit due to deceitful practices by her employer, who did not pay her wages. She then turned to a local, informal-work intermediary that provided jobs abroad in elderly care in exchange for a negotiated percentage of earnings. At the time, she was 19 years old.

During migration, her first work experience abroad in Germany was based on an informal agreement with the family of a woman who was over 80 years old. She lived in the house as the caregiver and became part of the family.

> *I stayed three years (with) that woman, and after that, she died. I felt very sorry for her. I was fond of her more than of my grandmother. She suffered (from) a little dementia, but no one took her to a doctor. I noticed this, but she was nice (even) with her dementia. (...) This changed my perception on life. I started to see that old people still have young souls. (...) It was the first time when I stayed with an old person, and I started to talk to her.*

After this work experience, she decided to return because she felt like she had a special relationship with this woman and could not take care of another old person. She moved back to her hometown for a short while, seeking employment without success.

Anna's next period working abroad was characterized by insecurity and stressful experiences. She started to look again for jobs in elderly care in Germany. Using contacts established during her first stay, she found a new job relatively easily. This time, the work experience was less pleasant, and she couldn't stay more than three months with an old woman who also suffered from dementia and who treated her badly. Using personal connections, she managed to find a new job for six months caring for another old woman who died suddenly when Anna took a short trip to Romania. She had to look again for work and found a married couple:

> *They were husband and wife. He was in advanced stages of dementia and was aggressive. He did not sleep (at) night, slammed the doors, and it was a catastrophe. His wife had some bleeding and damage on the brain, and she was half-paralyzed.*

She left this job after six weeks. After this difficult and tumultuous period, she found another old couple and cared for them for roughly four years. During this period of work security, she met a Romanian man who worked in seasonal agriculture in Germany, and they decided to get married. These years of financial stability (she bought a car and saved money in a bank) and her desire to return made her more confident that she could build a professional career back home. Her first step in this direction was to attend a nursing school in Romania. "I thought to invest in my future with this school, and I said that it is the moment to start to work legal."

> *This is not physical work; it is psychological work. The old people, in Germany, they take very good care of them. I had to keep them occupied all the time, I had to give them a schedule, a rhythm of the day… a lot of affectivity. So, you cannot be cold (distant) with them. You have to be calm, to smile, to take their hands in yours, to hug them, to praise them. (…) For me, it was satisfying, and I felt joy to see that they are enthusiastic to do something with you. I had to be there for them all the time, and only when they slept, I had some time for me.*

Anna decided *to return* when she became pregnant and decided that her type of work was not an appropriate environment for raising a child. At the time of the interview, she already started to explore job opportunities as a nurse locally because her maternity-leave period was about to end.

The working experience abroad convinced Anna that she had the necessary skills to become a professional nurse. Being unsatisfied with the precarity embedded in informal jobs abroad and thinking about her new motherhood situation, she decided the best option was to obtain a nursing diploma and build a career in Romania. In this case, the return context is slightly different from the origin because she now lives in a village near a relatively developed Romanian city, as opposed to her underdeveloped hometown.

The Dependency Model
This model departs from what we labeled "migration as a joint venture," in which women were at least somewhat pressured by their romantic partners to migrate, to keep or quit jobs, and to return. This model is one in which the migration experience heavily affects women's work trajectories because they are dependent on their husbands' work and migration trajectories. The structural determinants are mainly linked to the traditional model of family that embedded an unbalanced relationship between partners (the man is the provider model and the woman is mainly responsible for domestic tasks, even if she has a paid job). We unpack Rona's work trajectories as an example of this type of limited and dependent agentic choice. At the time of the interview, she was 38 years old.

To understand "migration as a family project," Rona offers a good example. She married immediately after she completed post-high-school education. At the time of emigration, she was 21 and had no work experience when she left with her husband for Italy.

> *At that moment, my links to Romania were quite broken up. If I remained in the country, certainly it would have been different. I mean on the professional part… I would not have left myself like that… I mean I was still in school. I could have continued with an internship; it would have been totally different.*

Although Rona had a certificate as a dental technician, she decided to put her professional life on hold and follow her husband abroad, even if her educational background did not constitute a competitive advantage in Italy's labor market.

Rona's decision to emigrate is a consequence of a couples' strategy in which the woman decides to follow her partner for his job abroad. Her first migration experience lasted eight years (1999–2007). Her work experiences during this time subjectively evaluated as being insignificant to the household budget.

I was the one who insisted (that I) work. If it was (up to) my husband, I could stay home because it did not make a difference; my salary was modest. I don't (mean to) say that 1,000–1,200 euro are not good, but this was not changing our life.

Elsewhere in her life, Rona applied this type of logic in several other circumstances. For example, in Italy, her husband "insisted" on having a child. At that time, she had a work contract at a hotel, but during the pregnancy, she had to go on medical leave because she encountered some health problems and a premature birth. After her maternity leave, she left her previous job to raise her child, although the decision to have a child was also rather imposed on her by her partner who "insisted that it is the time." When the child was one year old, they returned to Romania and stayed there for roughly three years (2007–2010). At that time, they wanted to test life in Romania and finish an already-started project of building a house. Her mother helped her take care of the child, and Rona enjoyed working for a year as a secretary for a public notary, but she had to quit when they decided to migrate again.

I was very fond of this job. I learned a lot of things. I felt sorry to quit because I learned many, many things. I really liked to work in the field of cadaster (official land-survey data), and I was very centered on this (…). Whenever I had the chance and some time, I was instructing myself. I was reading what we have to do because there are many rules.

Rona decided to migrate again because they did not finish their house, and her husband's work prospects in Romania were less lucrative than abroad. Her investments in skills and abilities in the field of *cadaster* were considered less important, and they returned to Italy for six more years (2010–2016). Even though Rona held several jobs in Italy (in a hotel, a restaurant, a bar), she constantly renounced her work opportunities because her husband was in a better work position. Even if this dynamic is encountered in other *gendered regimes*, migration seems to increase this type of inequality.

Nowadays, *upon return*, she is highly dependent on her husband's earnings, and her professional situation is rather uncertain. She is thinking about pursuing further education, as she shows little interest in working for a regular wage in Romania.

Today, we find ourselves a bit lost because we have nothing. We do not have (educational) basis; we have nothing. We are not connected. It is hard to be on your feet here. If you do not become something, I don't know, I don't see myself. Let's say that I will graduate a college, to have a new diploma or something. If not, you have to start your own business. I don't want to go to work here for 250 euro per month, certainly no... no.

During all these periods, in her family, the distribution of domestic tasks was unbalanced, and in her words, "My husband is responsible only of his job and to bring money home. The other responsibilities are all mine."

The Mixed Model
These two examples allowed us to explore two different work trajectories of women with extensive migration experience. The agentic model illustrates cases in which the woman's work trajectory is the result of her independent choices in the given contexts, from origin to destination and back. In contrast, the dependency model draws the main lines for understanding cases in which contextual determinants from origin and destination forced the woman to interrupt a work trajectory and forgo her career desires. Rona worked during her stay in Italy, even though her husband earned enough for the entire family. She invested in a secretary job she liked during her temporary return to Romania. Her unstructured desire to return to school can be seen as a struggle for autonomy—to build her own professional life. However, up until the time of the interview, the structural constraints were stronger than her actions. This very detailed tale enabled us to emphasize that a more nuanced approach must go beyond the dichotomic approach in terms of agency and structural constraints. Based on these considerations, we suggest a third model that incorporates features pertaining to both the previous models presented above.

The mixed model includes cases in which migration overlaps with a transition from the agentic model toward the dependent model or a transition from dependency to gaining independence, combining elements from the other two models. For example, even if a woman emigrates with her partner, during migrations, she loses or gains independence through work.

In general, the migration experience seems to increase the financial stability of the household, but if we look at women's work trajectories, there is high heterogeneity. The type of employment during migration that they find (mainly domestic services, in our case) is not sufficient to compensate for their low levels of education, and usually the human capital gained during migration is not directly usable in finding employment upon return.

Men's Work Trajectories

Male interviewees' subjective evaluations about migration's effects on their lives generally were positive. Our research benefited from an excellent analytical opportunity because our subjects emigrated during the first decade of transition, remained abroad for a relatively long period, and, in many cases, experienced transitions from not having the right to work (working informally) to gaining legal status, then returning after Romania joined the European Union. The average period spent abroad by men from our sample is about 12 years. Following their work trajectories, one can see at the individual level how migration ensures accumulation of economic resources, fortifies their position within the family context, and creates more fertile ground for entrepreneurial initiatives.

The Agentic Model (Migration as a Path to Entrepreneurship)
This model depicts migrants as agents who are actively looking for work opportunities using economic and human capital accumulated abroad. They creatively select investment opportunities and combine bits of knowledge to build an entrepreneurial career. We present a detailed profile of Sorin's work trajectory to illustrate how the migration experience represents a path to entrepreneurship. At the time of the interview, he was 43 years old.

Before migration, Sorin completed vocational school immediately after the collapse of the communist regime. Structural constraints of that period led to him exploring all kinds of work opportunities. He left his hometown and worked in Bucharest for a while but was fired after punching a supervisor. He then worked for short periods of time in construction in Yugoslavia and dabbled in small-scale trade with goods imported from Turkey.

> *I was, a few times, in Yugoslavia. You were (gone) two or three weeks (then returned). And after that, I left (for) Turkey. I was there for three weeks at work, and after that, I started to import goods. You were going and (could) bring some goods and sell them here. (...) After that, I left again (for) Yugoslavia, and I started to work with a team in construction. I worked with them for about five years. I was going from springtime to autumn, but I was still visiting home during these periods. I was very well-paid there.*

Sorin's decision to migrate was linked to his determination to explore all kinds of opportunities abroad (some of them not completely legal). He chose Italy, and after one week in Italy, he managed to obtain a job in agriculture. His migration experience was a period of work stability, even though he constantly looked to improve his earnings.

> *(The job) was in an orchard. First, I had to plant very small trees. After one year, I obtained a job as a tractor driver, and I stayed there for eight years. I can say that during these years, one could earn money and other things. (...) After five years, I (returned) for the first time to the [origin] country because only then I (could) obtain my papers.*

When he re(established) connections in Romania, he started to think about opportunities to earn money by helping other irregular Romanian migrants in Italy return to Romania. Some of his practices were not completely legal, but this provided him with increased financial resources. This lasted only for about a year, but it also increased his tolerance for risk.

After a few more years in Italy, Sorin was not satisfied anymore with the money earned in agriculture and decided to use some of his skills gained before migration.

> *I started to work in construction. I worked for a short while with a team, and after that, I was employed by a bigger company who worked with cranes at 30 meters from the ground. We made the front parts for buildings. (...) I worked there for one year and a half, and after that, I started my own company. This way was better for them because they were not responsible for you anymore. They paid you more, but they had no responsibility.*

He bought a house in Romania, started to invest in more land, and explored several additional investment possibilities. During his migration experience, he decided that the only way to have a good life was to be focused on work, so work gained importance in his life. Part of his migration experience also overlapped with personal changes. He married a Romanian woman he met in Italy, and this marriage lasted about nine years. They divorced, and he obtained custody of his son, who was four years old at the time. Upon his return, Sorin's mother helped him raise the child, while he continued to focus mainly on his work life.

Sorin started his entrepreneurial career during migration. Several factors must be taken into consideration to understand his work trajectory toward entrepreneurship. First, there were his previous informal trade activities (importing goods from Turkey and selling them in Romania), "helping" Romanians in Italy visit Romania, and pressure from an Italian construction company that preferred to work with self-employed people. Second, the migration experience allowed him to save up financial capital to start several small-scale businesses. Upon his return, he invested in various businesses (bakery, agriculture, car rental, construction), which he viewed as safety measures for securing the future of his family.

> *I opened the bakery (…) and I returned in the country. Here, you have to do everything to survive. I opened a farm with 100 pigs. Now I have about 70, but I decided to sell them… Then I started to buy cars for renting them, and now I extended this business a little bit (…). Nowadays, I also work in the construction industry [self-employed].*

The Dependency Model

This model is relevant for understanding a specific work trajectory determined by structural constraints from origin and destination countries. In contrast to the entrepreneurial model, which emphasized individuals' agency, the dependency model illustrates cases concerning those who were forced to emigrate and return by structural determinants in the labor market. Lack of agency is more visible upon return and can be illustrated by Romanians who lost their jobs abroad due to the recession started in 2008 and who were forced by circumstances to return to their home communities. This is in stark contrast to the *dependency model* for women, mainly because extra-familial factors are perceived as more significant. Our main example for this pattern is provided by Radu, a man who was 40 years old at the time of the interview.

Radu emigrated in 2001, and after a short period working in Germany (a few weeks), he moved to Spain to search for work. At the time of emigration, he had a job, but he was unsatisfied with his salary. He lived and worked in Spain for almost 15 years, and during this time, he changed jobs several times, got married, and had a daughter. He got married in 2011, and his wife joined him in Spain and occasionally worked in the domestic sector. Upon his return, their daughter was three years old. They returned after a period of work insecurity generated by the lack of labor opportunities.

> *At the moment of return, I had several experiences of intermittent employment and unemployment. I was in unemployment, and I have also had periods of assistance after unemployment. Exactly at the moment of return, I was again unemployed. So, during these periods of unemployment, money was low, it is not enough… and if you are also with the family—it is not enough, not even for*

rent and food for a single person... to survive (...). And this last time, I said that it is enough. I took the benefits from unemployment, and when the period after unemployment started, we decided to go and try in Romania. In Spain, it is very hard these days because they are recovering very slow after the crisis from 2008.

The Mixed Model
Positive outcomes in different aspects of individuals' life might be associated with an inconsistent work trajectory. During migration, individuals experience a period of stability (concerning financial and family dimensions of life), but upon return, they are often unable (and sometimes they don't want) to gain stable employment, and thereby prefer the flexibility associated with informal self-employment. This situation is rather specific for people who worked in construction abroad and who can use their new skills to compete in the local market for services in this sector. Marian was 36 years old at the time of this interview, and we briefly present his work life for a better understanding of this model.

Marian has only eight years of formal, primary education, and he also completed a short-term training course as a painter before migration. At an early age, he left school and worked for his father as a mechanic, accumulating practical skills and knowledge in this field. Immediately afterward, he changed informal jobs in his hometown. He thinks that this formative period as a worker was very important during his stay abroad because he already had good skills to work in the construction industry, and in his view, this was more important than returning to school.

He decided to emigrate because he was very disappointed with the wages in Romania and found job prospects lacking. Even if he was satisfied with the money earned abroad, he knew he could not adjust to the lifestyles there (Belgium, Denmark, and Spain). He lived for almost nine years in Spain and for a few months in Belgium and Denmark. He worked only in the construction industry informally during the entire period. He viewed the time he spent abroad as an essential transition to adulthood (through work) and as a period to accumulate financial resources to build a house. During migration, he married a Romanian who joined him in Spain, and they had two children. When the money abroad was the same as what he could earn in Romania, he decided to return to origin, but in a different village.

Upon return, he decided to work in the construction industry, but at the time of the interview, he was self-employed on the black market. His attitudes toward work changed because he was very affected by the experiences of overworking abroad. He wanted to reduce work hours to a minimum, so he could work on his apiculture business at home, while taking a temporary job in construction now and then from other people in his village. He decided not to search for stable jobs in Romania because he thinks being self-employed is the best work situation for him. There were no perceived advantages in the labor market upon his return, and his lack of formal qualifications is subjectively viewed as one of the main problems with reintegrating into the local workforce. Despite this, he does not plan to invest further in education. Lack of re(adaptation) to some structural aspects upon return, a negative attitude toward work due to his overwork experiences from abroad, and little interest in working for local employers are all exhibited by male migrants who fall into this model.

Discussion and Conclusions

This chapter's focus on work trajectories responds to the need for a detailed portrait of how migration affects individuals' life courses. The chapter argues for the usefulness of a gendered approach in analyzing individuals' work trajectories. For each gender, intricacies between two contrasting types of work trajectories are analyzed using a classical sociological distinction between individuals' agency and structural determinants.

Building on the perspective which emphasizes a limited capacity for improving work trajectories through migration for low skilled migrants, the paper illustrates, both cases of returnees who did and who did not enhance their professional career. Some of them subjectively evaluate their work trajectory mainly in optimistic terms and emphasize the positive outcomes of the migration experience, while others are in a complex condition with low levels of security, satisfaction, and agency. Further quantitative research can help to draw specific profiles for the group of returnees who benefited from the migration experience in terms of work trajectory, as well as for those who are in vulnerable positions after return. The chapter argued that gender and individual agency can represent important variables for understanding the work path of return migrants during all the relevant periods.

Table 5.1 presents a synthetic overview of several essential features of the evolution of Romanian returnees' work trajectories, in direct relation to the theoretical models introduced in the analysis part of the chapter.

Table 5.1 A gendered view of two contrasting types of Romanian returnees' work trajectories

		BEFORE MIGRATION	DURING MIGRATION	UPON RETURN
WOMEN'S WORK TRAJECTORIES	The agentic model	Independent decision to emigrate (adopted after a period of struggle trying to find a good job at origin)	Migration is perceived as a temporary strategy of financial accumulation through work (mainly financial autonomy)	Return is motivated by the desire for professionalization and gaining a better position in the labor market. There are also cases of pregnancy/childbirth.
	The dependency model	The emigration decision is perceived as a "joint venture" in which the man assumes the main role	A woman's work life is perceived as being less important compared with the man's due to earning power. Having children can interrupt their migration experience.	The decision to return is made mainly by the man, and upon return, the woman depends on her partner's earnings
MEN'S WORK TRAJECTORIES	The entrepreneurial model (agentic)	An individual emigration decision is adopted after a period of exploration of labor opportunities (at origin and abroad)	Migration increases individuals' tolerance for risk (e.g., through informality) and secures the necessary financial resources to pursue entrepreneurship	Return is linked to an entrepreneurial project (they are looking for opportunities for investments during migration and decide to return when their subjective evaluation leaves them confident that the business is sustainable)
	The dependency model	The migration decision is forced by circumstances (dependence on migration network also can be a factor)	They manifest a higher dependence on the social system of benefits at destination (e.g., repeated periods of unemployment)	Return is determined by structural factors (e.g., he lost his job at destination and was unable to find another one)

The gendered approach proves to be very helpful in understanding different migration pathways and destandardized work trajectories (before, during, and after migration). Each of these periods presents different types of challenges for women and men. Before migration, Romanian women and men were affected by the structural transformations related to the country's new market economy. At the individual level, we can see that the push factors are subjectively related to the low level of satisfaction with employment opportunities at origin. It is important to determine whether the decision to emigrate was taken independently by the woman or was part of a family "joint venture" because the first case could lead to increased autonomy, and the second creates premises for dependency.

Our empirical results can have direct implications on a policy agenda of return migration. Work paths of returnees are affected differently by the experience of migration, and as a consequence, policies designed to attract potential return migrants have to provide distinct mechanisms of support for men and women. For example, we can look at some return policies which aim to stimulate entrepreneurship among returnees, while literature emphasizes that a typical entrepreneur is rather a male with heroic character and bold personality traits (Hamilton 2013). As we already noted and exemplified above, men are more attracted toward entrepreneurship. In some cases, this type of program strengthens men agency and increases women dependency due to men's preference for family return instead of individual return. Then again, women who return are more attracted to continue their education and to gain new qualifications. Policies designed to reintegrate women returnees, especially those without tertiary education, in the labor market have to take into consideration the specificity of these needs.

During migration, we can note that structural determinants from the destination context have a major influence on obtaining formal or informal employment and that individuals are usually directed toward specific sectors where they can find employment more easily (e.g., domestic, construction). Individuals' lack of human capital and precarious conditions in the labor market influence migrants' work trajectories, according to interviewees' responses. On the one hand, migration can increase individuals' financial autonomy and tolerance for risk. On the other hand, we pointed out certain elements of an increased dependency on partners or state social service benefits. The decision to return is presented as a complex process in which work status, marriage, and childbirth are given different levels of importance depending on gender.

Upon return, one of the main differences between women and men's work trajectories is related to their attitudes toward accumulating formal human capital (higher education or job training). Women's subjective evaluations of their positions in the labor market indicated feelings of instability and vulnerability, and their response to this tended to lean toward furthering their education. During migration, their financial expectations increased, and upon return, they decided to invest in human capital to improve their chances in the labor market. An exception to this is represented by those cases in which, upon their return, their work trajectories are linked to family businesses. On the other hand, changes in expectations related to work make men more eager to become entrepreneurs, so the experience of migration encourages them to start a business upon return.

In terms of human capital, there are certain outcomes of the migration experience, and the long period spent abroad can be enough to increase proficiency levels in the language of the destination country. However, these abilities are used only sporadically upon return, and this is not perceived as a competitive advantage in the labor market. Other skills and competences gained abroad are associated with the transition to adulthood—and to a more stable life period.

The research has limits and some of these can be managed better in further studies. The research design can include a control group of people without any experience of migration but similar in other relevant features. This will be useful mainly for better delineating the role played by the constraints of society of origin and by the experience of migration itself in shaping individuals' work trajectories. For instance, one can ask whether events related to family formation and childbirth have different impacts on work trajectories of migrants or nonmigrants.

In a nutshell, this chapter followed the work experiences of a specific type of returnees and discovered that longtime migration experiences affected their work trajectories. Although our sample size is small, and caution is needed to interpret our findings, we offered several examples of individuals' agency, revealed in given contexts at origin and destination, paying special attention to the role played by gender in such a complex process.

References

Anderson, Bridget. 2010. Migration, Immigration Controls, and the Fashioning of Precarious Workers. *Work, Employment and Society* 24 (2): 300–317.

Anghel, G. Remus. 2008. Changing Statuses: Freedom of Movement, Locality, and Transnationality of Irregular Romanian Migrants in Milan. *Journal of Ethnic and Migration Studies* 34 (5): 787–802.

Bettio, Francesca, and Alina Verashchagina. 2009. *Gender Segregation in the Labor Market. Root Causes, Implications, and Policy Responses in the EU*. Luxembourg: Publications Office of the European Union.

Borjas, J. George. 1999. *Heaven's Door: Immigration Policy and the American Economy.* Princeton: Princeton University Press.

Charles, Maria. 2011. A World of Difference: International Trends in Women's Economic Status. *Annual Review of Sociology* 37: 355–371.

Constantinescu, Monica. 2004. The Importance of Weak Links in Migration. *Sociologie Românească* II (4): 169–186.

Diaconu, Laura. 2014. Education and Labor Market Outcomes in Romania. *Eastern Journal of European Studies* 5 (1): 99–112.

Duncan, Simon, and Birgit Pfau-Effinger. 2002. *Gender, Economy, and Culture in the European Union.* London and New York: Routledge.

Dustmann, Christian. 1999. Temporary Migration, Human Capital and Language Fluency of Migrants. *Scandinavian Journal of Economics* 101 (2): 297–314.

Dustmann, Christian, and Oliver Kirchkamp. 2002. The Optimal Migration Duration and Activity Choice After Re-migration. *Journal of Development Economics* 67: 351–372.

Evans, Karen. 2002. The Challenges of Making Learning Visible: Problems and Issues in Recognizing Tacit Skills and Key Competences. In *Working to Learn: Transforming Learning in the Workplace,* ed. Karen Evans, Phil Hodkinson, and Lorna Unwin. London: Kogan Page Limited.

Evans, Melvyn, Stephen Syrett, and Colin Williams. 2006. *Informal Economic Activities and Deprived Neighborhoods.* London: Department for Communities and Local Government.

Gurak, T. Douglas, and F.E. Caces. 1992. Migration Networks and the Shaping of Migration Systems. In *International Migration Systems. A Global Approach,* ed. Mary M. Kritz, Lin Lean Lim, and Hania Zlotnik. Oxford: Clarendon Press.

Hamilton, Eleanor. 2013. The Discourse of Entrepreneurial Masculinities (and Feminities). *Entrepreneurship & Regional Development: An International Journal* 25 (1–2): 90–99.

Hennebry, L. Jenna. 2014. Transnational Precarity: Women's Migration Work and Mexican Seasonal Agricultural Migration. *International Journal of Sociology* 44 (3): 42–59.

Lutz, Helma. 2008. When Home Becomes a Workplace: Domestic Work as an Ordinary Job in Germany? In *Migration and Domestic Work: A European Perspective on a Global Theme,* ed. Helma Lutz. Aldershot: Ashgate Publishing Limited.

Malyutina, Darya. 2015. *Migrant Friendships in a Super-Diverse City: Russian-Speakers and Their Social Relationships in London in the 21st Century.* Stuttgart: Ibidem-Verlag.

Mureşan, Cornelia, and Paul-Teodor Hărăguş. 2015. Norms of Filial Obligation and Actual Support to Parents in Central and Eastern Europe. *Romanian Journal of Population Studies* IX (2): 49–81.

Osella, Caroline, and Filippo Osella. 2006. Once Upon a Time in the West? Stories of Migration and Modernity from Kerala, South India. *Journal of the Royal Anthropological Institute* 12 (3): 569–588.

Perrons, Diane. 2007. *Gender Divisions and Working Time in the New Economy: Changing Patterns of Work*. Edward Elgar Publishing: Care and Public Policy in Europe and North America.

Pfau-Effinger, Birgit. 1998. Gender Cultures and the Gender Arrangement—A Theoretical Framework for Cross-National Gender Research. *Innovations* 11 (2): 147–166.

Qureshi, Kaveri. 2012. Pakistani Labor Migration and Masculinity: Industrial Working Life, the Body and Transnationalism. *Global Networks* 12 (4): 485–504.

Ruhs, Martin, and Bridget Anderson. 2010. Semi-Compliance and Illegality in Migrant Labour Markets: An Analysis of Migrants, Employers and the State in the UK. *Population, Space and Place* 16: 195–211.

Ryan, Louise. 2011. Migrants' Social Networks and Weak Ties: Accessing Resources and Constructing Relationships Post-Migration. *The Sociological Review* 59 (4): 707–724.

Sandu, Dumitru. 2006. *Living Abroad on a Temporary Basis. The Economic Migration of Romanians: 1990–2006*. Bucharest.

———. 2010. *Lumile sociale ale migrației internaționale*. Iași: Polirom.

Schierup, Carl-Ulrik, Aleksandra Alund, and Branka Likic-Brboric. 2015. Migration, Precarization, and the Democratic Deficit in Global Governance. *International Migration* 53 (3): 50–63.

Scrinzi, Francesca. 2008. Migrations and the Restructuring of the Welfare State in Italy: Change and Continuity in the Domestic Work Sector. In *Migration and Domestic Work: A European Perspective on a Global Theme*, ed. Helma Lutz. Aldershot: Ashgate Publishing Limited.

Șerban, Monica, and Bogdan Voicu. 2010. Romanian Migrants to Spain: In—Or Outside the Migration Networks a Matter of Time? *Revue D'études Comparatives Est-Ouest* 41 (4): 97–124.

Shelley, Toby. 2007. *Exploited: Migrant Labour in the New World Economy*. London: Zed Books.

Sundström, Eva. 2003. *Gender Regimes, Family Policies and Attitudes to Female Employment: A Comparison of Germany, Italy and Sweden*. Doctoral dissertation in Sociology at the Faculty of Social Sciences, Umeå University.

Thornton, H. Patricia. 1999. The Sociology of Entrepreneurship. *Annual Review of Sociology* 25: 19–46.

Tudor, Elena. 2017. Return Migration in a Csángós Village in Romania. In *Religions and Migrations in the Black Sea Region*, ed. Eleni Sideri and Lydia Efthymia Roupakia. Palgrave Macmillan.

Vianello, Francesca Alice. 2016. International Migrations and Care Provisions for Elderly People Left Behind. The cases of the Republic of Moldova and Romania. *European Journal of Social Work* 19 (5): 779–794.

Vianello, Francesca Alice, and Devi Saccheto. 2016. Migrant Workers' Routes to the Informal Economy During the Economic Crisis: Structural Constraints and Subjective Motivations. *Prakseologia* 158: 299–321.

Vlase, Ionela. 2013a. My Husband is a Patriot! Gender and Romanian Family Return Migration from Italy. *Journal of Ethnic and Migration Studies* 39 (5): 741–758.

———. 2013b. Women's Social Remittances and Their Implications at Household Level: A Case Study of Romanian Migration to Italy. *Migration Letters* 10 (1): 81–90.

Voicu, Malina. 2004. Work and Family Life in Europe: Value Patterns and Policy Making. In *European Values at the Turn of the Millennium*, ed. Wil Arts and Loek Halman. Leiden and Boston: Brill.

Williams, M. Allan. 2007. International Labor Migration and Tacit Knowledge Transactions: A Multi-Level Perspective. *Global Networks* 7 (1): 29–50.

Williams, M. Allan, and Vladimir Baláž. 2005. What Human Capital, Which Migrants? Returned Skilled Migration to Slovakia from the UK. *International Migration Review* 39 (2): 439–468.

Williams, C. Colin. 2009a. Formal and Informal Employment in Europe: Beyond Dualistic Representations. *European Urban and Regional Studies* 16 (2): 147–159.

———. 2009b. The Motives of Off-the-Books Entrepreneurs: Necessity—Or Opportunity Driven? *International Entrepreneurship and Management Journal* 5 (2): 203–217.

Williams, Fiona. 2012. Converging Variations in Migrant Care Work in Europe. *Journal of European Social Policy* 22 (4): 363–376.

CHAPTER 6

Fragmented Careers, Gender, and Migration During the Great Recession

Francesca Alice Vianello

In Italy, the economic crisis of 2008 hit migrant workers hard, rattling their already-precarious existence (Lewis et al. 2014) by interrupting their work paths, among other disruptions (Istat 2014). Drawing on longitudinal qualitative research based on Moroccan and Romanian migrant workers living in Northern Italy, this chapter analyzes the effects of employment fragmentation on other social-accomplishment lines.

I approach this subject from the Chicago School's conceptualization of *career* to understand migrants' routes in the labor market in relation to other dimensions of their life paths, such as gender identities and roles (Moen 2001), and migration careers (Martiniello and Rea 2014). This perspective allows me to provide a new contribution to studies on migrants' careers and their reactions to times of crisis. In the first case, my contribution concerns analysis of the gendered dimension of low-income migrants' careers, while in the second case, I add some insights into migrants' trajectories in times of crisis, considering both migration seniority and

F. A. Vianello (✉)
University of Padua, Padua, Italy

© The Author(s) 2018
I. Vlase, B. Voicu (eds.), *Gender, Family, and Adaptation of Migrants in Europe*, https://doi.org/10.1007/978-3-319-76657-7_6

settlement. In both cases, the life-course approach (Heinz and Krüger 2001) is crucial to understanding how the historical event of the Great Recession has produced multiple breaks in migrants' social-accomplishment lines. This perspective is rarely adopted in migration studies and is more common among studies on native populations (Edwards and Irwin 2010).

According to Everett C. Hughes, a career is a person's course through life, especially through that portion of life in which he or she works (Hughes 1997: 389). The concept of career includes the subject's point of view, since it is 'the moving perspective in which the person sees his life as a whole and interprets the meaning of his various attributes, actions, and the things which happen to him' (Hughes 1937: 409). Additionally, the scholar pointed out that historical events can break people's life trajectories, such as unemployment, wars, and technological innovations (Hughes 1950). Accordingly, the relationship between an individual's life and historical events can define people's careers, requiring continuous adjustments to subjective understandings of these careers.

Moreover, Howard S. Becker and Anselm Strauss (1956), who built on Hughes' analysis, argued that career movements are not necessarily linear and upward, given that 'some people never set foot on a work escalator, but move from low job to low job' (p. 260). Second, they stressed that workers' occupational positions can elicit different meanings depending on social stratification and subjective understanding; that is, attaining a certain position may be considered a success to one person but a failure to another.

Another important point stressed by Hughes is that even if the job is very important in defining individual's career, it cannot be understood apart from the whole: the career is by no means exhausted in a series of business and professional achievements. There are other points at which one's life touches the social order, other lines of social accomplishment—influence, responsibility, and recognition (Hughes 1937: 410).

Another crucial line of people's social accomplishment that Hughes (1937) marginally stresses is associated with the gendered life course, namely, the sequence of different roles and relationships expected of men and women at different life stages (Moen 2001). For an analysis of this topic in relation to migrants, it is necessary to first consider their ever-evolving reference models concerning the relationship between professional life and gendered institutional clocks and norms, which are shaped by their culture, class, education, and religion. Second, it is crucial to consider the conflicts that could arise when migrants face destination societies' fluid reference models and the negotiations and everyday practices they adopt to face this plurality of models and structural constrains, such as the economic crisis.

Very few studies deal with gendered working identities and careers in the migratory context and with the impact of the economic downturn on migrants' occupational routes. The literature analyzing migrants' careers with a gender perspective usually focuses on women and on a narrow conceptualization of career, understanding it as the upward mobility of migrants in destination countries' labor markets (Cuban 2009; Liversage 2009). These studies often deal with skilled and highly skilled migrations and the frequent misrecognition of migrants' skills and education. However, as I have pointed out elsewhere (Escrivà and Vianello 2016), social research rarely analyzes migrants nonlinear' careers in the lower sectors of the labor market and even more rarely investigates interconnections between occupational paths and gendered life courses.

Interesting exceptions worth noting are studies that analyze migrants' working lives in different sectors of the labor market, such as care and hospitality services, and their negotiations between different gender roles and care obligations (Batnitzky's et al. 2009; Doyle and Timonen 2010; Hagelskamp's et al. 2011). These studies show that to understand migrants' careers, it is important to identify and understand migrants' goals and their strategies for achieving them according to their gender and how they are defined in relation to the values and norms of both origin and destination societies.

The fragmentation of migrants' work careers elicits another important break in migrants' life courses, threatening their migration careers. According to Martiniello and Rea (2014), the concept of *career* is crucial to the study of migrants' trajectories, as it allows researchers to consider both legal-institutional and socioeconomic paths, as well as subjective meanings within migration routes, based on differences between initial expectations and real-life migration experiences. This analytical category is useful for going beyond studies on new mobility strategies adopted by migrants after the economic downturn—for instance, returning home or remigrating (e.g., Ahrens 2013; Kahanec and Zimmermann 2016)—with the aim of achieving a more comprehensive understanding of how migration trajectories have been reformulated during the recession by settled migrants with different legal status, migration seniority, and reproductive responsibilities (Herrera 2012).

Socioeconomic Context

An optimal example of a Great Recession situation affecting migrants can be found in Italy, in the Veneto region of Northeast Italy. The area is one of the richest and most industrialized in the country, with a high migrant population. Moreover, it was hit relatively hard by the global economic crisis in the second half of the 2000s (Sacchetto and Vianello 2013).

Even though foreign labor in Italy increased in absolute terms during the crisis, when analyzing relative measures, the recession particularly pummelled working conditions among low-skilled migrant men compared with those of both native men and migrant women, pushing them toward even more precarious positions and reinforcing occupational segregation (Bonifazi and Marini 2014). For migrant men living in Northern Italy and employed in the manufacturing or construction industries, the probability of shifting from employment to unemployment and remaining jobless is significantly higher compared with that of Italian citizens, especially if they are non-EU citizens (Istat 2014). Conversely, migrant women have been affected less than their male counterparts because they are employed in sectors of the labor market that are less vulnerable to economic crises, such as domestic, cleaning, and personal home care services (Farris 2014). Likewise, during 2011–2013, the only positive dynamic detectable in the Italian labor market was in low-skilled and manual jobs, especially services for families (Fellini 2015).

Although the impact of the economic crisis on migrants' employment has been pronounced, increasing their unemployment rates, it is also true that their levels of employment have remained quite high, as migrants are compelled to find new jobs in a short time (Reyneri 2010). The limited unemployment benefits for flexible workers tend to prevent long unemployment spells for migrants.

Data and Methods

This chapter reports on research that investigated the impact of the Great Recession on migrants living in Veneto, sponsored by the Regional Agency 'Veneto Lavoro' and the University of Padua. It elicited longitudinal research data from in-depth interviews with Romanian and Moroccan workers, who are among the largest foreign-national populations in Italy.

Between December 2010 and April 2011, the research group contacted, by phone, all unemployed Moroccan and Romanian migrants registered at two public job centers. We conducted 435 phone questionnaires, then 170 in-depth interviews with migrants who, after answering the phone questionnaire, agreed to face-to-face interviews. In 2014–2015, we contacted the same people again, asking them whether they were available for more interviews. We succeeded in collecting 176 phone interviews and 40 in-depth interviews from that effort.

However, this selection method has some limits. Although it allowed us to reach a large and diversified group of migrants, it was not representative. During the second round of interviews, we could only reach those migrants who remained in Italy despite the recession, while we could not contact those who returned to Morocco or Romania, or moved to other EU countries. Moreover, we realized that phone contact was problematic because many respondents mistrusted phone surveys and refused to participate.

The in-depth interviews lasted between 60 and 90 minutes each and were conducted in different kinds of settings—bars, parks, respondents' houses, and universities—according to interviewees' preferences. Usually, only the interviewer and interviewee were present during interviews, but when the meetings took place in domestic settings, other members of interviewees' families were present. The interviews were conducted in Italian, except some cases in which we used Moroccan Arabic because of some respondents' low Italian fluency. The interviews were transcribed and analyzed through the support of Atlas.ti.

This chapter's research results are based on a sample of 40 people (21 women and 19 men) who were interviewed twice: in 2010–2011 and 2014–2015. Most were between 30 and 50 years old, married, and parents. The majority of participants were long-term migrants: Romanian migrants began arriving between 2000 and 2006, while Moroccans, especially men, arrived between 1990 and 1999. Their migratory seniority is reflected in their legal status: some Moroccans have obtained Italian citizenship, and most hold long-term EU permits.

Gendered Life Courses and Working Careers

In Morocco, women historically were subordinate to men, which was strongly associated with the spatial separation between men and women, in accordance with the Arab-Muslim patriarchy. Women living in urban areas and those belonging to the middle and upper classes particularly had been segregated in the domestic–private sphere, while men had been associated with the public sphere. This strict public–private dichotomy changed from the 1960s onward, when urban women entered the formal labor market (in rural areas, women always have worked on family farms). After this radical transformation, Moroccan working women were called upon to accommodate two types of identities and self-fulfillments: that of paid workers with rights and responsibilities and that of wives and mothers (Sadiqi and Ennaji 2006). However, in Morocco, formal working women are still a minority, as women's employment rate is 23% (men 66%) and women's inactivity rate is 74% (men 27%) (ILO 2013).

In Romania, women's participation in the labor market and their gendered life course have followed a different path. Traditionally, in this country as well, the patriarchal organization of society was rooted in the sexual division of labor, providing to women the primary duty of taking care of the family and the house. Later, during communist times, women were incorporated into the labor market, but the traditional sexual division of reproductive labor persisted, imposing on women a double burden. This radical transformation changed men's social position as well, since they were no longer the main breadwinners, given that the typical family changed to a dual-earner model. After the fall of the Ceausescu regime, Romanian society underwent a deep social, political, and economic transformation that engendered a revival of the traditional family model and the return of women to the unpaid reproductive role (Voicu and Voicu 2002; Vlase and Preoteasa 2018). Indeed, the female activity rate has decreased sharply during the past two decades, from 57.4% in 1996 to 45.2% in 2015 (INSSE 2016).

Upon their arrival in Italy, Romanian and Moroccan migrant workers faced a society characterized by a persistence of gender inequalities despite the great feminist movement that took place in the 1970s. Women's inactivity rate is one of the highest in the EU, even if there are great disparities within Italy: the national rate is 46.5%, while in Veneto it is 40.4% (EU: 34.4%) (Istat 2012). The Mediterranean familistic welfare regime reproduces the patriarchal division of labor that relegates women to reproductive labor, both in the public and private spheres. Indeed, even if participation by women in the labor market has been increasing since the 1970s, women are segregated in more feminized sectors. Paid work has been a crucial aspect in the shaping of Italian men's conventional lockstep life course, based on the model of education, (continuous) paid employment, and retirement. Especially among Northern Italian women, the model of the double presence (Balbo 1978), which elicited a succession of entries and exits into and out of the labor market, was common. However, in recent decades, large societal transformations have been taking place in the economic and cultural fields, making the conventional gendered life course and lockstep career obsolete, even if they persist as reference models. Thus, gender roles are slowly changing, and new masculinities and femininities are emerging (Magaraggia 2013).

According to this brief overview, I suppose Moroccan and Romanian migrants in Italy can manage to carry out their gendered life courses and careers even if they face a society with different reference models. However, the Mediterranean welfare state and discrimination against foreigners can hinder the working ambitions of migrants, in particular of women. Regardless of migrants' jobs or education in their origin countries, in Italy, migrant people work in the lower-skilled areas of the labor market (Fullin and Reyneri 2011).

The vast majority of migrants in the study sample found manual jobs in the manufacturing or service sectors. Moroccans, who arrived in Veneto in the 1990s, experienced a period of solid employment opportunities in the manufacturing industry that ended with the Great Recession. Indeed, most of them—mainly men, but also some women—held long-term jobs at local factories, often with permanent contracts. Conversely, Romanians arrived in Veneto in the 2000s, when the effects of flexibilization of the labor market were underway. Thus, male Romanian migrants experienced more fragmented working conditions in the manufacturing and construction sectors, and for women, in the industrial and care/domestic sectors.

Analysis of the interviews indicated that migrant working trajectories between 2010–2011 and 2014–2015 were subjected to a process of pronounced precariousness. Throughout the working paths of the migrants interviewed, almost all alternated regular work with unemployment, during which they often worked irregularly. In other words, a portion of interviewees were in a 'gray' area consisting of a mix of short-term regular and irregular jobs. At the time of the second round of interviews, seven Romanians and four Moroccans, both men and women, defined themselves as unemployed. Moreover, there were four inactive women who were not looking for jobs because of reproductive duties: three Moroccans and one Romanian. Two Moroccans were inactive in 2010–2011 as well, while two were employed.

Career fragmentation takes different forms and is experienced differently according to gender. In the next sections, I reveal two main tendencies from the interview data that had a great impact on migrants' gendered life course and gender identity.

The Entrapment of Women in the Domestic Sphere

Migrant women in Italy who were employed in the manufacturing industry have been pushed out of the sector and led to the domestic sphere, where they perform both paid and unpaid work. The trajectories driving migrant women toward reproductive work are different according to their nationality and age. Some female interviewees, both Romanians and Moroccans, in their 40s and 50s, who arrived in Italy in the late 1990s and early 2000s, experienced a great rupture in their work lives because they had been working for a long period in the manufacturing industry. When they lost their jobs, they had to choose between looking for a new job in the domestic and care-services sectors or remaining at home until a new job opportunity in the industrial sector was available.

Other women, mainly Moroccans, tried to enter the labor market for the first time during the economic crisis because their husbands were unemployed or underemployed, but since the only available jobs were domestic, some decided to remain at home because it did not match their expectations.

Finally, there is a third category of young migrant women, both Romanian and Moroccan, in their 20s and 30s, who arrived in Italy a few years before the beginning of the recession. They were accustomed to dealing with high precarity, working in both blue-collar jobs and as domestic workers. Even if their flexible and intermittent work patterns made their work lives very precarious, their earnings were crucial for their families' income because often their husbands were intermittent workers as well. These women are proud of the fact that, for certain periods of time, they were their families' main breadwinners.

Karima is an emblematic case from the first group of women who, after a long work path in the manufacturing industry, experienced ruptures in their career trajectories and had to accept more precarious jobs that in many ways moved them closer to the domestic sphere. The informant (Moroccan, divorced, aged 58) arrived in Italy in 1992. In Morocco, she took vocational courses, but does not like to speak about her past life in her home country because she is divorced. After her arrival in Italy, she worked as a home-care worker for a while, then found a job at a textile factory, where she worked for 15 years. In 2011, the factory closed, and she failed to find another job in the manufacturing sector, so she started to work as a care and domestic worker. Reading her quotes, her frustration over her forced exit from the manufacturing sector in Italy remains, as she considers a factory job a proper job, while reproductive paid work is not:

Now I work by the hour. I work on-call. Sometimes in the hospital too. I find this work through acquaintances. People know me, I'm here a lot of years. But I don't have a steady job. I do everything: home-care worker, domestic jobs, I take care of people who are hospitalized during the night. Sometimes I also work for some restaurants. I prefer my previous job, but I also do these kinds of jobs. In Morocco, I studied. I took two vocational courses to be a seamstress and a nurse. I made a lot of effort, but now I'm without a proper job. (Karima 2015)

The case of Amal (Moroccan, married with three children, aged 32) represents the second category of migrant women—those who entered the labor market during the economic crisis because their husbands were unemployed. Amal grew up in a wealthy family and started law school, but because of migration, she did not graduate. In Morocco, she had never worked and migrated to Italy via family reunification in 2006. Until 2011, when her husband lost his job, she never thought of looking for a job because she had two children (aged 1 and 2) to care for and because her priority was to learn the language first, then look for a good job. However, after a while, she realized that the only job she could find was as a domestic worker, and she refused to do such a job:

It is difficult to find the work you would like. If you come from Morocco with your high school diploma or with your degree, you cannot clean, you feel discriminated. I'd like to work in a nursery or in a retirement home to be able to take care of my children too. If you work in the afternoon, how can you look after the children? Here, I don't have any relatives who can help me. In the end, you decide to stay home: for the language, because I haven't found a good job and because I didn't know to whom to leave my children. (Amal 2011)

Among Romanian women, I could not find similar experiences. Even among educated Romanian interviewees, they accepted underqualified jobs in the cleaning and care sectors with less frustration than Moroccan women. This difference can be explained by the diverse levels of interiorization of the wage-worker habitus characterizing Moroccan and Romanian women (Sadiqi and Ennaji 2006; Vlase and Preoteasa 2018). However, more research should be done to provide deeper and more appropriate analysis of this phenomenon.

Finally, Dana (Romanian, married with one child, aged 36, arrived in 2003) represents the third category. In Romania, she attended an economics and finance high school, then worked as a clerk and as blue collar in a factory. In Italy, she works occasionally through temporary agencies in the manufacturing industry, with her last contract lasting seven months. During unemployed periods, she takes care of the home and her child, and sometimes irons for some Italian families in the village. In 2014, she was unemployed and looking only for industrial jobs for two reasons: she liked the social aspects of the factory and because her husband did not want her working in bars or restaurants since he was jealous:

> *I worked three years in a factory, but when the crisis started... they did not renew my contract. Since then, I've worked through temp agencies. Now, I have been unemployed for one month. At home, I go crazy. I bring the child to school, I come back home, I clean, I go to pick the child up from school, I cook the lunch... nothing interesting.* (Dana 2014)

What associates these women's typology is not only that they live in uncertainty, but also that they have been pushed out of the manufacturing industry and isolated in domestic spheres. During the economic crisis, they were hit by a triple process of precariousness, downward mobility, and vulnerabilization, which hinders women's capacity to realize themselves. However, unlike Italian women,[1] precariousness and unemployment do not impede these women with respect to the social timing of certain life events associated with womanhood, such as marriage and having children. Nevertheless, the family dimension is only part of migrants' identity. Many interviewees present interiorization of a multifaceted model of self-realization, in which employment plays an important role in self-satisfaction. This finding resembles what was found by Hagelskamp et al. (2011) in their investigation on role-identity associations among low-income migrant women in New York: being fulfilled working mothers means being able to balance two independent areas of their lives—work and family—achieving fulfillment from both. The economic downturn engendered a process of feminization among female migrants (Ho 2006), driving them to feelings of isolation in the domestic sphere. Staying at home or working as domestic worker shattered their notions of how they want to be employed—doing 'proper' work.

Men in the Vortex of Intermittent Work and Dependence on Their Wives

Men continue to work, but most have more precarious working conditions. Indeed, during the recession, the number of permanent contracts decreased, especially in the economic sectors in which male migrants are often employed (Istat 2014). Interviewees worked mainly in factories or in logistical services. They report that labor contracts were shortened, confirming the national data on the progressive reduction of non-standard contract lengths (Istat 2014). Moreover, some of these men, mainly Moroccans, are experiencing long-term unemployment.

For these precarious workers, with work careers characterized by high discontinuity, their fulfillment of the conventional male-breadwinner ideal often is difficult to achieve. This is true particularly for men who arrived in the 1990s and were accustomed to a certain job continuity and security. The process of flexibilization forced them to rethink their careers and identities both as men and, as I will show in the next section, as migrants.

Brahim (Moroccan, married with two children, aged 46) attended the first three years of grammar high school in Morocco, then worked casual jobs until his departure in 1991. After 10 years working as a peddler in Sardinia, in 2001, he moved to Veneto and started working in the engineering industry. He thought that his economic position would be robust enough to reunify his family and support it, adhering to conventional gender norms. When he lost his job in 2010, he found other jobs in the same industrial sector, thanks to his diploma as a welder, but with worse conditions, so his family's financial well-being diminished. However, he remained attached to a traditional view of the gendered division of labor.

Q. Maybe your wife could look for a job in the domestic or care sector. In this period, it is easier for women. What do you think about it?
A. My wife, with an 8-month-old baby, cannot work. Those women with older children can work two or three hours a day. On the contrary, men want to work longer, even 10 hours a day, because they have to maintain the family. In particular, in our Islamic culture, the man must be the main breadwinner, while you cannot force women to work. (Brahim 2011)

Those who arrived later, like Ion (Romanian, married with two children, aged 42), who arrived in 2005, had to deal with work flexibility since the beginning, but according to his testimony, precarity further increased during the recession. This condition compelled Ion to rely on his wife, who is employed with a permanent contract at a big household electrical-appliance factory. Unlike Brahim, Ion recognized that the model of the main male breadwinner under which he was socialized was unsustainable, given that his wife's earnings were higher than his were and crucial to support the family. Ion's reflections indicated a different attitude from that of Brahim—an understanding of the challenges from economic transformations that have required shifts in conventional gender roles. Ion, indeed, is aware of the great conflict between what he learned during socialization and the everyday reality he is now living in Italy, where he performs domestic duties while his wife works:

> *I'm lucky that my wife has a good and secure job, but I feel guilty, since I should be in her place. I learned that the man must shoulder the burden of the family. When I don't work, I do the domestic chores. I'm not able to iron, but I clean, and I do the laundry. Sometimes I also cook, even if I don't like it. She arrives home exhausted and fed up. I feel bad, but I don't feel ashamed because there are a lot of men in my situation. It is the fault of the system. In Romania, there is the rule that the man has to bear the burden of the family, while the woman must stay behind. She must help him, but not bear the burden.* (Ion 2014)

Similarly, Farid (Moroccan, married with one child, aged 47) presents the relationship with his wife as equal and based on reciprocity. Before leaving Morocco, Farid attended one year of law school, then he travelled throughout Europe. In 1992, he arrived in Italy. After some casual jobs, he worked for more than a decade for an engineering factory, which closed in 2009. Since then, his wife became the main breadwinner. The interviewee said he doesn't view being supported by his wife as a problem because he believes a family should be based on reciprocity and cooperation. Indeed, he stresses that there were periods when he was the main breadwinner, but he doesn't feel that he's burdening his wife:

> *No, I'm not bothered that she works and me not. Before, I worked, and she didn't. [In that period,] I was very tired. When she arrived in Italy, she didn't work. Then she started to work. She had never worked in her life; she was studying. Now she doesn't burden me because she works. She doesn't mortify me by giving me pocket money...We have a banking account, and everyone can take money when needed. My money is her money.* (Farid 2014)

Finally, the last example is that of Nico (Romanian, single, aged 38, vocational school). Since 2004, when he arrived in Italy, he has been doing many different jobs, in both the construction and manufacturing industries. In 2014, he was unemployed and felt very frustrated, not only because of the persistency of economic insecurity but also since he was late in achieving the gendered expectations associated with this stage in life.

He recounted that he postponed settling down and starting a family for many years because of precarity, but he realized that precarity would be a permanent characteristic of his life and that deferring this life-changing event no longer made sense. Moreover, it is interesting how he argued for the economic efficiency of a couple, since the double income is a tool to cope with economic insecurity. This argument shows the interiorization by Nico of the double-earning couple model:

> *Now I am starting to look to create a family. Before, I didn't think about it because I had a precarious employment situation, but I see that this problem continues, it never finishes, so I have to go ahead. Now I want a family, a child. As a couple, it is easier. She could work. However, it is difficult to find a woman because I don't have the money to go out or to invite her out.* (Nico 2014)

An analysis of migrant men's working lives during the economic crisis shows a process of intense precariousness that affects men's gender identity because for them, professional/economic fulfillment is strictly tied to their capacity to be the family breadwinner. They are unable to fulfill the social expectations concerning gender roles and gendered timing: many who are single cannot get married, and married men are unable to be the main breadwinners or finance family reunifications, as they lack the necessary financial resources.

In conclusion, according to these interviews, we see that the de-gendering of care/domestic duties (Dyer et al. 2011) is not an automatic result of men's unemployment. Like other studies (Schmalzbauer 2011), it is apparent that in some cases, husbands' unemployment has little impact on gender ideologies and practices, while in other cases, it engenders transformative processes.

Migration Careers: 'Between a Rock and a Hard Place'

As I have pointed out in the methodological section, concerning selection bias, this research focuses on migrants who, despite the worsening of their working and living conditions, continue to live in Italy and to carry out their previous migratory endeavors. During the first interview in 2010–2011, they were waiting for the conclusion of the economic crisis to determine whether they can continue their migratory careers in Italy or whether they needed to rethink it. In 2014–2015, those who were still in economic trouble were starting to consider possible solutions.

For Moroccan interviewees who arrived in the 1990s, having experienced a period of regularity with steady jobs in the manufacturing industry, job insecurity from the economic crisis is viewed as a betrayal of their efforts to realize their migratory dreams of improving their lives. The new strategy they adopt to deal with this precarious situation—in which they risk losing their economic power as migrants, including their homes,[2] financial stability, and permission to stay in Italy and move freely—is the acquisition of Italian citizenship.

Farid, whom we met in the previous section, explained this perspective:

> *After 12 years in the same factory, you feel safe, with a permanent contract… now it doesn't exist anymore; you find yourself without anything. When the unemployment benefit finishes, nobody helps you, even if you have paid taxes and so on. If you live in a rented home, the owner evicts you. I know Italy. I've been living here for 23 years. The social policies are weak. If you go to France, this doesn't happen. Nobody remains without a house. They help you until you find a job. This is a big problem I went through. Last July, I became Italian citizen, so if the situation doesn't improve, I can go to another country, where you are not considered only a worker, but also a person.* (Farid 2014)

Farid and other interviewees in similar situations want Italian citizenship to have the right of free movement within the EU and, thus, the chance to find more work opportunities and better-developed welfare states. In these cases, which are quite common among both Moroccans and other non-EU migrants (Danaj and Çaro 2016; Della Puppa and Sredanovic 2017), the experience of unemployment played a crucial role, as migrants realized the deficiencies in the Italian welfare state.[3]

Furthermore, Moroccan migrants want to become Italian citizens not only for freedom to enter other EU countries but also to extract themselves from the rule of immigration law, particularly from the strictures of the residence permit. For non-EU citizens with permission to stay for working reasons, being unemployed or employed with short-term contracts undermines their legal status because if they are employed only for a few days or months, or if they are unemployed, they can obtain only a short-term visa that must be renewed every year.[4] Moreover, those holding a long-term permit cannot start the procedure for naturalization if they work only for short periods or off the books, since they are unable to satisfy the economic requirement.[5]

Brahim explained that flexibilization of the labor market and unemployment presented a real threat to people's migration careers:

> *Even if you have the citizenship, you continue feeling that you are not from here. I did it for documents because you cannot always stay in front of police headquarters. Moreover, now they don't renew the permission to stay to those who don't work. A person who has been living here for 20 years, do you send him away? With children, with family...Where do you send him? It's not good for me.* (Brahim 2014)

These interviews highlight that Italian citizenship is a way to affirm the right to have rights: social rights, the right to go elsewhere in the EU, and the right to stay regardless of employment. Here, migrants claim full citizenship and the right to equality. Their actions are acts of citizenship (Isin 2008), given that they are informed by a marked political understanding of the 'Thought of the State' concerning migration and the relationship between individuals and work.

The economic crisis and the fragmentation of working careers not only threatened the right to stay and to move, but also interrupted other dimensions of migrants' careers, particularly family reunifications, which are strictly tied to the gendered life course. Many men, for instance, could not afford reunifications with their wives and children, which demonstrate to the community back home that these migrations were successful and that these are adult men who can support their families (Della Puppa 2014). Women who cannot reunify with their children feel like they are betraying the idea of motherhood. Aicha (Moroccan, married with one child, aged 42) recounted her frustration and pain due to the impossibility of bringing her daughter to Italy, given her economic problems:

> *We have a daughter in Morocco; we need to send her money. I had a nervous breakdown because I didn't have enough money to go to visit my daughter. I left my daughter in Morocco because it was important for me that she learned the Arabic language at school. Then, my idea was to bring her to Italy. But then the problems started.* (Aicha 2014)

Thus, for Aicha, precariousness means that her career as a mother was interrupted and she could not fulfill the mother's role. As other studies already have demonstrated, transnational mothers live a conflicted existence concerning their duties as mothers, pushing them to redefine their understanding of motherhood to justify their absence (Hondagneu-Sotelo and Avila 1997).

Romanian interviewees are in a different position. They benefit from EU citizenship and the right of free movement, so they do not fear losing resident permits. However, like Moroccan migrants, they fear losing other achievements connected to migration, such as their homes, spending power, and the hope for a life free of poverty and insecurity. Most are deeply rooted in Italy and do not want to move. Nevertheless, a few of them are starting to think that it is not worth the trouble anymore and are considering returning home, something that was not contemplated for years.

Adelina's (Romanian, married with two children, aged 42) narration is quite representative of this minority perspective among this specific sample. She had been working in a plastic factory until 2011. Since then, she only has worked for very short periods in some small factories. Adelina and her husband are considering returning home, even if they continue to postpone this event, depending on whether job opportunities in Italy surface and the job climate in Romania:

> *We are happy here, but times are changing. We don't know how long we are able to resist because we have to pay the bills, and we need money. In Romania, we have at least our house; we don't have to pay rent. [...] But now [in Romania], there is less money. Those who were building houses stopped. Everything is stopped. Like here, there it is even worse. So, it is difficult to return. It is difficult to find a job, and if you find it, they pay you 200 euro, but food costs like here, the prices are the same. How can you live? We find ourselves between a rock and a hard place. We don't know what to do. Going to another country… you don't know the language, you don't know anybody… we have already been there 14 years ago. My husband doesn't want to. He says that he wants to stay here until they fire him. Now, I hope to find a job. It would be a breath of air.*
> (Adelina 2015)

To summarize, migration careers in Italy have been bulldozed during the Great Recession. Migrants have been forced to rethink their migratory existence and adapt to these new conditions if they expect to survive. However, migrants' strategies differ according to their nationality, given that on the one hand, legal-institutional and socioeconomic structures frame their paths and opportunities differently, and on the other hand, they have different expectations based on how long they have been migrants.

For Moroccans, naturalization, which wasn't an issue before the recession because they felt safe and confident with their socioeconomic and legal positions in Italy, became a solution to save their migration careers: some establish deeper roots in Italy, others embark on onwards migrations. Moreover, legal and economic constraints hindered their realization of migration career achievements that are deeply linked to the reinforcement of gender identity, especially family reunification, which represents successful migration and life courses for both men and women.

Unlike Moroccans, Romanian migrants are in a better position because they need not deal with legal constraints, being citizens of an EU member nation. However, the precariousness that has marked their life trajectories—from the political and economic transition in Romania to their migration experiences—has made them much more determined to continue their migration careers in Italy, with only a few in the study considering a return to Romania.

In general, work insecurity disrupts interviewees' migration careers. They are figuring out how to reshape their careers to preserve their achievements and give sense to their life.

Conclusions

In this chapter, following the Chicago School's *career* definition, I sought to explore how the Great Recession produced deep fractures in migrants' occupational careers, as well as initiated a process of redefining gendered lines of social accomplishment (Moen 2001) throughout their migration careers (Martiniello and Rea 2014).

The chapter contributes to the advancement of social-science knowledge on two levels. First, it develops studies on gendered migrants' working careers. It provides innovative insights into the analysis of interrelations between gender roles and the careers of migrants who work in the lower-skilled levels of the labor market, with unemployment periods being a typical stage of precarity along working paths. With respect to the scarce studies on this subject matter, my findings confirm the strong ties between work and gender identity that need to be analyzed in relation to both destination and origin countries. The comparison between men and women of two different nationalities, an aspect missing in other studies that focus on only one gender, allows researchers to understand how the economic downturn touched migrants' working paths and how career fragmentation affected their gender identity.

For migrant women, the recession increased their entrapment in the domestic sphere and in care and domestic jobs, which some interviewees viewed as downward mobility, given that, unlike what emerged in Doyle and Timonen's (2010) study, they prefer factory jobs, which they consider legitimate work. Furthermore, as underlined by Hagelskamp et al. (2011), maternity is not the only source of self-fulfillment for Moroccan and Romanian women. Because of the transformations of gender identities and roles occurring in countries of origin, most female informants identify themselves in the model of working women, and they feel mortified by their current positions, characterized by economic dependence and downward mobility. Thus, the fragmentation of their working careers produced a process of feminization like that engendered by Chinese women migrating to Australia, as analyzed by Ho (2006). This process appears to be stronger for Romanian women than for Moroccan women, who seem to be less attached to paid work. However, more research should be done on this topic.

As for what concerns migrant men, the fragmentation of their work careers impedes them from having a comprehensive view of their life courses and feeling satisfied about their work and migration careers. We have seen economic insecurity hinders their capacity to satisfy gender norms associated with both male professional careers—based on the idea of economic power, financial self-sufficiency, and social recognition—and typical male life courses requiring that men be heads of households. Some migrant men depend on their wives' paychecks. This experience of dependency and vulnerability triggers a reflexive process that drives some of them to challenge conventional gender norms, as some interviewees confirmed what is becoming a new model for gender roles: double-earning couples (Dyer et al. 2011). Therefore, compared with what was found by Batnitzky et al. (2009), it is not only the migration experience and the kind of work performed by migrant men but also the experiences of precariousness and career fragmentation that create space for the emergence of different masculinities and for the renegotiation of gender identities. However, this challenge to conventional gender norms has not resulted in widespread, immediate changes to everyday practices and may even produce a reaffirmation of the conventional gender order (Schmalzbauer 2011).

The second stream of research I contributed to concerns the analysis of migration in times of crisis. Adopting a life-course perspective and the analytical concept of migration careers (Martiniello and Rea 2014), I showed how migrants are reframing their migration careers to give them a new coherence. The comparison between two national groups allowed for identifying different strategies to cope with the recession, according to legal status, a variable that has been stressed by other studies, and migration seniority, a less-studied variable. This last analytical dimension is useful, particularly to understanding the point of view of settled migrants, who do not want to return to their country of origin or emigrate to another country.

From the study of the impact of precariousness on migrants' work careers during the recession, it has emerged how the fragmentation of these careers results in diverse ruptures in the gender and migratory lines of social accomplishments. Future investigations should carry on the longitudinal analysis of migrants' life courses and careers, developing a deeper intersectional examination and comparing migrants and natives' paths. This approach can provide an important contribution to sociological knowledge concerning the relationship between gender identity and the careers of low-income and flexible workers, as well as the settlement processes of migrants.

Notes

1. In Italy, there is a great scientific debate around the obstacles faced by young Italian working women in starting a family because of labor insecurity (Fantone 2007; Modena, Sabatini 2012).
2. 80% of Italians live in their own homes. Immigrants are in a more precarious situation, with 62.8% renting, 19.1% owning (usually with mortgages), 8.3% living at their workplaces, and 9.8% living with relatives (Caritas Migrantes 2016).
3. For an analysis of Italian welfare state policies, see Lynch (2014).
4. One year for those who have short-term contracts, two years for those who have permanent contracts (Dlgs 286/98).
5. In Italy, citizenship applicants must demonstrate that in the past three years, they had an income higher than 8500€ per year (Dlgs 286/98).

References

Ahrens, Jill. 2013. Suspended in Eurocrisis: New Immobilities and Semi-Legal Migrations Amongst Nigerians Living in Spain. *Journal of Mediterranean Studies* 1: 115–140.
Balbo, Laura. 1978. La doppia presenza. *Inchiesta* 32 (8): 3–6.

Batnitzky, Adina, McDowell Linda, and Sarah Dyer. 2009. Flexible and Strategic Masculinities: The Working Lives and Gendered Identities of Male Migrants in London. *Journal of Ethnic and Migration Studies* 35 (8): 1275–1293.

Becker, Howard S., and Anselm L. Strauss. 1956. Careers, Personality and Adult Socialization. *American Journal of Sociology* 62 (3): 253–263.

Bonifazi, Corrado, and Cristiano Marini. 2014. The Impact of the Economic Crisis on Foreigners in the Italian Labour Market. *Journal of Ethnic and Migration Studies* 40 (3): 493–511.

Caritas Migrantes. 2016. *Immigrati: il protagonismo nel mercato immobiliare*. http://www.dossierimmigrazione.it/docnews/file/Focus%20su%20casa%20-%20Dossier%202016(1).pdf

Cuban, Sondra. 2009. Skilled Immigrant Women Carers in Rural England and Their Downward Mobility. *Migration Letters* 6 (2): 177–184.

Danaj, Sonila, and Erka Çaro. 2016. Becoming an EU Citizen Through Italy: The Experience of Albanian Immigrants. *Mondi Migranti* 3: 95–108.

Della Puppa, Francesco. 2014. Men's Experiences and Masculinity Transformations. In *Migration, Diaspora and Identity*, ed. Tsolidis Georgina. Springer.

Della Puppa, Francesco, and Djordje Sredanovic. 2017. Citizen to Stay or Citizen to Go? Naturalization, Security, and Mobility of Migrants in Italy. *Journal of Immigrant & Refugee Studies* 15 (4): 366–383.

Doyle, Martha, and Virpi Timonen. 2010. Obligations, Ambitions, Calculations: Migrant Care Workers' Negotiation of Work, Career, and Family Responsibilities. *Social Politics* 17 (1): 29–52.

Dyer, Sarah, McDowell Linda, and Adina Batnitzky. 2011. Migrant Work, Precarious Work-Life Balance: What the Experiences of Migrant Workers in the Service Sector in the Greater London Tell Us About Adult Worker Model. *Gender, Place and Culture* 18 (5): 685–700.

Edwards, Rosalind, and Sarah Irwin. 2010. Lived Experience Through Economic Downturn in Britain—Perspectives Across Time and Across the Life-Course. *Twenty-First Century Society* 5 (2): 119–124.

Escrivà, Angeles, and Francesca Alice Vianello. 2016. Late-Career International Migration and Reproductive Work. A Comparison between Peruvian and Ukrainian Women in the Southern Europe. *Investigaciones Feministas* 7 (1): 89–113.

Fantone, Laura. 2007. Precarious Changes: Gender and Generational Politics in Contemporary ITALY. *Feminist Review* 87 (1): 5–20.

Farris, Sarah R. 2014. Migrants' Regular Army of Labour: Gender Dimensions of the Impact of the Global Economic Crisis on Migrant Labor in Western Europe. *The Sociological Review* 63 (1): 121–143.

Fellini, Ivana. 2015. Una via bassa alla decrescita dell'occupazione: il mercato del lavoro italiano tra crisi e debolezze strutturali. *Stato e Mercato* 105: 470–508.

Fullin, Giovanna, and Emilio Reyneri. 2011. Low Unemployment and Bad Jobs for New Immigrants in Italy. *International Migration* 49 (1): 118–147.

Hagelskamp, Carolin, Diane Hughes, Hirokazu Yoshikawa, and Ajay Chaudry. 2011. Negotiating Motherhood and Work: A Typology of Role Identity Associations Among Low-Income, Urban Women. *Community, Work & Family* 14 (3): 335–366.

Heinz, Walter R., and Helga Krüger. 2001. Life Course: Innovations and Challenges for Social Research. *Current Sociology* 49 (1): 29–45.

Herrera, Gioconda. 2012. Starting Over Again? Crisis, Gender, and Social Reproduction Among Ecuadorian Migrants in Spain. *Feminist Economics* 18 (2): 125–148.

Ho, Christina. 2006. Migration as Feminisation? Chinese Women's Experiences of Work and Family in Australia. *Journal of Ethnic and Migration Studies* 32 (3): 497–514.

Hondagneu-Sotelo, Pierrette, and Ernestine Avila. 1997. I'm Here, but I'm There: The Meaning of Latina Transnational Motherhood. *Gender and Society* 11 (5): 548–571.

Hughes, C. Everett. 1937. Institutional Office and the Person. *American Journal of Sociology* 43 (3): 404–413.

———. 1950. Cycles, Turning Points, and Careers. Lecture at the *8th Annual Conference of Theology in Action*, Adelynrood, South Byfield, MA.

———. 1997. Careers. *Qualitative Sociology* 20 (3): 389–397.

ILO. 2013. *Morocco*. ILOSTAT.

INSSE. 2016. *Labour Force in Romania. Employment and Unemployment*. Bucarest: National Institute of Statistics.

Isin, Engin F. 2008. Theorizing Acts of Citizenship. In *Acts of citizenship*, ed. Engin F. Isin and Greg M. Nielsen. London: Zed Books.

Istat. 2012. *Tasso di inattività*. NoiItalia.

———. 2014. *Rapporto annuale*. Roma: Istat.

Kahanec, Martin, and Klaus F. Zimmermann. 2016. *Labor Migration, EU Enlargement, and the Great Recession*. Berlin: Springer.

Lewis, Hannah, Dwyer Peter, Hodkinson Stuart, and Louise Waite. 2014. Hyper-Precarious Lives: Migrants, Work and Forced Labour in the Global North. *Progress in Human Geography* 39 (5): 580–600.

Liversage, Anika. 2009. Vital Conjunctures, Shifting Horizons: High-Skilled Female Immigrants Looking for Work. *Work Employment & Society* 23 (1): 120–141.

Lynch, Julia. 2014. The Italian Welfare State after the Financial Crisis. *Journal of Modern Italian Studies* 19 (4): 380–388.

Magaraggia, Sveva. 2013. Tensions Between Fatherhood and the Social Construction of Masculinity in Italy. *Current Sociology* 61 (1): 76–92.

Martiniello, Marco, and Andrea Rea. 2014. The Concept of Migratory Careers: Elements for New Theoretical Perspective of Contemporary Human Mobility. *Current Sociology* 62 (7): 1079–1096.

Modena, Francesca, and Fabio Sabatini. 2012. I Would if I Could: Precarious Employment and Childbearing Intentions in Italy. *Review of Economics of the Household* 10 (1): 77–97.

Moen, Phyllis. 2001. The Gendered Life Course. In *Handbook of Aging and the Social Sciences*, ed. Robert H. Binstock and Linda K. George, 179–196. San Diego, CA: Academic.

Reyneri, Emilio. 2010. L'impatto della crisi sull'inserimento degli immigrati nel mercato del lavoro dell'Italia e degli altri paesi dell'Europa meridionale. *Prisma. Economia Società Lavoro* 2: 17–33.

Sacchetto, Devi, and Francesca Alice Vianello. 2013. *Navigando a vista. Migranti nella crisi economica tra lavoro e disoccupazione*. Milano: Franco Angeli.

Sadiqi, Fatima, and Moha Ennaji. 2006. The Feminization of Public Space: Women's Activism, the Family Law, and Social Change in Morocco. *Journal of Middle East Women's Studies* 2 (2): 86–114.

Schmalzbauer, Leah. 2011. Doing Gender, Ensuring Survival: Mexican Migration and Economic Crisis in the Rural Mountain West. *Rural Sociology* 76 (4): 441–460.

Vlase, Ionela, and Ana Maria Preoteasa. 2018. Gendered Life-Course Patterns in Post-Socialist Romania: An Illustration from Households Situated in Precarious Prosperity. *Journal of Balkan and Near Eastern Studies* 20 (1): 31–48.

Voicu, Mălina, and Bogdan Voicu. 2002. Gender values dynamics: Towards a common European pattern? *Romanian Journal of Sociology* 13 (1–2): 42–63.

PART III

Gender and Family

CHAPTER 7

Immigration, Transition to Parenthood, and Parenting

Anca Bejenaru

Transitions to parenthood and human parenting, although influenced by biological factors, are rather the outcome of parents' developmental history and interactions with different sociocultural backgrounds. In traditional communities in which mobility is reduced and parental models are limited, parenting methods were transmitted as such or with little variation from one generation to the next. Nowadays, increased access to information and parents' geographical mobility provide exposure to a much wider variety of parenting models. This is even more obvious in the case of immigrant parents. They bring into a fledgling family new coupling and child-rearing patterns that may overwrite traditional ones.

A great challenge in researching transitions to parenthood and parenting practices among migrants is considering the influence of multicontextual factors (Ochocka and Janzen 2008). Many studies have addressed migrants' parenthood and parenting practices through the lens of the acculturation process (Berry 1997; Birman and Trickett 2001). Other scholars have investigated how such patterns are passed down from one

A. Bejenaru (✉)
'Lucian Blaga' University of Sibiu, Sibiu, Romania

© The Author(s) 2018
I. Vlase, B. Voicu (eds.), *Gender, Family, and Adaptation of Migrants in Europe*,
https://doi.org/10.1007/978-3-319-76657-7_7

generation to the next and how they are influenced by the sociocultural context of adults' childhood (Chen and Kaplan 2001; Serbin and Karp 2003; van Ijzendoorn 1992). Both approaches offer a limited understanding of the context and factors influencing migrants' transition to parenthood and their child-rearing practices.

In this chapter, we contribute to the debate and document it further. To do so, we adopt a life-course perspective to show how transitioning to parenthood, on the one hand, and parenting practices, on the other, are negotiated and adjusted under the influence of both migrants' childhoods and migration contexts. Some mechanisms of parenting formation and transformation were identified by using both inductive and deductive procedures for data analyses. These methods elicited novel information on how women change during migrations with respect to child-rearing and familial patterns.

In the first part of the chapter, we provide a brief review of the literature that defines and explains the transition to parenthood and the formation of parenting values and behaviors. Then, on the basis of existing studies, we outline a portrait of Romanian parents as a basis of comparison for the results of our study. Original findings resulting from a qualitative survey are depicted in the most extended part of the chapter. In the discussion, we assert how the findings contribute to existing literature on migration and parenthood, as well as to the life-course perspective in general.

Transitions to Parenthood

A transition is a period of change, instability, and internal conflict about gains and losses that result in the reorganization of the inner life and behaviors (Cowan 1991; Falicov 1991). The transition to parenthood usually spans from the beginning of a pregnancy until the baby's first few months (Goldberg 1993). It is considered a normative life event, meaning that, in general, it is expected and predictable (Easterbrooks 1993). Even so, it imposes both risks and opportunities for individuals, as well as for families. An important factor that contributes to the adjustment to parenthood is the transition's timing (Cowan 1991).

For the transition to parenting to be in time, most authors think it should happen in a certain age bracket and in some synchrony with other life transitions and trajectories (Goldberg 1993). These sequences of events and transitions are socioculturally and historically defined. Currently, Romanian mothers first give birth, on average, when they're 26.3 years old, with a significant difference between the average age of mothers in rural and urban areas. Consistent with Romanian National Institute of Statistics data, mothers in urban areas tend to have their first child at 28.5 years, while in rural areas, it's 24.6 years. Differences in level of education also are recorded. Less-educated women are more likely to start a family and become mothers immediately after leaving the education system (Muresan 2014). Higher education is associated with birth postponement (d'Albis et al. 2017). Highly educated women tend to delay marriage and motherhood until they consolidate their careers and economic situations (Baetică 2015). The transition to motherhood in highly educated Romanian women in urban areas tends to dovetail with the profiles of women in EU member states (European Commission and Eurostat 2015). The same cannot be said about the profiles of less-educated women in rural areas. A question arises: *When and in what sequence will young Romanian women from the last category* (low educational level, from rural areas) *who migrate to countries in Western and Southern Europe transition to parenthood?* Another question is: *Will these women adapt to their new countries' parenthood transition patterns or will they retain the home-environment model?* Existing literature provides some useful explanations in this regard, which are discussed later. Before that, we'll discuss parenting practices. The transition to parenthood contributes to the success of the parental career, but it is not the only factor.

Parenting Practices

Parenting encompasses a range of attitudes and behaviors aimed at providing children with biological, physical, psychological, and social development (Hoghughi 2004). Diane Baumrind was among the first authors to describe parenting behavior, which she defines using two dimensions: demandingness and responsiveness. Responsiveness means, in her view, being warm, supportive, and concerned about the development of children's individuality and assertiveness. Demandingness includes behavior regulation and control, direct confrontation, and supervising children's activities (Baumrind 2005).

Considering these dimensions, Baumrind described four parenting styles. Authoritative parents are both highly demanding and responsive. They set high standards for their children, and they support them as they pursue goals that rise to these standards. Authoritarian parents are highly demanding, but have a lower level of responsiveness. They ask for obedience and enforce clear regulations on children's behavior. Permissive parents, however, provide a high level of responsiveness, but are not demanding, while disengaged parents are neither demanding nor responsive. The latter tend to neglect their children (Baumrind 1991).

While acknowledging in her research the importance of sociocultural context in the manifestation of parenting, Baumrind does not establish a clear connection between this factor and parenting styles. Kâğıtçıbaşı (1996) addresses this shortcoming. He adopts Baumrind's models and integrates them into a sociocultural and family context. A "general model of parenting" is proposed, encompassing three specific forms. *The model of interdependence* is characteristic of a culture of relatedness, usually rural, traditional communities based on subsistence, with high birth rates and low woman status. Parents who adopt this style inculcate loyalty and both emotional and material interdependence among generations. The child has utilitarian value for the family. These parents take an authoritarian style, as Baumrind (1991) defines it. *The model of independence* is characteristic of Western, industrialized, urban, or suburban societies. Specific to the nuclear family, the model is characterized by lower fertility and higher woman status. Dominant social values lead to separation of generations and independence among family members. A permissive parenting style is adopted, with an emphasis on autonomy and self-reliance. *The model of emotional interdependence* is a combination of other models, entailing loyalty and emotional interdependence among family members, combined with autonomy. The parenting style most likely adopted is authoritative. This model is frequently encountered in more developed, urban communities, among middle-class, educated families.

Recent studies assessing parenting patterns in Southern and Western European countries indicated that they demonstrate a high level of child acceptance and parental involvement, specific to authoritative and indulgent parenting styles (García and Gracia 2014; Moscardino et al. 2011; Otto and Keller 2016). The difference between the two styles, as we have shown above, is the level of control. In this sense, in Southern European countries, especially in Spain, the indulgent, and therefore less-coercive style, is preferable by parents and children (García and Gracia 2014), while in Western countries (e.g., Germany), the authoritative style, in which parents are more strict but still engaged and affectionate with children, is preferred (Otto and Keller 2016).

Presently, little is known about the parenting styles adopted by Romanian parents (Moscardino et al. 2011; Robila 2004). Synthesizing the existing research data, we can say that in Romania, the child is a central part of the family, making it complete (BOP 2008). Responsibility for care is largely incumbent on mothers (Robila 2004). Parents are responsible for transmitting values and shaping behaviors. Romanian parents aim to instill personal responsibility, hard work, and respect for others in their children (Voicu 2012). Punitive practices are still common among parents (Tudor et al. 2013; Voicu and Tufiș 2016). However, according to the most recent studies, parenting models generally have become more democratic and increasingly child-centered (Nesteruk and Marks 2011). Given these differences between parenting practices in Romania and those in Southern and Western Europe, we are interested in identifying what kind of parenting practices Romanian migrants adopt. *Will they keep their practices acquired in Romania, or will they adopt the practices learned in the host country?*

Transition to Parenthood and Parenting Practices of Returning Migrants: Some Explanatory Models

As we noted in previous sections, our focus is on migrants returning to their country of origin. In most of their cases, we talk about highly destandardized life paths characterized by discontinuity in their experiences, caused by multiple transitions and contact with other sociocultural backgrounds. The way in which these issues affect different life trajectories and coping behaviors has been explained in various ways in the literature. The most useful explanations are presented and discussed below. For a comprehensive view, we will try to identify both the mechanisms of initial behavioral patterns and those that facilitate their transformation because of successive transitions and contact with other cultural environments.

The first patterns of behavior are formed in childhood during the socialization process. Two mechanisms seem to be important from the perspective of social psychology, explained by social learning theory and attachment theory (Madden et al. 2015; van Ijzendoorn 1992).

According to attachment theory, in the child's interactions with his or her primary caretaker, cognitive representations of himself or herself and others are formed. These representations are known as internal working models (Bowlby 1969). In its simplest form, the theory assumes that the parent's early experiences with his or her own caretakers will be reflected in that parent's own parental practices. To illustrate, an adult who has built an unhealthy, insecure relationship with his or her own caregiver will tend to perpetuate it with his or her own child. In the migration process, these working models are important from two perspectives. On the one hand, they can influence migrants' adaptive skills to a new culture, thereby influencing their mental health. By extensively documenting this relationship, Oppedal (2006: 101) proposed the acculturation development model. According to her, working models are the basis of sociocultural competencies that allow migrants to adapt to new cultures. On the other hand, a new sociocultural environment perceived as favorable, and positive experiences with significant others in the migration country, can moderate the effect of adverse experiences and unfavorable circumstances encountered in childhood (Belsky 1984; van Ijzendoorn and Bakermans-Kranenburg 1997). These can lead to a change in internal working models and can cause a disruption in the transmission of parenthood models and parenting practices. In this respect, Oppedal (2006: 108) suggests that the frequency of contact with majority society members is not as important as the quality of these relations.

The social learning theory assumes that human behavior is influenced by exposure to models offered by the sociocultural environment. In the case of migrants, exposure to new patterns of transition to parenthood and parenting practices in the host country may result in a transformation of the models originally acquired, through the process of acculturation. White et al. (2008) formulated the hypothesis of exposure, which assumes that the more immigrants are exposed to the host country's environment, the more they adapt.

Berry (2007), taking into account migrants' desire to maintain their cultural identity in their countries of origin and to actively participate in the social lives of their host countries, defines four strategies of acculturation: integration, assimilation, separation, and marginalization. The most praised, from Berry's point of view, is integration because it enables the preservation of one's own identity and, at the same time, includes participation in the cultural, social, and economic lives of the receiving country. In their study, Moscardino et al. (2011) show that Romanian immigrants in Italy tend to value the interdependence of family members, similar to parents in Romania, but at the same time, they stimulate cognitive development, autonomy, and self-fulfillment of their children, similar to Italian parents. The assimilation strategy assumes that immigrants seek interactions with others and tend to assimilate to the norms and values of the host country. Assimilation is not a linear process. It involves learning, negotiation, and accommodation, processes that vary with individual factors and are contingent on the family-life stage during which migration occurs (Hernandez and McGoldrick 1999). Keeping the values of the home country and avoiding cultural interaction in the host country implies, from Berry's perspective, adoption of a separation strategy (Berry 2007). A range of studies indicates a tendency among first-generation immigrants to adhere to the private, familial environment—the cultural norms and values of the country of origin—when deciding the transition to parenthood, number of children, and parenting styles (Kahn 1994; Milewski 2010; Sobotka 2008). The stagnation of migrants in the culture of their origin country makes them adopt parenting models that often contrast with most parents' styles in the host country (de Haan 2011). Two causes are more obvious: (1) parents' fear of losing their power in the family by adopting modern parenting models, which emphasize children's independence and their involvement in decisions that concern them, and (2) parents' inability to adapt to the new setting (de Haan 2011). The marginalization strategy, identified by Berry (1997), characterizes those who are not interested in keeping their own culture, or in assimilating to the host country's culture.

These strategies should not be viewed as mutually exclusive but rather as complementary. The adoption of any of them depends on many factors related to sociodemographic characteristics, such as motivation for migrating, stage in life when they migrate, and so on. For instance, Berry (2006) believes that the strategy of marginalization is specific to people excluded from society and/or discriminated against in their host country. In their case, researchers tend to observe an increase in births in the destination country (Kulu et al. 2017). For them, children often represent a source of income, rather than a domain of parents' investment. Regarding youth migrants motivated by economic goals and professional fulfillment, demographers have advanced the disruption hypothesis to explain their behavior. They suggest that immediately after migration, migrants' efforts to invest in the realization of these financial and career goals may result in the postponement of the transition to parenthood, resulting in fewer births (Kulu and Milewski 2007). Several studies confirm this hypothesis (Mussino and Strozza 2012; Nedoluzhko and Andersson 2007).

All these previous explanations concerning adaptation strategies demonstrate that the transition to parenthood and parenting practices involves complex processes, contingent on the interplay of individual attributes, personal development, structural context, historical time, and cultural environment. Although existing literature provides some useful explanations of the transition to parenting and the parental behavior of migrants, it does not fully cover research questions. Our empirical research sheds more light, as we explain, in the following sections.

CURRENT STUDY

In the present study, we adopt a life-course perspective, allowing us to integrate, temporally, various explanations on the impact of different contexts and factors on the transition to parenthood and parenting practices (see also Evans et al. 2009). Our purpose is to highlight the influence of both origin and migration contexts on these processes and to study the mechanisms that facilitate the formation and transformation of various attitudinal and behavioral patterns. More specifically, we address the following questions: *When and in what sequence do young Romanian women who migrate to countries in Southern and Western Europe achieve the transition to parenthood? Will these women adapt to the host country's pattern of transition, or will they retain the home country's model? How are parenting models acquired in childhood reshaped? How do immigrants change their representations about themselves and others in the context of migration? How are these changes reflected in child-rearing values, aspirations, and practices?*

Responding to these questions, we aim to extend knowledge on the parenthood-transition patterns and parenting practices of migrants who have returned to their home country or are planning to do so soon. Past studies on parenthood, mostly carried out in migration countries, focus on migrants adapting to the new environment. An important driver of migrants' acculturation is, according to Ochocka and Janzen (2008: 86), the loss of the social structure that sustains the values, beliefs, and parenting strategies acquired in their country of origin. But if their migration is intended to last only for a limited period of time, and they intend to return, are they still as open to change?

Romanian immigrants can provide a good test case to answer such questions for some important reasons. Romanian migration is a recent phenomenon, rising significantly between 2000 and 2010, both in terms of migrant numbers and migration patterns (Șerban 2011; Șerban and Voicu 2010; Vlase 2015). Bradatan (2014) reported an increase in migrant couples and children involved in the migration process. Romania has a very low birth rate, but a relatively young age at the time of marriage, and the birth of the first child, particularly in the case of migrants with a low level of education in rural areas, can complicate the migration process, with problems related to the transition to parenthood and the raising of children (Bradatan 2014). In this context, migrant women who have been socialized in family environments with traditional values, as is the case in Romanian villages (Popescu 2008), are facing new family and parental patterns in their countries of migration.

Participants

The research data reported here were gathered from the project *"Migrants' life courses: dealing with uncertain, highly de-standardized biographies in Romania."* A purposive sample was used, consisting of 40 Romanian immigrants, both men and women. All subjects worked abroad for a minimum of five years. Currently, they have returned to Romania or plan to do so in the near future. For purposes of this study, we selected nine participants, exclusively women, who had at least one child at the time of the interview. The exclusive choice of women was motivated by the fact that parenting is a gendered activity (Videon 2005), and that men and women unevenly share parental responsibilities. Hence, our selection was guided by evidence that women are more likely to be providing the most childcare in families (Sharma et al. 2016) and discursively engage and reflect upon their caretaker role. Applying the maternity criterion, 15 subjects were selected in the first phase, of which six were successively excluded. Of the latter, four were eliminated because they had children at the age of maturity when they started their migration process. Another participant was excluded because she migrated in her early childhood, so she was socialized in the host country. The final excluded informant belongs to the upper class—the only one in this category, with the rest falling into the lower working class. The exclusion of these subjects from the sample is based on previous research showing that both migration timing (Glick et al. 2012) and parents' social class (Sherman and Harris 2012) influence the transition to parenthood and parenting practices. Although the resulting sample is small, we contend that the richness of narrative accounts of the nine informants in the sample—concerning their childhood, migration, and parenting experiences—gave us a deeper understanding of the studied topic (Patton 2002).

The resulting sample includes: 01_F_40 (born 1977, returnee from Italy, one child), 03_F_33 (born 1984, migrant in Italy, one child), 06_F_38 (born 1979, returnee from Germany, one child), 09_F_38 (born 1979, returnee from Italy, one child), 10_F_46 (born 1971, returnee from Italy, one child), 15_F_36 (born 1981, returnee from Spain, two children), 22_F_31 (born 1986, returnee from Germany, one child), 31_F_49 (born 1968, returnee from Germany, five children), 33_F_36 (born 1981, returnee from Spain, one child).

Procedures

The method used for data collection was life-story interviews. The aim was to capture the important events experienced throughout their lives, the major transitions, and the meanings assigned to them by interviewees. To facilitate the narration, each interview was structured in two parts: one in which participants were encouraged to speak freely about their life trajectories and a second part that, based on a semi-structured interview guide, deepened and clarified the chapters set by the interviewees. During the narration phase, each interviewee was encouraged to adopt "the form, shape, and style that was the most comfortable" for her (Atkinson 1998: 8). The interviews were conducted either at the interviewee's residence or at a neutral place, depending on each interviewee's preference. The interviews were audio-recorded, ranging from 70 minutes to 127 minutes (the average interview lasted 94 minutes). The recordings were transcribed in full.

Data Analysis

A common method of analyzing qualitative data is thematic analysis. For this study, we followed the phases proposed by Braun and Clarke (2006). The coding process was performed using NVivo 10. In the first phase, we used an inductive procedure for coding. The data coding was followed by the systematic development of the themes and subthemes, then by their definition and association in a unitary model. The procedure was similar to that proposed by Ochocka and Janzen (2008) (see Fig. 7.1). The main components of the model are *the context and experiences of childhood; the context of migration; the transition to parenthood; and the adjusted parental model.*

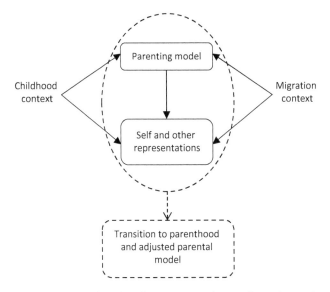

Fig. 7.1 Mechanisms for the formation and transformation of parenting practices

The Resulting Model

The model shows how the values and parental beliefs of migrants returning to their country of origin were formed, transformed, and translated into behaviors. To this end, the model integrates social learning theory, attachment theory, and life-course perspective.

Childhood is the first context in which parental models and values are learned and internalized, and an internal working model of self and others is developed. In the absence of a contextual or relational disruption, these values, models, and representations formed in childhood are transferred into later parental behaviors. But for migrants, the context of the host country offers new values and parenting models that can replace or change the old ones. At the same time, new experiences and relations that are set in this environment can transform the internal models of self and others' representations. This way, we can expect a change in the process of transition to parenthood and parenting practices.

Findings: 1. The Context and Experiences of Childhood

Most interviewees went abroad around the age of 20, after following their educational paths to completion, usually vocational or high school. For most, the end of childhood and the transition to adulthood were marked by migration. The childhood chapter occupied a large space in their life stories and provided rich information for our purposes.

Socioeconomic Context of Childhood

All nine interviewees come from lower-working-class families. Except for one migrant who was an only child, the rest came from families with at least three children. The profiles of these migrants' mothers are very similar. Their main occupation was being a housewife or a low-skilled worker.

Social and Family Values in Childhood

Our interviewees described their childhood community as "closed," dominated by traditional, heavily rooted values. In the family environment, the interviewees identified a range of values that we grouped into two categories: moral-religious values and values that promote independence or interdependence among family members (see Kâğıtçıbaşı 1996).

In the category of moral-religious values lies faith in God, frequently mentioned by the informants, but also honesty, fairness, self-respect, and respect for others. For example, a 36-year-old migrant from a rural area said:

> *My mother is a simple country woman, but she taught me some essential things in my life: be afraid of God (…), be honest, and be clean (33_F_36).*

A 49-year-old interviewee from a small urban area said:

> *They taught us to be honest. So, this was a very strong value. We have tried like all the children to lie, but for this, we have been severely punished. Yes. To be honest, to be hard-working, and to be polite (31_F_49).*

Concerning the second category of values, the interview data support a strong orientation among migrant families toward economic and emotional interdependence among their members. Children were taught to obey adults and to be responsible and helpful to the family. Our interviewed women were involved very early in their childhoods with household activities or in agriculture. For example, a migrant remembers that she was withdrawn from school because she was no longer productive for the family. She said:

> *I now seem to hear my mother saying: "You are no longer productive. We have to pay for your transport subscription. You are every day at school; you come home and you have lessons to learn. So, you can't help us with the household chores. You will not go to high school anymore!" And in the 11th grade, first quarter, they took me out of high school. Today, being mature, being a mother, I wonder why I didn't defend myself? So, I didn't say, "No, mother!" I didn't even think of defending myself. So, I'm getting more and more aware of how we (she and her same-age peers) were otherwise raised. So ... I don't know ... I don't want to say submissively, but maybe obedient ... but I think in a negative manner, meaning without the right of decision (31_F_49).*

This interviewed woman amends the model of family interdependence and the authoritarian style used by her parents. Throughout the interview, she returned to and highlighted the negative effects of these parenting practices on her personality.

Parental Models in Childhood

Analyzing the two dimensions proposed by Baumrind (1991), responsiveness and demandingness, we found that most interviewees were raised in an authoritarian style. They described a reserved, even Spartan, attitude from both or one of their parents, with little evidence of sensitivity and appreciation for the child. One respondent, aged 40, described her parents as follows:

> *They were very distant. My mother did not hug me, didn't kiss me, didn't tell me I was beautiful. These words didn't exist for them. (...) My father was very distant, too. He read instead. But I never understood why he never expressed his love for me. Probably, in turn, he did not get it (01_F_40).*

The lack of responsiveness is associated with strict parental behavior. The parents made decisions for children, imposing their will, and exerting severe control. For example, a 31-year-old migrant woman talks about how she chose a male profession because her father demanded that she do so:

I (took) the capacity exam, and I could choose another specialization. I never wanted to become an electrician. But because that's what dad wanted me to do, so he decided, (and) I wanted to listen. I and my sister, both of us (31_F_49).

For the parents of our informants, a child's education was viewed as his or her swift path into the labor market. In this way, the child became useful to the family by contributing with his or her wages at a fairly young age.

In a few cases from our sample (three out of nine), the informants described one or both parents as being sensitive. However, we cannot categorize them as authoritative. Like the other parents described above, they showed rigid behavior with strict rules, failing to help the child shape his or her own aspirations and follow them.

In the description of her parents, a 40-year-old respondent talked of disengagement from them. She had two young parents, without material resources, who worked in shifts. So, she was raised by her grandparents in an abusive environment without being able to build a secure relationship with anyone. She said:

They did not know how to show me love because they worked in three shifts. I can now cry for my childhood. What I remember about my childhood are sad things. If I ever had to be a child again, I would not want it anymore (01_F_40).

Among the above interviews, we can identify two predominant parenting styles: authoritarian and disengaged. Here, it should be noted that our informants spent their childhoods during the last 10–15 years of Soviet communist rule, a period characterized by economic recession and lack of adequate support measures for families with children. The economic precariousness forced rural families to put children to work at very young ages, and families living in urban areas at a time of high industrialization and expansion of shift work were forced to temporarily abandon their children, leaving them with grandparents. Under these circumstances, it is easy to understand why dominant parenting styles prevailed during the childhoods of our informants.

Self and Others: Representation in Childhood

Seven of the nine informants talked about how they perceived themselves before the migration and about the factors that favored the construction of this self-image. The seven women described themselves in very similar ways: fearful, introverted, insecure, and with low aspirations. A 38-year-old migrant presented herself as follows:

Before going to Germany, I was rather shy, quite inhibited ... I felt rather inferior. I didn't trust myself (...) (09_F_38).

Some of our informants traced the foundations of these self-images to their parents' discouragement, frequent criticism, and disregard for their welfare. Relevant to this is the perspective of a 49-year-old woman. She said her parents emphasized her weaknesses rather than her strengths, and even blamed weaknesses on supposed character flaws:

They did not point out what we know well or what we can (do). On the contrary, they continually showed us what we don't know. So, we were scolded a lot for our mistakes. In my opinion, the mistakes were much emphasized and associated with my identity—"You are bad, or it's you" not "You did something wrong." So, regarding my identity ... I even had problems with this because I have never had the courage to hope that I can succeed, that I can do it. I've often heard "You can't" (31_F_49).

Other respondents spoke about unsatisfied basic needs (e.g., food, security) in the family environment, which prevented one informant from building self-fulfillment aspirations.

I was a very silent child. Growing up in a family with physical and verbal violence, I was a child who wanted very little. (...) I didn't have anything to eat. I was moved around ... What should I desire? I never dreamed of being anywhere (01_F_40).

Another aspect that contributed negatively to the construction of their self-images was the communities they grew up in and the attitudes of people in these communities. Many respondents talked about limited opportunities for interaction with the world outside the community and about the lack of role models to facilitate aspirations.

We have no aspirations, we were so.... We were held there. We had nothing. We did not know much. We're not communicating. The kids around you were raised just like you. You did not see much. Later, I saw some smarter, more emancipated children ... In high school, I realized I had a delay in many ways. An educational delay... and so on (09_F_38).

Some informants described people in the community as uncommunicative, envious, distant, and unwelcoming toward others. Several interviewees expressed their gratitude for being able to leave that environment:

Because people judge you, they look at you, analyze you ... how are you dressed ... if you possess something or not; who are your parents ... I was glad to get out of there (22_F_31).

FINDINGS: 2. THE CONTEXT OF MIGRATION

New Parenting Models in the Host Country

In the informants' narratives, there are relatively few references to parental or familial patterns in the migration countries. Apart from four interviewees who have worked in family settings in their host countries, for example, as babysitters, caretakers for the elderly, or housekeepers, there is little evidence that most informants had contact with and were under the direct influence of parental models in host countries. The four women who have directly interacted with families in their migration countries did not build a convergent picture of any observed parenting practices. However, some of the migrants working in family settings said they did observe and appreciate parents' investment in their children's education, their overall efforts to foster children's development, and children's freedom to make choices. Speaking about what she has learned and what she wants to convey to her own children, 31_F_49 states:

That's what I'm telling my children: learn, try, see what is yours, what is your gift, what you want to do! That you will do well and with pleasure.

Among the negative aspects raised by interviewees about family models in their countries of migration, we identified lack of cohesion, family instability, and the birth of children outside of marriage. All of these were perceived by interviewees as negatively affecting the children's mental health. A 31-year-old interviewee who cared for elderly people said:

My last family, where I stayed four years, where I met my husband, was a good family. The husband and the wife, both doctors, and five children. All children were students, and they were very close. Very nice. A very good example. But otherwise (...) O, Lord, how many relationships ... and children with other partners. And I saw the kids because it affects them too. Because they do not have a stable family, I've seen them with psychological problems, the poor of them (22_F_31).

Another issue discussed by some of our informants was the early independence of children in countries such as Germany, Spain, and Italy, compared with Romania, and the resulting differences in the shape of life courses.

The Self and Others: Representation Redefined

Our interviewees appreciate the culture in their countries of migration, regardless of their belonging to Western or Southern regions (e.g., Italy, Spain, Germany). We also identified migrants' approval of everyday life and ways of being and behaving in the mainstream population in the receiving countries. Thus, a returnee, age 31, said:

> ... I like the society there. I like people. I like how they think. I like how they behave. For me, it was a pleasure to leave Romanian society and go to the society there (22_F_31).

In the same spirit, a 38-year-old woman said:

> And maybe I was fortunate enough to have very good people in Spain who did not disappoint me. Being they neighbors, bosses ... did not disappoint me (22_F_31).

An important gain from migration, observed by most interviewees, was the redefinition of self. Our informants strongly believe that they made a good impression and have been valued in their host countries. Seven interviewees said contact with their new cultures contributed to their personal education and development. For example, a 40-year-old informant talked about her changing mentality, attitudes, and behaviors:

> It influenced me in the good sense because there, you begin to educate yourself. Things are so clear. You learn a lot from strangers. First, living with them, thinking like them. There is no way to apply a spoken language to a different Romanian mentality. You learn to eat; there are beautiful things that happen to you. You cannot be different from them living there. Society forces you to be just like them (01_F_40).

Feeling appreciated and valued contributed to this boost in self-confidence among our informants, who felt empowered and determined to exceed their personal boundaries. Here are some eloquent excerpts:

And when I went there and met other people, my perception of life changed. I got more trust in me. I met people who appreciated my work, my way of being. Much more than I appreciated myself before. Before I was, I do not know ... I was just a kid; just my experiences so far have not been so pleasant. So, I appreciated it. I was very happy that those people saw something in me. They always say: "Wow, you are so intelligent. You have to do something." Everyone urged me to go to school. "You have to do nursing school or cooking school." Everyone knew I had the pleasure of cooking (09_F_38).

Or:

About life, so I said, were other people who saw me with other eyes. And they gave me confidence, and I got rid of shyness and who ... Before I was, I just felt that way. That helped me (22_F_31).

Although for the most part, this positive redefinition of self-representation implied an awareness and gradual internalization of new relationships, there also were women who needed specialized support. One person talked about how confronting a new socioeconomic context in her country of migration led her to disregard herself through personal devaluation. She remembers saying: "*I was nothing. I say, 'I am nothing,' then I fell.*" The need for counseling help led her to return home for a while. Another migrant has lately become aware, after the birth of her children, of the need to change herself:

I was wrong in this matter and my mother too. (...) I thought I was not important. And I have never learnt this, to take care of me (...). And then I was in Germany for 10 months, in a psychiatric clinic, where I did psychotherapy and counselling, I learned a lot about how I think, and why I think like that and then I let everything go (31_F_49).

FINDINGS: 3. TRANSITION TO PARENTHOOD

The Maternal Age at First Birth and the Synchronicity of Parenting with Other Life Trajectories

The age of migrant mothers in the study for their first births was between 27 and 36 years, with the average being 30.3 years. All women were married when they got pregnant. By the time they got pregnant with their first child, the nine interviewees spent a minimum of three years in the host country. Of the nine mothers, two returned to Romania to give birth to their children, then went back to the country of migration for different periods of time. One returned during pregnancy and remained in Romania. When they got pregnant, all the women were employed, and some had more than one job. Over the course of their pregnancies, many of our informants gave up their jobs partially or totally. In six out of nine cases, the pregnancies were unplanned, generating a wide range of emotions, mainly internal conflicts. Thus, some of them considered themselves immature and psychologically unprepared to assume child-rearing responsibilities, although they all exceeded the average age at which mothers in Romania have their first child. For example, 06_F_38, aged 35 when she first became pregnant, said:

> ... Now, honestly, when I was thinking of having my children, being pregnant, I felt very unprepared to be a mother. I don't know. I had the impression I would not know what to do. How should I raise a baby?

Or 15_F_36, age 27, concerning her first pregnancy, said:

> First, I didn't feel ready because I felt like a child.

These experiences have been associated, in most cases, with the perception of asynchrony between parental and professional trajectories. Leaving work for motherhood meant a loss to most migrants and a move away from the purpose for which they were in the country of migration, namely to gain economic comfort. In this respect, one informant said:

> Secondly, I had a very, very good job, and I did not want to lose it. I knew a child came with responsibilities. Great responsibilities. Before I had a baby, I was working from 8 a.m. to 8 p.m. in the evening. Of course, with a child, you cannot do that anymore. So, I was not prepared from any point of view. (15_F_36)

Another loss associated with the parental role was that of personal and couples' freedom. 09_F_38 said:

> Eeee ... I was not really ready. I was 27 years old, and we (she and her partner) were accustomed to the comfort of independent living. (...) We came home when we wanted to... We did not have a schedule ... We wanted to wake up at 4 a.m. (?) ... and I woke up at 4 to go to work before the girl was born. (...)

With the child, I did not agree to have one, but instead, my husband, he wanted to. Not that he forced me, but he insisted that it was time. And then, thinking about it, I saw around us that our friends were having children. And then she was born. And it was beautiful. It was very beautiful.

The difficulty of accepting pregnancy is also reflected in maternal behaviors during pregnancy. 01_F_40 received no affection from her parents and, at the age of 29, aborted a baby at the request of her husband. When she got pregnant again, unplanned, at age 32, she had difficulty being sensitive to her unborn baby. She states as follows:

Many pregnant women say, 'Wow, I'm pregnant' and talk to their baby ... but I could not be so emotional, so romantic. I couldn't.

The Experience of the Child's Birth, and the Mother's Accommodation in the First Few Months After the Childbirth

Between the onset of pregnancy and the birth of the child, we identified a major transformation in the perception of the parental role, and of the child. These mothers began to identify the advantages and benefits of this role. Most spoke about having their babies as the happiest moment of their lives:

It's nice to be a parent (...) It's something you cannot describe, uttered. (06_F_38).

This positive transformation of parental perception was not always easy. For example, an interviewee asked for specialized help. She told her story this way:

I involuntarily became a mother. That's how it was to be ... to go to the psychologist. Because of no ... no matter how much the world would advise you until you convince yourself, you don't have that peace. And I decided to go to the psychologist. (...) Then I went to the psychologist for two or three sessions and helped me a lot. And then I went this way. It was very difficult for me, but when I assumed and assimilated everything, I changed radically. It is said that a child comes with an open tap, or I don't know ... I realized that the real happiness comes, with the birth of the child. When you have two what to say (...). Life is totally different. Honestly, I tell you. (15_F_36).

Making adjustments right after giving birth was not easy for all these mothers. Some faced health problems, while others felt overwhelmed. Most have only received informal support from family members. The mothers who gave birth in host countries relied mainly on help from their husbands. An immigrant describes the experience of the first few days after giving birth in Italy:

> *The experience has been very difficult. After birth, I felt terrible. I've had three days of all sorts ... it was very hard. But I had my husband, who pulled me up because I was very demoralized at that time. I left the hospital, and the baby stayed there for another three weeks in the incubator. And going home without the baby is not easy. ... Why are you going home? What for? The next day, as I was, I went 60 km to see my baby. My husband was working away then ... (09_F_38).*

Women who chose to give birth in Romania have benefited from the support of other family members—their own mothers or sisters. In most cases, the aid was needed during recovery, in the first days or weeks. We, therefore, tend to view this help as instrumental.

> *It was very difficult at first (smile). I did not know what it was, I wanted my baby, and I had it at a fairly old age, that is, 30 years old. But I didn't know what it means to care for me. Fatigue ... I have to wake up at night and so ... However, it was a great joy. Now that time has passed, I have become more experienced. DL (her daughter) has grown and is not that difficult. Mom helped me. So, she came to my house and stayed for the first two weeks (22_F_31).*

In a retrospective assessment, becoming a parent generated positive changes for marital partners and for their relationships.

FINDINGS: 4. PARENTING MANIFESTATION

Motherhood Values

The values of the interviewed mothers that guide their children's education were grouped in the same two categories previously presented. Most of them want to convey to their children the moral-religious values that have been inspired by their own parents. Faith in God is common, and respect for oneself and others has been mentioned frequently. The major difference between them and their own parents is the emphasis they put on valuing the child's independence. For example, 01_F_40, explaining how her parenting behavior differs from her mother's, says:

> *Yes, my daughter has the right; she can tell me what she likes or what she doesn't like. She can speak freely, and I'll accept her choices (01_F_40).*

Hard work and responsibility are still important values for migrant mothers. However, these values are considered strictly as a path to personal self-actualization. The child no longer exists for its economic value to the family. He or she now provides emotional value, and family unity is more valuable than before. The aspirations and independence of the child are no longer stifled. He or she is no longer responsible for the welfare of family members. As one mother states:

> *It is said that parents are obliged to give wings to their children, to let them leave… Definitely, I would not keep her attached to me. I would like her to choose to stay with me, to study in Romania. But, of course, if she tells me she wants to study in another country, I would certainly let her go, though it would surely break my soul. I would not want to clip her wings (33_F_36).*

Mothers' Aspirations for Their Children

Mothers speak with some reticence about what they want for their children. Everyone admits they have aspirations for them, but children's desires and choices are primordial. As shown in the first part of this analysis, mothers followed the aspirations dictated by their own parents. They do not repeat this practice with their children. Many of them are committed to directing, supporting, and even following their children to fulfill their dreams.

> *It is very important for a young man to choose his job or his own way, and in this sense, we, as parents, should help them, not order them. We should feel them; let them do it. I'm not saying to tell them "do what you want" (…) because the child will unbalance. But that moment when I'm imposing and say (missing), you should now learn! She disagrees and damages my relation with her. And for me, it's more important that my relationship with her to succeeds … when two fight, two lose. That's my principle. And then as a mother, I try to be close to her, to be like a fence, not of safety, but of support (31_F_49).*

Parenting Behaviors and Attitudes

Transferring these values into parenting practices means, in most cases, the adoption of a democratic, or even permissive, parenting style. Common to both styles is the high level of responsiveness. Although most of them were deprived of affection in their own childhoods, these mothers' discourses show a lot of availability, sensitivity, and support for their own children. Most desire for their offspring a different childhood from theirs—childhood in which children do not feel the fear of mistakes or lack of support to fulfill aspirations. 01_F_40 presents "a life philosophy" that she applies to her daughter's education:

> *What philosophy guides me in life? ... Life has a one-way sense. You should pass and live all the moments at their time. Unfortunately, the leaps I've done were not good, if I could give advice to someone. My daughter went to kindergarten as she was supposed to, with everything that it was, with mistakes, excursions, with all that it was. I want her to go to school and do her mistakes...even get the mark 4, do everything. In adolescence, if she wants to have a life, to love, I'll let her do it, I won't do as my parents did. There was a "no" without explanations. We should live life differently, with all the experiences, not with fear, the fear that I had the fear to make mistakes, the fear of tomorrow. No, this is not life (01_F_40).*

Some of the mothers spoke openly about their transformations, from rigid, severe, and closed people—as they were socialized in their own childhoods—to calm, tolerant, serene, and sensitive in relation to their own children. For some of them, the change was possible through self-education and control. Others needed specialized help.

> *Having the experience behind, I tend to drive her too much, to say it is not good. I have to let her make mistakes (01_F_40).*

Regarding the second dimension of the parental style, the data in the interviews indicate moderate control of children's behavior. The emphasis on relationships and trust weakens the need for strict control. The parent has become a resource that facilitates new experiences, provides direction, listens, and provides feedback while refraining from imposing on their children their own ideas, choices, or aspiration.

Discussion

This study raised a range of questions about the transition to parenthood patterns and parenting-practices models among Romanian migrant mothers, who have returned or plan to do so in the near future.

The data lend support to the disruption hypothesis when we analyze the transition to parenthood. In all nine cases, we recorded a removal from the Romanian model of transition to parenthood, specific to the lower class, characterized by early marriage after the completion of studies, followed shortly by the birth of children (Baetică 2015; Muresan 2014). What seems to be straying from the traditional Romanian model is the rise in births outside of marriage.

There is no strong evidence for the assimilation of the patterns in the host country, even if the age of migrants for their first births is very close to the age of mothers in Southern and Western European countries (European Commission and Eurostat 2015), and the birth rate is relatively low. Delaying first pregnancy is mainly explained by the incompatibility that migrants set between professional and parental trajectories. These results are consistent with those obtained by Mussino and Strozza (2012), showing that Romanians are very unlikely to give birth to a child in the first 18 months after migration.

Being perceived as a burden that hinders the achievement of the main goal of migration, pregnancy has generated a series of internal conflicts. In contrast to non-migrant mothers who generally find emotional support from their families, some migrant mothers have sought specialized help. In all cases, from the onset of pregnancy to the birth of the child, there was a radical change in attitudes toward children and the parental role.

The life-story interviews enabled migrants to reflect on their own childhoods and to identify differences in their own parental behaviors compared with their parents' parenting styles. What they have preserved from their own parents are moral-religious values. In contrast, child-rearing values and parenting behaviors have changed considerably. From traditional values that emphasized obedience, unyielding respect for adults, and the economic and emotional interdependence of family members, we see a transition to values that emphasize children's independence. The child is free to aspire, to decide his or her path, and the parent offers support and development opportunities. We noticed a transition from authoritarian behaviors that involve strict child control, associated with few expressions of affection and support, to authoritative, even permissive styles.

Although we have been tempted to believe that these parental models are adopted from the country of migration because they are similar to them (see above García and Gracia 2014; Moscardino et al. 2011;

Otto and Keller 2016), the data do not indicate a direct connection. At the same time, there is no evidence that mothers were constrained to adopt a certain parental model, either from the country of migration or in the country of origin, once they returned. In many informants' narratives, we have identified an association between changing the parental models learned in their own childhoods and developing a better self-image. Self-appreciation in the migratory country, through the trust and self-esteem given to them by those with whom they have interacted in the new context, generated positive changes in self-image. This positive relationship with oneself, and significant others, appears to have translated into parental values and practices. Our empirical data suggest that self-change in the case of young migrant mothers has gradually developed through awareness of one's own qualities and internalization. This evidence is in line with the mechanisms of resocialization explained by attachment theory and discussed previously. These results show that understanding of acculturation requires a deeper analysis of psychological mechanisms. Explaining acculturation through social learning as a result of exposure to new patterns of behavior does not seem to be sufficient. For the observed patterns to be assimilated, they must come from people whom they respect. Our informants reported in their stories about such people, who changed their perspectives on themselves and others.

Future studies should consider these aspects and should inform the development of social services aimed at supporting migrant adaptation. The process of transforming the self is not smooth. Some of our informants acknowledged that their inner tensions were so acutely felt that they could not cope with them without specialized support. Therefore, this study shows that migrants need not only educational services, for learning the language and culture of the host country, but also support in the process of internalizing new experiences and redefining themselves.

Without a claim to data generalization, this study has given us the opportunity to thoroughly examine the ways in which the context of migration has generated a discontinuity in the transmission of parental patterns acquired in childhood. The life-course perspective adopted in this study has proven to be very useful in understanding how many sociocultural and psychological factors combine to explain the transformations generated by migration.

References

Atkinson, Robert. 1998. *The Life Story Interview*. Thousand Oaks, CA: Sage Publications.
Baetică, Radu. 2015. Romania Between Modernism and Traditionalism. *Eurostat—Statistics Explained*.
Barometrul de Opinie Publica (BOP). 2008. București: SOROS Foundation.
Baumrind, Diana. 1991. The Influence of Parenting Style on Adolescent Competence and Substance Use. *The Journal of Early Adolescence* 11 (1): 56–95.
———. 2005. Patterns of Parental Authority and Adolescent Autonomy. *New Directions for Child and Adolescent Development* 108: 61–69.
Belsky, Jay. 1984. The Determinants of Parenting: A Process Model. *Child Development* 55 (1): 83–96.
Berry, John W. 1997. Immigration, Acculturation, and Adaptation. *Applied Psychology* 46 (1): 5–34.
———. 2006. Contexts of Acculturation. In *The Cambridge Handbook of Acculturation Psychology*, ed. David L. Sam and John W. Berry. Cambridge: Cambridge University Press.
———. 2007. Acculturation Strategies and Adaptation. In *Immigrant Families in Contemporary Society*, ed. Jennifer E. Lansford, Kirby D. Deater-Deckard, and Marc H. Bornstein. New York: Guilford Press.
Birman, Dina, and Edison J. Trickett. 2001. Cultural Transitions in First-Generation Immigrants: Acculturation of Soviet Jewish Refugee Adolescents and Parents. *Journal of Cross-Cultural Psychology* 32 (4): 456–477.
Bowlby, John. 1969. *Attachment and Loss. Vol. 1. Attachment*. New York: Basic Books.
Bradatan, Cristina E. 2014. The Interplay Between Family and Emigration from Romania. *Migration Letters* 11 (3): 368–376.
Braun, Virginia, and Victoria Clarke. 2006. Using Thematic Analysis in Psychology. *Qualitative Research in Psychology* 3 (2): 77–101. https://doi.org/10.1191/1478088706qp063oa.
Chen, Zeng-Yin, and Howard B. Kaplan. 2001. Intergenerational Transmission of Constructive Parenting. *Journal of Marriage and Family* 63 (1): 17–31.
Cowan, Philip A. 1991. Individual and Family Life Transitions: A Proposal or a New Definition. In *Family Transitions*, ed. Philip A. Cowan and E. Mavis Hetherington. Hillsdale, NJ: Lawrence Erlbaum.
d'Albis, Hippolyte, Angela Greulich, and Ponthière Grégory. 2017. Education, Labour, and the Demographic Consequences of Birth Postponement in Europe. *Demographic Research* 36: 691–728.
de Haan, Mariëtte. 2011. The Reconstruction of Parenting after Migration: A Perspective from Cultural Translation. *Human Development* 54 (6): 376–399.

Easterbrooks, Ann M. 1993. Effects of Infant Risk Status on the Transition to Parenthood. In *The Transition to Parenthood: Current Theory and Research*, ed. Gerald Y. Michaels and Wendy A. Goldberg. New York: Cambridge University Press.

European Commission and Eurostat. 2015. *Short Analytical Web Note: Demography Report*. Luxembourg: Publications Office.

Evans, Bronwynne C., et al. 2009. Utility of the Life Course Perspective in Research with Mexican American Caregivers of Older Adults. *Journal of Transcultural Nursing* 20 (1): 5–14.

Falicov, Celia Jaes. 1991. Family Sociology and Family Therapy Contributions to the Family Development Framework: A Comparative Analysis and Thoughts on Future Trends. In *Family Transitions: Continuity and Change Over the Life Cycle*, ed. Celia Jaes Falicov. New York: The Guilford Press.

García, Fernando, and Enrique Gracia. 2014. The Indulgent Parenting Style and Developmental Outcomes in South European and Latin American Countries. In *Parenting Across Cultures*, ed. Helaine Selin, vol. 7, 419–433. Dordrecht: Springer Netherlands.

Glick, Jennifer E., et al. 2012. Migration Timing and Parenting Practices: Contributions to Social Development in Preschoolers with Foreign-Born and Native-Born Mothers: Migration Timing and Social Development. *Child Development* 83 (5): 1527–1542.

Goldberg, Wendy A. 1993. Perspectives on the Transition to Parenthood. In *The Transition to Parenthood: Current Theory and Research*, ed. Gerald Y. Michaels and Wendy A. Goldberg. New York: Cambridge University Press.

Hernandez, Miguel, and Monica McGoldrick. 1999. Migration and the Family Life Cycle. In *The Expanded Family Life Cycle: Individual, Family, and Social Perspectives*, ed. Elizabeth A. Carter and Monica McGoldrick. Boston: Allyn and Bacon.

Hoghughi, Masud. 2004. Parenting—An Introduction. In *Handbook of Parenting: Theory and Research for Practice*, ed. Masud Hoghughi and Nicholas Long. London: Sage Publications.

Kâğıtçıbaşı, Çiğdem. 1996. *Family and Human Development Across Cultures: A View from the Other Side*. Mahwah, NJ: L. Erlbaum Associates.

Kahn, Joan R. 1994. Immigrant and Native Fertility during the 1980s: Adaptation and Expectations for the Future. *International Migration Review* 28 (3): 501–519.

Kulu, Hill, et al. 2017. Fertility by Birth Order among the Descendants of Immigrants in Selected European Countries: Fertility by Birth Order Among Descendants of Immigrants. *Population and Development Review* 43 (1): 31–60.

Kulu, Hill, and Nadja Milewski. 2007. Family Change and Migration in the Life Course: An Introduction. *Demographic Research* 17 (2007): 567–590.

Madden, Vaishnavee, et al. 2015. Intergenerational Transmission of Parenting: Findings from a UK Kulu Longitudinal Study. *The European Journal of Public Health* 25 (6): 1030–1035.

Milewski, Nadja. 2010. Immigrant Fertility in West Germany: Is There a Socialization Effect in Transitions to Second and Third Births? *European Journal of Population/Revue européenne de Démographie* 26 (3): 297–323.

Moscardino, Ughetta, Costanza Bertelli, and Gianmarco Altoè. 2011. Culture, Migration, and Parenting: A Comparative Study of Mother-Infant Interaction and Childrearing Patterns in Romanian, Romanian Immigrant, and Italian Families. *International Journal of Developmental Science* 5 (1–2): 11–25.

Muresan, Cornelia. 2014. Postponement of Motherhood in Romania: The Role of Educational Attainment. *Revista de Cercetare și Intervenție Socială* 47: 137–149.

Mussino, Eleonora, and Salvatore Strozza. 2012. The Fertility of Immigrants After Arrival: The Italian Case. *Demographic Research* 26: 99–130.

Nedoluzhko, Lesia, and Gunnar Andersson. 2007. Migration and First-Time Parenthood: Evidence from Kyrgyzstan. *Demographic Research* 17: 741–774.

Nesteruk, Olena, and Loren D. Marks. 2011. Parenting in Immigration: Experiences of Mothers and Fathers from Eastern Europe Raising Children in the United States. *Journal of Comparative Family Studies* 42 (6): 809–825.

Ochocka, Joanna, and Rich Janzen. 2008. Immigrant Parenting: A New Framework of Understanding. *Journal of Immigrant & Refugee Studies* 6 (1): 85–111.

Oppedal, Brit. 2006. Development and Acculturation. In *The Cambridge Handbook of Acculturation Psychology*, ed. David L. Sam and John W. Berry. Cambridge: Cambridge University Press.

Otto, Hiltrud, and Heidi Keller. 2016. Is There Something Like German Parenting? In *Contemporary Parenting: A Global Perspective*, ed. Guerda Nicolas, Anabel Bejarano, and Debbiesiu L. Lee. New York: Routledge.

Patton, Michael Quinn. 2002. *Qualitative Research and Evaluation Methods*. 3rd ed. Thousand Oaks, CA: Sage Publications.

Popescu, Raluca. 2008. Family Values in Romania and in Europe. In *The Values of Romanians: 1993–2006. A Sociological Perspective*, ed. Bogdan Voicu and Mălina Voicu. Iași: Institutul European.

Robila, Mihaela. 2004. Families in Eastern Europe: Context, Trends and Variations. In *Families in Eastern Europe*, ed. Mihaela Robila. Amsterdam: Elsevier.

Șerban, Monica. 2011. *Dinamica migrației internaționale: un exercițiu asupra migrației românești în Spania*. Iași: Lumen.

Șerban, Monica, and Bogdan Voicu. 2010. Romanian Migrants to Spain: In- or Outside the Migration Networks—A Matter of Time? *Revue D'études Comparatives Est-Ouest* 41 (4): 97–124.

Serbin, Lisa, and Jennifer Karp. 2003. Intergenerational Studies of Parenting and the Transfer of Risk from Parent to Child. *Current Directions in Psychological Science* 12 (4): 138–142.

Sharma, Nidhi, Subho Chakrabarti, and Sandeep Grover. 2016. Gender Differences in Caregiving Among Family—Caregivers of People with Mental Illnesses. *World Journal of Psychiatry* 6 (1): 7.

Sherman, Jennifer, and Elizabeth Harris. 2012. Social Class and Parenting: Classic Debates and New Understandings: Social Class and Parenting. *Sociology Compass* 6 (1): 60–71.

Sobotka, Tomáš. 2008. Overview Chapter 7: The Rising Importance of Migrants for Childbearing in Europe. *Demographic Research* 19: 225–248.

Tudor, Elena, Mihaela Manole, and Gabriela Alexandrescu. 2013. *Child Abuse and Neglect: National Sociologic Study*. București: Save the Children.

van Ijzendoorn, Marinus H. 1992. Intergenerational Transmission of Parenting: A Review of Studies in Nonclinical Populations. *Developmental Review* 12 (1): 76–99.

van Ijzendoorn, Marinus H., and Marian J. Bakermans-Kranenburg. 1997. Intergenerational Transmission of Attachment: A Move to the Contextual Level. In *Attachment and psychopathology*, ed. Leslie Atkinson and Kenneth J. Zucker. New York: Guilford Press.

Videon, Tami M. 2005. The Impact of Marital Dissolution on Mothering and Fathering: Parenting Practices Before and After Dissolution. In *Contemporary Issues in Parenting*, ed. Melissa J. Kane. New York: Nova Science Publishers.

Vlase, Ionela. 2015. Migrația și revenirea românilor în țară. Implicații. In *Este România altfel? Societatea si sociologia ... incotro?* ed. Bogdan Voicu, Horațiu Rusu, and Adela Popa. București: Tritonic.

Voicu, Bogdan. 2012. Measuring Child-Rearing Values. A Research Note. *Social Change Review* 10 (1): 47–70.

Voicu, Bogdan, and Claudiu Tufiș. 2016. *In-Depth Assessment of the Social, Health, and education Status of Children and their Families in Target Areas of the Bacău County*. București: UNICEF.

White, Stephen, et al. 2008. The Political Resocialization of Immigrants: Resistance or Lifelong Learning? *Political Research Quarterly* 61 (2): 268–281.

CHAPTER 8

Women's Stories of Migration: Youth, Personal Agency, and Linked Lives

Ana Maria Preoteasa

International migration stands as a visible sign of a global age (Castells 2001) and often is studied in relation to topics such as gender (Piperno 2012; Vlase 2013; Tyldum 2014), family (Kofman 2004; Cong and Silverstein 2012), education (Pitkänen and Takala 2012), and work (Anderson 2010; Favell 2008; Damelang and Haas 2012). The intricate interconnections among these fields carry deep implications for individual lives, as well as society as a whole, requiring careful societal arrangements and sometimes tailored social policies or programs.

This chapter documents the construction of women's narratives about their migration trajectories by considering their stage in life at the time of migration, their education level, career status in origin and destination countries, and the role played by family members in shaping their decision-making in respect to migration and return. Family and social networks become important triggers for migration, career, and return decisions (Șerban 2011; Damelang and Haas 2012). To depict and explain these all-

---

A. M. Preoteasa (✉)
Research Institute for Quality of Life, Romanian Academy, Bucharest, Romania

© The Author(s) 2018
I. Vlase, B. Voicu (eds.), *Gender, Family, and Adaptation of Migrants in Europe*,
https://doi.org/10.1007/978-3-319-76657-7_8

encompassing processes, the chapter builds on the analysis of accounts from eight informants' case studies and considers the biographical facts, feelings, and attitudes accompanying the narratives of their life events. The analysis follows a deductive and inductive approach (Saldana 2011; Green and Thorogood 2004; Willis 1942). The chapter starts by reviewing the literature on the main reasons for migration and the interconnections among migration trajectory, family, and education. Next, I introduce the migrant women's case studies to illustrate their migration trajectories and their perspectives as women on these migration paths. This chapter's main goals are to document these women's personal/individual reasons for migration and depict how women construct their life-course biographies through their choices and actions, considering opportunities and constraints, as well as the role of linked lives, in explaining their decisions (Elder 1995).

To offer a preview example, let's take the case of Andreea, a Romanian woman whose dream is to continue her college education. Due to her disadvantaged family's socioeconomic situation, she decided to work as a housekeeper in Germany to earn enough money for college. She migrated for six years between Germany and Romania, where she completed her graduate and postgraduate studies. However, her case is not unique. Although Romanian migrant women are most often depicted as caregivers and housekeepers abroad, their life situations are much more complex, and the satisfaction they derive from economic gains often is jeopardized by conflicts with other life dimensions (e.g., marital relationships, parental and/or filial responsibilities, or downward mobility in their professional careers). Romanian women's migration has been studied extensively in the context of unskilled migration, disproportionately focusing on the caregiver category, especially in destination countries such as Spain and Italy, at the expense of other categories of migrant women. There is also a tendency to picture women's migration as a personal sacrifice for the sake of meeting family needs (Tyldum 2014), while pushing aside their personal aspirations.

The present research goes beyond addressing the economic drivers of migration and delves into more intimate mechanisms that underpin women's decisions by also considering the individual desire for education and personal growth, the role of family situations, and the difficult balance between personal aspirations and the necessity to meet family needs. All eight study participants completed their higher education during migration or immediately upon return. In all cases, the main migration drivers are situated at the individual level, and migration is considered a route toward achievement of professional skills and competencies to meet personal aspirations. Contrary to most research on women's migration, this study shows that, regardless of their origin families' economic situations, these women's decisions were made in a context in which their personal needs occupied a central place and were not necessarily disregarded or subordinated to family concerns.

This chapter provides perspectives from women migrants, including their narratives on moving and return decisions (in the case of those who repatriated). While considering the interdependence among time, place, and family in women's migration decisions and the consequences of their life paths, this study intends to expand understanding in at least two directions. On the one hand, migrant women fall into different categories, depending on their life goals. On the other hand, the study focuses on the differences in their freedom to make decisions on family and personal levels, and the findings indicate that these women play multiple roles.

Circular migration, or seasonal migration, such as the various commuting patterns between Romania and other European countries, seems to be, for young Romanian migrant women, a strategy to achieve their life goals. The present analysis includes the participants who migrated to attain their own objectives, which may refer to a wide range of necessities, including access to better health care, enrollment in European universities, employment opportunities, or accumulated savings to complete educational trajectories in their home country.

Empirical evidence illustrates the ways in which migrant women negotiate their personal objectives against other commitments and obligations attached to their family situations (e.g., marriage and motherhood) and career (e.g., employment status, education, and training). Three research questions are addressed: Which are the individual-level drivers that led these women to migrate? How did their migration trajectories intersect with educational paths? How were their migration trajectories linked with romantic lives, families, and marriages?

To answer these three research questions, Romania offers an excellent context. Migration has risen steadily in recent decades, from almost nothing to one of the highest rates in Europe (Bîrsan et al. 2008). The transition from communism generated high social and economic inequalities among age, class, and gender among Romanians, with deleterious effects on the standard of living for a significant share of the population (Mărginean 2013). Developments in the labor market led to redundancy in many former qualifications gained during communism, leaving many people unemployed or forced to take lesser jobs (Preoteasa et al. 2016). The economic inequalities also are reflected in the disparities in access to education. Poor economic conditions in the origin family could prevent access to formal higher education (Neagu 2007). Romania inherited an educational system that is very similar to those in other post-Soviet Eastern European countries. Despite changes during the transition years, the nation's education-system quality did not substantially improve, as it ranked among the lowest in Europe, based on PISA (Programme for International Student Assessment) data (Voicu 2005), while its investments in education still trail most other European countries (Neagu 2015). Access to higher education remained financially difficult in the 1990s for most Romanians, though women were more frequently seen as university students than men, and they are generally present in the labor market there (Voicu 2005). This created a fertile environment in which the migration-education-career-family mix can be studied.

Why Do Women Migrate? Agency and Linked Lives: Some Answers from Literature

The existing literature dealing with Eastern Europeans' reasons for migrating to Western European nations postulates a general desire to achieve a better life, usually economically, through higher incomes and more job security. However, connected reasons—such as employment opportunities, a chance for better health care, and/or improved access to quality education—are scarcely studied. The motivation for migration is not always easy to determine (Geist and McManus 2012) and is linked largely to the economic situation of the country of origin and the differences and opportunities offered by the destination country. The difficulty in understanding migration triggers becomes even more pronounced when using a quantitative approach since "the motivation underlying the move is not generally known, so researchers are forced to make assumptions" (Geist and McManus 2012: 198). Several reasons could explain the decision to move, including a desire for a better lifestyle or climate (Gauld and Horsburgh 2015); cultural motivations, such as those of Western citizens who move to other Western European countries (King et al. 2016a, b); and highly skilled Eastern Europeans' desire for better working conditions and access to new technologies (Petroff 2016).

Migration is an individual phenomenon, but it also manifests itself as a collective one, through couples, extended families, organized groups, or networks. Gender differences regarding migration refer to the motivation for migration, migration strategies, or occupations in destination countries (Pessar and Mahler 2003). The concept of gender goes beyond biological differences, takes on a cultural dimension, and is often studied as a process, including the gender differences that are created and perpetuated by social norms (Pessar and Mahler 2003). Gender differences in the labor market are reflected in the discrepancies in migration trajectories between women and men. The literature talks about the feminization of migration, including a higher rate of migration among women. Feminization occurs due to family reunification, family migration, and individual women's migration (Marchetti et al. 2014).

Migration from Eastern Europe often has been viewed as rather feminized, due to the employment options available in destination nations, including domestic jobs such as care for the elderly, children, or people with disabilities. For instance, in the case of 2011 Italy, 76% of migrants from Ukraine and 65% from Moldova were women (Marchetti et al. 2014). The migration population from Romania is more balanced, with 54% women, while Polish migrant women stand at 65% (Marchetti et al. 2014). Scholars invariably describe the migrant women from Eastern Europe as migrant caregivers (King et al. 2016a, b) and emphasize their transnational ties with family members who remain in origin countries (Bahna 2014, 2015; Piperno 2012; Tyldum 2014). Based on qualitative research carried out with Romanian women migrants in Italy, as well as their family members in Romania, various compensatory mechanisms for the absence of mothers were considered, including regular visits home, daily phone calls, and economic remittances (Piperno 2012). These phenomena signal the onset of a "transnational motherhood" process, with caregiving for children left behind partly or entirely taken over by significant others, such as grandmothers, aunts, fathers, or older siblings, especially if the latter are daughters and are considered responsible and mature enough to take care of younger siblings (Piperno 2012; Vlase 2013; Ducu 2014).

Regarding individual migrant women, the main reasons cited in literature are a quest for better economic conditions and a desire for higher education (Ghosh 2009). For example, in France, in 1996, 56% of new international students were women; Northern African women attended French universities to escape oppression in their home countries. A study that used a qualitative approach investigated the mobility of Romanian and Bulgarian undergraduate students in the UK and Spain (Marcu 2015), concluding that migration often is used as a strategy to improve career and family prospects. While the students who chose the UK were motivated by its prestigious universities, those who studied in Spain were migrants' children or returning migrants. Emancipation is defined as being able to make one's own choices, having attained legal and financial independence, as well as shared family care (Daly 2002; Kirk and Suvarierol 2014; Ghorashi 2010).

Educational emancipation of migrant women is one of the effects of migration (Ducu 2014; Oleinikova 2015), alongside material prosperity and boosted self-confidence. Literature on education levels post-migration highlights the transition from the status of labor migrant to education migrant, in terms of host country and the positive social and economic effects (Lee and Johnstone 2017). The post-migration education phenomenon also was studied by considering the socio-demographic characteristics of migrants enrolled in school after migration and the policy implications of inequalities among migrants viewed as human capital (Calvo and Sarkisian 2015).

Even in the case of individual women migrants' trajectories, their migration or return decisions are tied to their romantic or family lives. Family plays an essential role in decisions to leave, acting as an important driver of international migration. Household migration is tied to economic factors, including employment opportunities (Geist and McManus 2012), as well as children's education, while women's reasons for migrating generally are subordinated to men's goals, as men tend to be the main breadwinners and heads of households. Women who migrate with their husbands leave their employment in their origin country to follow men as tied movers (Lersch 2015; Geist and McManus 2012). In the case of couples' migration, the choice of destination is made by considering the possibility that both partners can finds jobs (Nisic and Melzer 2016). A quantitative study carried out in Albania shows that female migration is more sensitive to negative events at the household level (Stecklov et al. 2010:957). For instance, a health-related problem in a household decreases the chances for female migration, while economic strains (property losses) have the opposite effect. Returning Romanian migrants scarcely have been studied, the phenomenon being relatively new. Other countries' studies demonstrated that decisions to return often are influenced either by changes in marital status (Bijwaard and van Doeselaar 2014), fertility factors (Bertoli and Marchetta 2015), or poor economic outcomes in host countries (Saarela and Rooth 2012).

Despite the large number of studies devoted to women's migration and its relationship to career, education, and family, research that considers all three triggers simultaneously is scant in relation to life cycle, and in their interdependency as part of multiple migration, remigration, and return-migration decisions. This is the gap that this study fills in addressing the life-course perspective in migration studies. Also, this chapter looks to migration drivers and interconnections among career, education, and family by considering these eight women's narratives on their migration experiences.

DATA AND METHODS

Life-story interviews were conducted within the MIGLIFE project, also described in other chapters in this volume (see, for instance, Vlase, Bejenaru, or Croitoru). The research paid special attention to the meanings attached to different experiences that accompanied life events and transitions, and to the feelings the informants expressed while narrating their experiences. All informants received pseudonyms to protect their anonymity. For purposes of the present study, eight interviews were selected based on specific criteria: women who migrated in their youth (around age 20), who were unmarried and enrolled in higher education after migration.

The analysis followed a sequential, single-case analysis approach (Apitzsch and Siouti 2007), while presenting illustrative cases for each pattern at the intersection of migration, career, education, and professional trajectories. The analysis was carried out in three steps: thematic analysis (coding), structural description of cases, and comparisons among them, as described by later authors. The biography offered the opportunity to link individual narratives with different social and cultural contexts, such as origin and destination countries, time of migration, and time of return.

The interviews were gathered following purposeful sampling procedures, with the women having at least five years of migration experience. They moved abroad at different times: before 2002 (preceding the removal of European Union (EU) visa requirements), between 2002 and 2006 (before Romania entered the EU), and since 2007, when Romania became an EU member. The participants experienced different migration pathways (e.g., length of time in host countries, migration countries chosen, type of migration). They migrated while young—less than 26 years old—and the study's case-selection criteria were that the migration decision had to have been made by the woman, not by her origin family. The eight women migrated in different eras: four before 2001, two between 2002 and 2006, and the final two since 2007.

The analysis of case studies followed a common framework to present migrant women's biographies. The main dimensions considered were: life events (e.g., marriage, divorce, parents' death, childbirths, etc.), migration trajectory, education path, employment events, and return. Our analysis considered those who migrated while young, with personal motivations for doing so, either for education, health, personal development, or as a route to autonomy. Family and community factors were examined by considering family relationships and social networks. The cases were rich in information and provided much diversity concerning the intersection of education, family, and migration paths. Looking through life-course lenses, the analysis considers the intersection of various life events—family events, transitions, and other main drivers of migration and return. It explores the interdependence among time, place, and family in women's migration decision-making and on their life paths. The education trajectory and its intertwining with migration pathways were the principal focus of my analysis to understand how female migrants struggled to increase their social status and become emancipated.

The presentation of findings below seeks to portray the stories as they were reported by the participants by considering the deployment of the educational trajectory as it intersected other life trajectories, such as family and careers during migration, and contributed to different life outcomes and uneven paths to emancipation.

Findings

The eight women in this study had different employment situations when they migrated: four worked in domestic or caregiver jobs, one worked as a skilled worker, another left Romania as an international student who once worked in restaurants (in Italy) during her graduate studies, one worked on various research projects while enrolled in a Ph.D. program, and the last one was a student who worked abroad on a farm during a university summer holiday. All spent time as students during their stays abroad. Furthermore, we establish migration/education patterns by illustrating each pattern through a representative life story: working at unskilled jobs abroad while enrolled as a student in Romania, converting work experience into higher education at a later age, education upon return, and becoming an international student as a first step toward economic and family migration.

Working at Unskilled Jobs Abroad While Enrolled as a Student in Romania

Andreea (38, economist) experienced difficult years as a teen. When she was 15 years old, her mother passed away after suffering from an incurable disease. Her father then abandoned the family, leaving the children to fend for themselves. Andreea and her older sister were left to take care of their younger brother. During adolescence, Andreea started to work in the mornings as a janitor for three blocks of flats; then in the afternoon, she attended high school classes. Her discourse revealed her pride in her ability to achieve good grades despite harsh living conditions:

> *I have never done my homework at home. Once I received homework that 10 minutes break was all I needed to do my homework and let my exercise-book travel around for the entire class. Everybody copied (small grin). As for learning...again, I did not learn. I paid attention during the class and succeeded to read, or rather not and that's why...oh, how sorry I am.*

She describes her childhood as "neither good nor bad," but emphasized that she was forced to become a grown-up earlier than others her age. Her reported transition to adulthood came suddenly with her mother's disease and subsequent death and her father's abandonment.

After high school, she decided to continue her education, but her poor economic situation led her to postpone her higher education for eight years. The recurrent-education model is more flexible than the standardized one (before work life), allowing individuals coming from lower-income families to access higher education (Kallen and Bengtsson 1974). After high school, she had various unskilled jobs, including as a wholesaler and a waitress at a café. Her first migration experience came five years after completing high school. She went to Germany with her boyfriend, a German citizen, and this period was a good chance for her to learn the German language. They spent three years in Germany until the relationship ended. She amassed nine years of migration experience in Germany, plus a four-month stay in Italy with her sister and a few months in Ghana.

Migration allowed her to earn money for university expenses in Romania. She then started to travel between Germany and Romania:

> *And then... I've worked for about six years while I attended college in the long-distance program in Romania. During these six years, I worked for... as a housekeeper and looked after elderly, for three months, then returned for a*

> *month, which was the rule then, if you did not have the required documents to remain abroad. That's how I did my higher education. I came, attended the examinations, went abroad again, worked again, and spent money here (grin). And, again, between high school and faculty, I had about eight years as a break, and only after that, I enrolled to faculty. After two years of faculty, I wanted to move there at the faculty, so up I went to ask about it. They told me that… I can transfer, as they acknowledge my studies. Then I was in the second year as the accounting chair. I suppose here is another system… I can opt for something else. They said they recognize my studies and I can transfer there. I came here, transferred to tourism, again economy and since then I finished. But then the education system changed a bit as well, as those…compulsory were decided, so I made five years of faculty and with compulsory master's. So, I did my master's as well. Oh, well…that's how that period of Germany-Romania went by.*

She said this period of commuting between countries was a very difficult one and, looking back, Andreea thinks it was not a very good decision. When she migrated first, before Romania joined the EU, Romanian migrants had better chances of finding good-paying jobs. With the benefit of hindsight, her experience becomes a lesson learned that she is willing to share with the younger generation to prevent other family members from repeating what she views as a mistake.

> *If I would have been clever, I believe I would have abandoned faculty in Romania (laughs) and worked without any other fuss because then one could earn well; money did have value. So, in that time, if you worked abroad and came again in the country, you could build your own house in a few years and achieve something. You know, it was at the beginning. Now, it's not that easier anymore; money no longer has the same value in Romania. And… to make a long story short, if I would have been clever, I would have caught then a contract and worked for the entire year. Now, if a child would ask for my opinion, say, my niece, I would advise her to work for a year and come to take the exams in the re-examination sessions. You understand? She should learn there for the entire year and during the re-examination sessions, she can solve all problems. So, I believe she would make more money than me, more than this…what I have achieved. Plus, in that time, I didn't have that much mind…what I earned abroad, I spent here. It's just that all young people hit the wall and only thereafter grow up.*

She met her husband through friends during one of her visits to Romania and decided to settle down and start a family in Romania. She describes her husband as her soul mate and "the most perfect in the world." However, he seems reluctant to consider migration to Germany, as he doesn't know German and his work at a Romanian construction company brings him enough rewards in their home country. She views her family as the main accomplishment in her life. They have a very young daughter and plan to have another child in the near future. Andreea's trajectory was influenced by critical life events, including her mother's death, father's abandonment, and her first romantic breakup. She considers herself lucky, having had a mother who educated her and her siblings well, and who was very kind to them, but severe at the same time. Her mother, a Baptist, was very devout, and she transmitted Christian morals and values to her children. When Andreea decided to have her own children, she asked herself whether she could be as good a mother as hers was. Despite her difficult childhood, she has wonderful memories of her mother. She remains optimistic and has found positive aspects in all dimensions of her life, even at the most difficult moments; for example, her mother's death forced her to grow up early and become responsible. Her father was a negative influence, and she is glad she did not inherit his character and only has some of his physical attributes.

In her life story, migration seems to be important not only for coping with financial difficulties and helping her family but also for nurturing her personal development by acquiring a formal education. Her migration experience contributed to her enhanced self-esteem, allowing her to develop the social skills needed to work with others. She perceives that others value her since her migration experience. She views her return to Romania as successful because of her young family, but her professional trajectory and economic outcomes are not very satisfying because her entrepreneurial attempts fell short. She tried three times to start a business (commerce and transportation) but was unsuccessful due to various difficulties in adapting to Romanian economic conditions. She instead worked for a few years for a transportation company.

At the time of the interview, she was on maternity leave, taking care of her very young daughter and seemingly very focused on her new motherhood role. Regarding future job prospects, Andreea says her family's economic situation may require more migration soon, but her husband's inability to speak German remains a roadblock. Thus, their future is uncertain (Saarela and Rooth 2012), but migration remains on the table if Romania's economy doesn't improve. Employment issues have dominated her life trajectory, with an increase in standard of living remaining an inviting incentive to migrate anew. Whatever happens, her new family provides her with fulfilment and balance, which she lost in her childhood.

Migrant as Caregiver and Social-Work Education: Converting Informal Caregiving Experiences into Formal Credentials

Viorica started her circulatory migration story in 2000 at the age of 19. Her migration career includes stints in Austria and Germany, interspersed with returns to Romania. Her first trip began with a newspaper ad: A family in Austria was looking for a babysitter for a six-month-old baby. She told her parents about her decision to migrate and left very happy and confident. Her origin family lives in a rural area. She described herself as very immature, having just graduated from high school and dreaming of traveling to places she saw on TV. "I've never gone to Germany…so I was thrilled. I imagined going to another world. I've never seen…I think, now, I was going there and and I dreamed I'd eat many sweets there." Her enthusiasm soon faded, as her first migration experience was traumatic, humiliating, and oppressive:

> *The problems began right at the beginning with the mother of the child, who was very, very…oh, she was a pharmacist, and had some ideas like: "Don't kiss the child." "Don't hold him close to you!" Very strict. She kept following me. She didn't trust me. In turn, the child loved me a lot. That's why the child grew slowly attached to me, and she was jealous that the child loved me that much, and in time, as weeks went by, she started shouting at me for anything she disliked. Moreover, something else came up: There was no food. They told me when we were at my parents that I can have all the food I want, and that the fridge is at my disposal. But the fridge was empty. A cold wind blew through it. So, I was hungry there. Never in my life have I suffered that much hunger as in that time. It was my ambition to stay; otherwise, I would have returned.*

The isolation and denial of her basic rights could be described as modern slavery (Hoerder et al. 2015). However, she said this first migration experience was a step toward adulthood that created prospects for her empowerment. In hindsight, she said personal ambition was the only reason why she endured such a situation. She views herself as someone with a solid plan, ready to make all the necessary decisions to achieve self-actualization and professional goals upon her return to Romania, despite fewer opportunities and regressive attitudes (including from her family and community). She graduated from a cooking school and worked for six months in a restaurant in Cluj-Napoca until she resigned because the owners were not paying employees' salaries.

However, she soon resumed her migration experience and worked in a succession of German caregiving jobs in elderly home care. She discovered her natural ability to work with people in need of care, such as those with dementia. She was not qualified but acquired much experience and, in her narrative, she highlights what she learned, including a better understanding of her skills and career aspirations. Nevertheless, causality cannot be inferred, as we cannot tell whether her new outlook on life would not have been achieved in the absence of migration. However, her discourse highlights the positive effects in terms of knowledge, and she attributes her career growth to migration. She was very young when she started working with the elderly, and her discourse includes her views on the aging process and the changes in her own perceptions of old age. Referring to working with the elderly after her return, she notes:

> *Still, it changed my life outlook. I began noticing that elderly have young souls still. I've never seen age like a thing…I could not imagine, and only thought; ow…it's an old person. I didn't grow up with elderly, and I didn't sit with my grandparents for a long time. They lived on the same street with us, but they didn't care much about us. I was not attached to them. And this was the first time I sat with an elderly person, and began talking with this person. They enjoy talking about their life experiences, how they lived, how were the war times, and I enjoyed listening. How it was because her husband was deported to Russia, how she waited for him to return, how she managed alone with four children. She kept telling me these stories, again and again. But I noticed: She was still young.*

At the same time, without any training in working with people who have dementia, she formulated her own methods that provided results. She was very creative and demonstrated innate qualities such as empathy, patience, and communication skills:

> *Always, I had to keep them (with) something to do. I had to make a program for them, a certain run of the day. This means a lot of affection. It's like this: You cannot give them the cold shoulder. They need you to be calm, to smile at them, to take them by the hand, to hug them a bit, to praise them: "Oh, wonderful what you managed to do!" or "Oh, how …" whenever they did something. What they could do. They kept helping me all the time; all the time, I tried to encourage them not to sit like vegetables. Not the "I'm old, so I won't do anything!" He, the old man, was the one emptying the trash bin and let the curtains down. The old lady cleaned the potatoes, or an apple. I made some pastries, and she was so happy that she had made some.*

Her openness and attitude toward working with elderly people who have difficult health conditions contributed to an increase in her self-esteem. Shy and inhibited was how she described herself at age 19, before migrating, but her clients' appreciation for her abroad fortified her self-image. In Germany, Viorica found her first job with the help of another Romanian national who formerly had recruited Romanian women and placed them in caregiving jobs there. She soon developed very good relationships with her clients' families, who referred her to other clients. She stayed in Germany for ten years. In Germany, Viorica met her husband-to-be, also a Romanian migrant from the same region where she grew up, who was a temporary worker harvesting vineyards. They were married in 2012, but she continued working in Germany for various stints while her husband returned on a permanent basis to Romania. She kept circulating between the two countries, and her period of migration provided them with the income necessary for a decent life in Romania. Her new family is based mainly in Romania, in a rural area, where they live on a farm. She gave birth to her daughter in 2013. Viorica started nursing school in Romania, as her previous attempt to enroll in a similar school in Germany was not possible due to language barriers and difficulties getting Romanian education certificates recognized. Her path was marked by her agency—a migration path that was personal, with her family prominent in her narrative, a landmark accomplishment that's ever present in Viorica's story. She also referred to her parents' opinion throughout her experience. She described her mother as a very good friend to whom she confides. Her older sister, who also worked as a caregiver for the elderly, was instrumental in helping her find a job in Germany. In Viorica's case, the role of her new family (husband and child) was essential in her decision to return (even for only a brief period of time). During her travels, she discovered her skills at working with people in need, and she continued her formal education in this field. Viorica left Romania looking for personal accomplishment, but she chose to return to fulfill her role as a woman and mother. Romania's economic conditions had driven her to leave, and migration was a chance to overcome her initial status and build career credentials and experience.

Education upon Return

Silvia is the fourth child in her family. She grew up in the countryside and did housekeeping chores since she was in first grade. She said she was overwhelmed by household responsibilities—an important factor in her decision to leave home and enroll in high school in a different city in her early adolescence. Her father decided that her high school career specialization would be primary school teacher. In her narrative, the father image appears as authoritarian and difficult to oppose. One of her sisters graduated from the same high school that she did; her father considered it crucial to have a profession upon high school graduation. After high school, her father decided she should go to college. In 2002, she migrated to Spain for a few years to earn money to continue her education. Her decision to migrate appears to be a reaction to her father's interdiction, but she also benefitted from her older migrant brother, who was living in Spain by that time and who helped her with accommodations and gave her information about local culture and jobs. She worked as a babysitter for several families. Silvia narrates her work experience in Spain from the perspective of lessons learned and in contrast with her life and work experiences in Romania:

> However, abroad it's not as one thinks, or hears. There's no Promised Land, and no money hanging out from trees. If you are honest, trustworthy, and work, then you earn, you earn decently…If not, it's just like here. You must be very dutiful. Working time is working time, what you must do, you do. Nobody distracts you from work; nobody comes with any extra claims. Nobody disregards you because you are beyond his class or because they are above you, no. There, everybody's equal, all people are respected, all have rights but also duties. You should know, there, people are more focused on their duties than on their rights.

Migration also elicited a change in her marital status. In Spain, she met her husband, who also is Romanian, and they have two daughters, both born in Spain. She notes the help she received from her brother and other Romanian migrants. In turn, she felt obligated to help other Romanian newcomers. They soon decided to rent a bigger apartment to accommodate migrant guests:

> In fact, when we moved into a flat, we've moved into a five-room flat. That is, that if I return….there, one must help each other. Someone else comes, family, or the like, so we've got rooms, and we had to pay about 3,000 euros rent.

They returned to Romania in 2015, mainly due to the economic situation. In Romania, they could afford to buy an apartment, which was not possible in Spain. Traditionally, in Romania, as in other Eastern European countries, homeownership is a strong norm, thereby explaining this participant's desire to return over housing issues. In Romania, about 95% of houses were owned, without a mortgage, in 2016, while in the EU as a whole, the rate is about 42.5% (Eurostat 2017). Simultaneously, in Romania, housing quality is one of the lowest in Europe, with the highest overcrowding rate.

Moreover, Silvia considers the educational system in Romania superior to Spain's and wanted to enroll her older daughter in Romanian schools. In Romania, she found a job as an instructor in the educational system. She also has continued her education as a student at College of Education and Teaching at the university. Her life trajectory reveals an early transition to adulthood, with education postponed due to her conflicts with her father and her precarious economic situation. Her agency made her achieve her goals: starting a family, having kids, and entering university at age 36. Silvia comes from a traditional rural Romanian family, where a father's position is dominant in most family matters, including children's choices of professional careers. Her father is a strong presence throughout the interview, manifested as someone positioned against all her wishes but who did not deter Silvia from following her dreams. Relying on familial networks (like her brother) helped her adapt to her migrant status, smoothing the transition. Settling down and starting a family also was a way to fulfill her needs for affection, security, and belonging. Her discourse revealed someone attached to family values, and despite conflicts with her father, she still considers him very important in her life. During her migration period, she was an active member of the Romanian community in Spain, which provided support during her difficult period in the beginning. She has tried to reciprocate the help she received by renting out a large apartment to accommodate Romanian migrant newcomers in Spain. Overall, her migration experience provided her with the tools for a successful transition to adulthood, and simultaneously, her repeated migratory behavior was a consequence of changes in her familial and self-fulfillment needs. Migration provided her with the resources to achieve independence, own a house, and continue her formal education.

Becoming International Student as First Step in Economic and Family Migration

Elena left Romania at age 20, with the first wave of immigrants, soon after the collapse of the communist regime in 1990. She already was a student in Romania at that time. She was orphaned at age 15, and her decision was spontaneous. She received a scholarship for summer school in Italy and prolonged her stay there, registering as a student in college. Her choice was related to her preference for Italian culture, as she had learned Italian as a child from an uncle. She graduated in seven years instead of five because of intricacies in her romantic and educational lives, compounded by her status as a migrant. Wanting to increase her employability, Elena took several courses on secretarial skills, marketing, and management. Working for a living was uneven in her narrative, and she described various jobs she took reluctantly:

> I assure you that for a communist child, like me, searching for work was at least a shame or between shame and panic, and you never knew what you've got. It was an issue about fighting myself. I've worked in a pizzeria; I worked in the mornings when I went to school. At lunch, I went to the pizzeria, then back to school till 11 o'clock at night, and you had to have energy to be marketable. No, after the pizzeria, I worked as a secretary, and after that, I worked as…I don't know, I did a lot of training for mathematics, and I taught everybody who needed it.

Concerning her family life, during her first years in Italy, she married an Italian citizen for three years and described their breakup as very painful:

> It was a nasty episode for me because I've lost a child with a malformation, and thereafter, we both went into some kind of psychic and emotional isolation, and I left him and we split, but thereafter, I remained tied because of the red tape, as divorce in Italy in those times lasted three years, and when I finished faculty, I finished also the divorce, I believe almost the same week, then I left for France.

The loss of the child and the subsequent marriage dissolution dramatically disrupted her educational, family, and work trajectories in Italy, and she needed to change this path by migrating to France, which was possible through education again. She started a master's program in Paris and planned to pursue a Ph.D. but could not obtain a scholarship. She still lives in France today, using her language skills to work as an authorized translator for a public institution. Her trajectory was split between two countries: Italy and France. In her discourse, she compares and contrasts the two countries in many respects. Regarding gender, Italy is described as very misogynistic:

What I disliked in Italy was that the woman is not regarded but as woman and only thereafter as operator…or any other profession. It used to drive me crazy because Italians are very evasive from this point of view, even if it's only a game, and so I was permanently stressed, a fact that never happened in France, even for a second…In France, you have a code of working relationships with the others, not nationality, not name, not…only competencies. How stupid that communist education was, but it still seemed to me according to the communist propaganda that men and women should be equal and to think about competencies and so on.

She appreciated France better, particularly its health-care system, as well as the welfare provided for families with children. Her second husband is Italian, and their two children are trilingual. When Elena lost her parents as a teen, she learned from a very young age to be responsible for herself and was able to make decisions to improve her life and exert agency to overcome her family losses.

Returning to Romania was a recurrent theme in her life. In 2005, she moved with her family (including, at the time, her Italian husband and their daughter) to Romania for nine months. The decision was mainly emotional, a return to her childhood, to her small town, surrounded by forests. Even so, the town's economic woes and the lack of social life and medical insurance drove them back to France, ahead of her impending delivery of her next child. Elena's intricate life path was dominated by her agency, constrained by the structural conditions offered by migration countries and by her multiple intersections of educational and familial arrangements (including lack of family of origin, failed first marriage, remarriage).

Conclusions

Looking at migrant women's paths through life-course lenses, we offered an in-depth perspective on eight women's lives. Their employment paths differed, from researchers and domestic workers to pizzeria workers and elderly caregivers. However, they all had a common desire to achieve higher-education degrees, and migration was the only possible strategy. The path I explored in the analysis differs based on several aspects: migration wave, education status, origin family, and education level. In all cases, their strategies have a common point: the move abroad. At the same time, migration led to different paths for their educational careers. Pursuing higher education occurred either during migration, after return, or by commuting back and forth between migration countries and Romania.

I selected women for this study who decided to migrate alone, at a very young age. Therefore, the analysis is limited to this demographic category of migrant women starting their migration journeys for individual reasons after varying life events. This assumed from the beginning certain individual characteristics of women, such as agency and the ability to make decisions alone at an early age. They demonstrated a strong self-determination in their decisions to migrate, but also to stay abroad, despite the harsh living conditions they encountered upon arrival. The Romanian migrants' communities and origin family members, some having migrated themselves, offered them various types of material or emotional support to help them adapt to destination-country conditions. Employment chances, education, or health care are cited as the principal reasons why they began their migration journeys. On the other hand, their difficult situations in their origin families, and a lack of means to pursue education, acted as push factors. Different situations such as loss of parent(s), repeated conflicts with parents, overly authoritarian parents, or precarious economic situations in their families are important factors in migration decisions. Moreover, their situations with their origin families empowered them and made them even more responsible with their lives.

The intersection of migration and education generates trajectories that could be defined by two major directions: education post-migration or migration for education. Their education trajectory post-migration mainly was dominated by an early transition to adulthood due to a difficult family context or personal financial difficulties. Their education was postponed and continued during migration through transnational commuting, or else they resumed higher education after their return. In these cases, they all continued their education in Romania either by commuting or after their return. In their narratives, they considered attending universities abroad, but due to language barriers in destination countries, they considered them less accessible. Other reasons for not attending universities in host countries were related to differences between educational systems and fear of not being able to adapt and cope. Continuing education is a chance for personal development, and in certain cases, the opportunity to formalize a professional experience for which they were not qualified (for those working as caregivers). All four women featured here passed through unskilled jobs (caregivers, nannies, or housekeepers) during migration, and their present situation finds them in superior professional positions. They managed to overcome their status through education and experience.

The third research question looked at the interconnections among migration paths and romantic and family lives and identified the different family roles of women on migrant-life courses. On the one hand, the migration decision was fueled by origin-family situations. On the other hand, the existence of already-migrant relatives represented an important factor for migration decisions. Finding a romantic partner for marriage during migration is very common to our cases, especially due to their young ages. All participants made this decision to start families. Their narratives revealed their determination to live up to family life, marry, and have children. The destination countries' labor-market challenges (such as the increase in Spain's unemployment rate) and financial crises were mentioned as secondary in driving their decisions to return.

There were many similarities between the four cases, with similar starting points—all experienced various deprivations in their origin families. They migrated to different European countries (Germany, Spain, Italy, or Austria), with differences in their educational or occupational trajectories. The most important effect of migration is that it facilitated their transition to financial independence. The study's findings open the floor for further study on the links between migration and education, and they reveal a need for public debates on education needs in Romania. The issue of access to scholarships for students coming from poorer populations is also implicitly stressed. The present analysis constitutes an exploratory attempt to investigate women's migration for personal development. We consider it important to design future research to study education patterns post-migration. Such research could explore, in depth, migration as a means for personal development in the case of women who migrate as unskilled workers and continue their education paths to expand their chances for employment and increase their standard of living. Furthermore, this study calls for comparative research on this topic that could include both men and women who followed educational careers through migration.

REFERENCES

Anderson, Bridget. 2010. Migration, Immigration Controls, and the Fashioning of Precarious Workers. *Work, Employment & Society* 24 (2): 300–317.

Apitzsch, Ursula, and Irini Siouti. 2007. *Biographical Analysis as an Interdisciplinary Research Perspective in the Field of Migration Studies*. Frankfurt am Main: Johann Wolfgang Geothe Universität.

Bahna, Miloslav. 2014. Slovak Care Workers in Austria: How Important is the Context of the Sending Country? *Journal of Contemporary European Studies* 22 (4): 411–426.

———. 2015. Victims of Care Drain and Transnational Partnering? *European Societies* 17 (4): 447–466.

Bertoli, Simone, and Francesca Marchetta. 2015. Bringing It All Back Home: Return Migration and Fertility Choices. *World Development* 65: 27–40.

Bijwaard, Govert E., and Stijn van Doeselaar. 2014. Impact of Changes in the Marital Status on Return Migration of Family Migrants. *Journal of Population Economics* 27 (4): 961–997.

Bîrsan, Maria, Romana Cramarenco, Wilfred Campbell, and Monica Savulescu-Voudouri. 2008. Women's Migration from an Eastern European Perspective: The Case of Romanian Women Migrants in Northern (The Netherlands, Denmark) and Southern Countries (Greece, Spain). *Studia Universitatis Babes-Bolyai Sociologia, Studia Europaea*, LIII 1: 645–659.

Calvo, Rocío, and Natalia Sarkisian. 2015. Racial/Ethnic Differences in Post-Migration Education Among Adult Immigrants in the USA. *Ethnic and Racial Studies* 38 (7): 1029–1049.

Castells, Manuel. 2001. *The Internet Galaxy Reflections on the Internet, Business, and Society*. Oxford: Oxford University Press.

Cong, Zhen, and Merril Silverstein. 2012. Parents' Preferred Care-Givers in Rural China: Gender, Migration and Intergenerational Exchanges. *Ageing and Society* 34 (5): 727–752.

Daly, Mary. 2002. Care as a Good for Social Policy. *Journal of Social Policy* 31 (2): 251–270.

Damelang, Andreas, and Anette Haas. 2012. The Benefits of Migration. *European Societies* 14 (3): 362–392.

Ducu, Viorela. 2014. Transnational Mothers from Romania. *Romanian Journal of Population Studies* VIII 1: 117–141.

Elder, Glen H., Jr. 1995. The Life-course Paradigm: Social Change and Individual Development. In *Examining Lives in Context: Perspectives on the Ecology of Human Development*, ed. Phyllis Moen, Glenn H. Elder Jr., and Kurt Luscher, 101–139. Washington, DC: American Psychological Association.

Eurostat. 2017. Distribution of Population by Tenure Status, Type of Household and Income Group—EU-SILC Survey (ilc_lvho02). http://appsso.eurostat.ec.europa.eu/nui/show.do?dataset=ilc_lvho02&lang=en

Favell, Adrian. 2008. The New Face of East-West Migration in Europe. *Journal of Ethnic and Migration Studies* 34 (5): 701–716.

Gauld, Robin, and Simon Horsburgh. 2015. What Motivates Doctors to Leave the UK NHS for A 'Life in the Sun' in New Zealand; And, Once There, Why Don't They Stay? *Human Resources for Health* 13 (75): 2–9.

Geist, Claudia, and Patricia A. McManus. 2012. Different Reasons, Different Results: Implications of Migration by Gender and Family Status. *Demography* 49 (1): 197–217.

Ghorashi, Halleh. 2010. From Absolute Invisibility to Extreme Visibility: Emancipation Trajectory of Migrant Women in the Netherlands. *Feminist Review* 94: 75–92.

Ghosh, Jayati. 2009. Migration and Gender Empowerment: Recent Trends and Emerging Issues. *Munich Personal RePEc Archive*. http://mpra.ub.uni-muenchen.de/19181

Green, Judith, and Nicki Thorogood. 2004. *Qualitative Methods for Health Research*. London: SAGE Publications.

Hoerder, Dirk, van Nederveen Meerkerk Elise and Neunsinger Silke. Towards a Global History of Domestic and Caregiving Workers. Brill: Leiden, 2015.

Kallen, Dennis and Jarl Bengtsson. 1974. *Recurrent Education: A Strategy for Lifelong Learning*. Organization for Economic Cooperation and Development, Paris (France): Centre for Educational Research and Innovation.

King, Russell, Aija Lulle, Francesca Conti, and Dorothea Mueller. 2016a. Eurocity London: A Qualitative Comparison of Graduate Migration from Germany, Italy, and Latvia. *Comparative Migration Studies* 4 (1): 2–22.

King, Russell, Aija Lulle, Laura Morosanu, and Allan William. 2016b. *International Youth Mobility and Life Transitions in Europe: Questions, Definitions, Typologies, and Theoretical Approaches*. Sussex. https://www.researchgate.net/publication/303896092_International_Youth_Mobility_and_Life_Transitions_in_Europe_Questions_Definitions_Typologies_and_Theoretical_Approaches

Kirk, Katherine Margaret, and Semin Suvarierol. 2014. Emancipating Migrant Women? Gendered Civic Integration in the Netherlands. *Social Politics* 21 (2): 241–260.

Kofman, Eleonore. 2004. Family-Related Migration: A Critical Review of European Studies. *Journal of Ethnic and Migration Studies* 30 (2): 243–262.

Lee, Eunjung, and Marjorie Johnstone. 2017. A Production of Education Migrants: A Case Study of South Korean Transnational Families in Canada. *International Social Work* 60 (2): 307–320. http://journals.sagepub.com/doi/pdf/10.1177/0020872814539987.

Lersch, Philipp M. 2015. Family Migration and Subsequent Employment: The Effect of Gender Ideology. *Journal of Marriage and Family* 78 (1): 230–245.

Marchetti, Sabrina, Daniela Piazzalunga, and Alessandra Venturini. 2014. Does Italy Represent an Opportunity for Temporary Migrants from the Eastern Partnership Countries? *IZA Journal of European Labor Studies* 3 (1): 1–20.

Marcu, Silvia. 2015. Uneven Mobility Experiences: Life-Strategy Expectations Among Eastern European Undergraduate Students in the UK and Spain. *Geoforum* 58 (Jan.): 68–75.

Mărginean, Ioan. 2013. *Territorial Profiles of Quality of Life*. Bucharest: Romanian Academy Publishing House.

Neagu, Gabriela. 2007. Accesul la Educație al Copiilor din Medii Defavorizate. *Calitatea Vieții* XVIII (3–4): 307–319.

———. 2015. Tinerii, Educație Și Ocupație În România. *Calitatea Vietii* XXVI (1): 16–35.

Nisic, Natascha, and Silvia Maja Melzer. 2016. Explaining Gender Inequalities That Follow Couple Migration. *Journal of Marriage and Family* 78 (4): 1063–1082.

Oleinikova, Olga. 2015. Migrants' Life Strategies and Opportunity Structures: Focus on Post-Independence Ukrainian Labor Market. *Italian Sociological Review* 5 (3): 323–348.

Pessar, Patricia R., and Sarah J. Mahler. 2003. Transnational Migration: Bringing Gender In. *International Migration Review* 37 (3): 812–846.

Petroff, Alisa. 2016. Turning Points and Transitions in the Migratory Trajectories of Skilled Romanian Immigrants in Spain. *European Societies* 18 (5): 438–459.

Piperno, Flavia. 2012. The Impact of Female Emigration on Families and the Welfare State in Countries of Origin: The Case of Romania. *International Migration* 50 (5): 189–204.

Pitkänen, Pirkko, and Tuomas Takala. 2012. Using Transnational Lenses to Analyze Interconnections between Migration, Education and Development. *Migration and Development* 1 (2): 229–243.

Preoteasa, Ana Maria, Rebekka Sieber, Monica Budowski, and Christian Suter. 2016. Household Role in Coping with Precarious Work. Evidence from Qualitative Research in Urban Romania and Switzerland Household Precarious Work Romania Switzerland. *Social Change Review* 14 (142, Winter): 177–201.

Saarela, Jan, and Dan Olof Rooth. 2012. Uncertainty and International Return Migration: Some Evidence from Linked Register Data. *Applied Economics Letters* 19 (18): 1893–1897.

Saldana, Johnny. 2011. *Fundamentals of Qualitative Research: Understanding Qualitative Research*. New York, NY: Oxford University Press.

Șerban, Monica. 2011. *Dinamica migrației internaționale: un exercițiu asupra migrației românești în Spania (International Migration Dynamics: An Exercise on Romanian Migration to Spain)*. Iași: Lumen.

Stecklov, Guy, Calogero Carletto, Carlo Azzari, and Benjamin Davis. 2010. Gender and Migration From Albania. *Demography* 47 (4): 935–961.

Tyldum, G. 2014. Motherhood, Agency, and Sacrifice in Narratives on Female Migration for Care Work. *Sociology* 49 (1): 56–71.

Vlase, Ionela. 2013. Women's Social Remittances and Their Implications at Household Level: A Case Study of Romanian Migration to Italy. *Migration Letters* 10 (1): 81–90.

Voicu, Bogdan. Penuria Pseudo-Modernă a Postcomunismului Românesc Volumul II Resursele. Editura Expert Projects, 2005.

Willis, Jerry. 1942. *Foundations of Qualitative Research*. 2007th ed. Thousand Oaks, CA: Sage Publications.

CHAPTER 9

Men's Migration, Adulthood, and the Performance of Masculinities

Ionela Vlase

This chapter examines the ways migration shapes men migrants' adulthood transitions, their performance of masculinities during migration and upon their return, and their narratives of adult male identity. The chapter documents the socially constructed nature of adulthood and provides evidence on the ambivalences and ambiguities that men migrants experience regarding adulthood and manhood as a result of their long-term migration. Tensions involving the duration of stays abroad after migration—12 years, on average—on the one hand, and the difficulties in settling down and establishing unequivocal benchmarks of manly adulthood while living in different cultural and structural contexts, on the other hand, result in unsettling migrants' prior beliefs and goals concerning age and gender identities.

This study uses qualitative research encompassing life-story interviews with 12 Romanian men in their early and middle adult years who have lived, on average, more than a decade in different European countries,

I. Vlase (✉)
'Lucian Blaga' University of Sibiu, Sibiu, Romania

especially in Italy and Spain. Regardless of the age they were when they migrated; their education, marital, and family status; their destination country; and their length of stay abroad, men migrants have experienced life events that have impacted their sense of adult identity and the development of their masculine identities. The empirical evidence shows that men migrants' subjectivities are deeply shaped and transformed by the very experience of migration and its attendant residential, relationship, and occupational changes. Some men migrants find themselves in situations trying to outperform in the areas of adulthood and masculinity, while others struggle to cope with threatened masculinity after negative life events (e.g., divorce, unemployment) or a lack of milestones in life (e.g., parenthood, homeownership), prompting them to discursively resecure their sense of adult-male status by framing their experiences transnationally, in a broader sociocultural context of both home and host countries.

Interplay of Adulthood and Manhood in Economic Male Migration

This section aims to examine the intricate patterns of manhood and adulthood developing within men migrants' time spent abroad during their early and middle adult life stages. Manhood acts as a crucial aspect in understanding the gendered selves and individuals' hierarchical positionalities (Schrock and Schwalbe 2009), while also capturing the contradictory locations of individuals alongside crosscutting axes of gender and age identity (Anthias 2012). To understand the challenges that migration imposes on progress toward becoming an adult male, anthropological and sociological scholarship has started to address the unsettled relationship between migration and the passage to manly adulthood (McKay 2007; Liu 2010; F. Osella and C. Osella 2000; C. Osella and F. Osella 2006). Historical records and worldwide empirical evidence illustrate that migration is *par excellence* a male process (Thomas and Znaniecki 1920; Monsutti 2007; French and Rothery 2008; Qureshi 2012), as it requires material resources that men can more easily mobilize at the household and community levels, as well as personal attributes most often associated with masculinity (e.g., courage, physical strength, risk-taking). There is, however, less straightforward evidence on how migration impacts young men's masculinity and their ability to achieve adult status in accordance with culturally desired trajectories toward reaching male adulthood. On the one hand, such culturally praised trajectories in both sending and receiving societies may overlap, differ, or oppose each other, which may result in different adaptation strategies on the part of men migrants who seek to reduce the tensions and ambiguities of their adult-male perspective, while being exposed to the host country's normative expectations for a considerable length of time. On the other hand, young economic migrants might enter new gendered worksites, often taking up unskilled jobs in construction and agriculture, and living in various residential arrangements, sometimes exclusively homosocial, which can subject their masculinity and adulthood to permanent negotiation and contestation (Cohen 2006).

Apart from the different gender regimes of sending and receiving societies that migrants need to reconcile, migration may interrupt, precipitate, or cancel life transitions expected to take place at certain ages. Significant stays abroad may result in men migrants facing multiple challenges regarding the achievement of full-fledged adult status. As C. Osella and F. Osella (2006: 118) noted, "migration may accelerate an individual's progress along a culturally idealized trajectory towards mature manhood," especially through an enhanced relationship with money earned abroad that becomes the most valued resource, conferring high prestige on men migrants within sending communities. Nonetheless, migration does not always accelerate, or even facilitate, the achievement of adult-male status and may even thwart the process of becoming an adult (Liu 2010). It can even precipitate the aging process upon exposure to health-damaging work conditions and lack of proper safety protection for immigrants working in heavy industrial conditions (Qureshi 2012).

The existing literature documents various cases in which men migrants' masculinity is threatened during migration through different work regulations, restrictions on interactions with host-country natives, and complex positions within other networks of relations. For instance, Gallo (2006) illuminates the processes of contestation and redefinition of masculine identity among Malayali men married to women working in the domestic sector in Italy. Her ethnographic study accounts for the ambivalence of masculinity that these men are facing. On the one hand, they are experiencing downward mobility given their limited work opportunities outside feminized domestic work, in which their spouses are usually employed. On the other hand, these husbands are experiencing opportunities to construct a respectable adult-male status owing to the marital bonds with domestic employees who are in relationships of trust and dependency with their middle-class Italian employers. The sympathy and trust that Italian employers have for their female domestic servants partly carry over to the male spouses who enter this domain. This could further be used as a means whereby these men gain legal status in Italy, while enabling the reassertion of their sense of masculinity and respectability, despite being placed within the highly feminized domestic work realm—a perception in both sending and receiving societies. Other research addresses men migrants' anxieties over state policies' representations and enforcement of their masculine subordination. For instance, McKay (2007) examines the narratives on masculinity among Filipino seamen. Such narratives are created as a way for them to cope with their threatened masculinity in a highly hierarchical labor niche in which the state, in its desire to secure remittances' flows, promotes its citizens' employability by depicting them as disciplined, obedient, and adaptable to changing work environments. These sailors' narratives become a source of agentic power through which they deconstruct the state's view of them, while portraying themselves as exemplars of masculinity by emphasizing their heroism and sacrifice for the sake of their family needs. Similarly, the narratives of Mexican male peasants migrating to the US under Bracero Program regulations epitomize the traditional male role as provider as a way to counter program regulations' assault on their masculine subjectivity. By living and working in extremely homosocial spaces, braceros—as these men migrants are labeled—find their claims to their identity as (heterosexual) men and their positions as patriarchs undermined and resolutely struggle to recoup their identity as proper adult men (Cohen 2006).

Recent Conceptualizations of Masculinity and Adulthood

Over the past few decades, the concept of masculinity has been redefined by many scholars as part of their efforts to understand the tensions and anxieties that men face in relation to work, family, health, aging, sports, and countless other life domains, yet its theoretical conceptualization remains unsatisfactory, partly because of this very pattern of generating knowledge about masculinity by addressing the links between men and life aspects (Schrock and Schwalbe 2009). These scholars suggest that a more helpful strategy to address masculinity, while avoiding the risk of reifying it by highlighting sex-appropriate and static personality traits, is to focus on manhood acts, that is, to look at what men actually do to claim their membership in the dominant gender group, to be approved as a member of this group, and to resist being controlled and exploited. In accordance with this view, for men to be socially recognized and culturally valued, individual males need to master "a set of conventional signifying practices through which the identity 'man' is established and upheld in interaction" (Schrock and Schwalbe 2009: 279). Men's acts and their narratives reflecting upon these acts are central to men's practical and discursive consciousness that constitutes their identity as men.

The idea that masculinity refers to the cultural practices that socially and economically advantage men's position in society at the expense of women's position by institutionalizing gender inequalities within various settings (e.g., family, work, state, global politics) is old, but the existence of power relations responsible for a hierarchy of masculinities was recognized in the mid-1980s (Carrigan et al. 1985). From the 1980s onward, scholars acknowledged that masculinity is plural and that the cultural and historical variants of masculinities are not equally celebrated at the local, national, and regional levels. As Connell and Messerschmidt (2005) put it, hegemonic masculinities, although emulated by a minority, embody the most revered ways of being a man, while other men who depart from this hegemonic ideal—because of either their bodily attributes or lack of necessary skills and material resources—are placed in subordinate masculine positions:

> *Hegemonic masculinity was not assumed to be normal in the statistical sense; only a minority of men might enact it. But it was certainly normative. It embodied the currently most honored way of being a man, it required all other men to position themselves in relation to it, and it ideologically legitimated the global subordination of women to men.* (Connell and Messerschmidt 2005: 832)

Although the initial formulation of the hegemonic-masculinity concept received a large amount of criticism, its current reformulation by Connell and Messerschmidt (2005) enables us to adequately frame masculine identities by retaining the concept's core dimension, namely the underlying reality of power differential, while adding new elements, such as the geography of masculinities. The latter refers to the interactions among local, regional, and global ideals of hegemonic masculinity, allowing for the understanding of masculinity as geographically contingent, complex, and fluid. This can be easily applied to the study of men migrants, as they navigate multiple masculinities at home and abroad, and their masculine performances could be informed by different—even contradictory—models of masculinities.

Another aspect that emphasizes the contingency of masculinity is its inherency among various strands of identity, such as age and class, and its embedding in certain social, cultural, and economic contexts. Recent studies on youth transitions rightfully argue that the construction of masculinities is contingent on the mobilization of class signs and leisure lifestyles that profoundly differ between young men from working-class backgrounds and those from families facing intergenerational unemployment (Nayak 2006). Alongside class, age is critical in shaping the growth of masculinities. The passage from boyhood to manhood captures the progress of masculinity from childhood to adulthood and its attendant transformations in values, aspirations, practices, and experiences. These transformations are responses to different societal expectations regarding the enactment of masculine identities at young and adult ages. This affirmation is not, however, unproblematic since the validation of masculinity through the realization of certain age-graded and clear-sequenced life transitions—including school completion, labor-market entry, departure from parents' home, marriage, and parenthood—is nowadays questioned under the current economic restructuring and the advent of liquid modernity (Bauman 2000), characterized by a perennial uncertainty and a lack of stable yardsticks to assess social roles' fulfillment. The life-transitions framework applied to the study of adulthood indeed has been criticized in the light of current evidence substantiating the claim that adult identity is narrowly and simplistically defined through individuals' achievement of social qualifiers associated with adulthood (e.g., obtaining full-time jobs, settling down, and becoming parents).

Another definition of adulthood considers both the variable societal structures that condition the timing and sequencing of adult transitions, as well as individuals' planful competence, understood as "the self's ability to negotiate the life course as it represents a socially structured set of age-graded opportunities and limitations" (Shanahan 2000: 675). Since migrants' life trajectories are presumably more dramatically impacted by societal conditions, given their exposure to different cultural norms and structural contexts, and because migrants' transnational living may affect their planful competence (e.g., low prospects to pursue a professional career, choose a stable partner, and cultivate and maintain relationships), migration, as a life event, appears likely to further disturb the achievement of adulthood.

Mary (2013) argues that for a better understanding of the achievement of adult status, one needs to include a broader view of adult identity, one that supersedes the conventional approach of considering the structuring power of the normative age-graded adult transitions by giving credence to individuals' voice and subjective experiences, as well as the derived psychological maturity that constitutes their adult identities. Following her argument, the present study adopts Cohler's (1982) idiographic approach to life trajectory that privileges the understanding of human development through the discursive analysis of personal narratives that individuals dynamically construct in their struggle to position themselves in relation to a master narrative of adulthood that is culturally shaped by specific circumstances varying in time and space. Building on Cohler's (1982) work, Hammack and Toolis (2014) emphasize that adulthood is not a clearly demarcated stage within the life span, but entails a dominant cultural discourse that mirrors normative expectations about proper adult status. However, norms can be tighter or looser in different societies, and individuals' transgressions against such norms happen more or less often depending on nature and the harshness of conditions inflicted upon those whose life courses depart from the norm.

Migration as a strategy to cope with underemployment in one's own country or region involves not only a physical separation from one's family and friendship networks, but it also can dissolve some of these relationships, as well as pressure migrants into allegedly adult transitions that can jeopardize their achievement once the social control of the origin society loosens during the migrant's prolonged absence. Acknowledging the impacts that migration can have on adult transitions, it becomes necessary to address migrants' self-perceived definitions of their position in their life trajectories. Another argument supporting this method of examining adulthood comes from youth studies. Panagakis (2015) brings empirical evidence of a variation in self-perceived adulthood between and within groups of 30-year-old individuals living in the US. Even those individuals who share similar gender aspects and education levels were found to differ in their subjective evaluations regarding the achievement of full adulthood. The explanation lies in the fact that individuals evaluate the timing of transitions and the nature of their ensuing social roles by referring to the normative standards set by their peer group, not through direct reference to societal norms that could appear too distant and abstract. In this view, having the same chronological age and having realized the same marital, residential, and professional milestones do not necessarily translate to similar perceptions of age identity because of the mediation of peers. In the same way that local hegemonic ideals of masculinity shape masculine identities during face-to-face interactions, relative age plays a more important role in shaping age identity through assessing one's own age by referring to the progress toward adulthood made by friends and other acquaintances of the same chronological age. One should not, however, ignore the reality that the process of growing up entails changes and transitions in several life domains (e.g., school, work, family) and that one may experience these transitions at varying paces.

Building on these conceptualizations of adulthood and manhood, we see the maturing of gender- and age-based identities not as separate projects that one aims to accomplish over the life span but as inextricably linked and in constant flux, while also subjected to permanent demonstration and validation elicited by changing social contexts and expectations. This view enables us to consider migrants as agents of their life projects, as they deal with uncertainties that pervade all their choices, aspirations, and personal achievements. For migrants who left their countries of origin at an age when the most important life transitions are expected to take place, migration can alter the pursuit of some gendered and age-related life goals that are central to their concept of meaningful lives. These lives correspond to specific cultural expectations about what the shape of their adult lives should look like to gain full recognition as proper adult men. Such expectations are institutionalized within families through upbringing at home, socialization at school, exposure to mass media, expectations among peer networks, and workplace values. We acknowledge that for various reasons, life outcomes do not always match prior expectations because of complex factors, such as social constraints, limited resources, life vagaries, and ongoing evaluation and redefinition of prior life plans. To assess the realization of life expectations, participants in this study were asked to narrate their childhood and adolescent aspirations, then to compare their current (post-migratory) positions with prior expectations and reflect on the perceived impact of migration. The presentation of our empirical data that follows will provide evidence that migration affects migrants' objective perspectives (constraints and opportunities), as well as their subjective evaluations of their satisfaction with their lives. It is through migrants' individual definitions of meaningful lives that we will seek to establish patterns of manly adulthood in the sample of 12 Romanian men who lived abroad for as many as 22 years.

Romanian Labor Migration: Gender and Age Structuring

The Romanian migration, as it developed from the early 1990s onward, showed a clear gender and age pattern. Before outlining these features, some facts about the context of its onset and an estimate of migrants' presence may serve to create a better understanding of the processes under scrutiny here. The breakdown of communism in Romania was followed by a series of dramatic economic, political, and social restructuring processes that never have been fully achieved (Stoica 2004; Gherghina and Miscoiu 2013). An upsurge in inequalities, rising unemployment, political crises, and economic turmoil in the labor market led many Romanians to seek solutions to their economic hardships and insecurity through migrations abroad for work by drawing on their agentic power to take advantage of gaps in restrictive regulations at the national and international levels to contain such mobility (Culic 2008). As of 2013, the National Institute of Statistics reported that at least 2.3 million Romanians have lived abroad for more than a year, with the top destinations being Italy, with 1.1 million, followed by Spain, with 796,000 Romanian immigrants (OCED 2015: 240). By all accounts, these are underestimations of the actual numbers of Romanians currently living outside their country of birth since neither receiving nor sending countries can accurately capture the size of this phenomenon, characterized by irregular border crossings or regular entries with visa overstays; seasonal participation of migrants in poorly regulated work domains; and migrants' reluctance to notify local authorities of their arrival and departure. Faced with rising unemployment due to the bankruptcy of large state-run factories after 1990, men were likely to respond to household economic crises first by engaging in circular and seasonal migration to nearby destinations, and then, starting in the mid-1990s, turning to long-term migration to more remote European countries, such as Italy, Spain, Germany, and France (Sandu 2006). The early 1990s were marked by migration flows to neighboring countries (e.g., Turkey, the former Yugoslavia, and Hungary) to find work in agriculture, construction, or petty trade, but the legal status of Romanian immigrants remains affected by different degrees of irregularity, given the restrictive policies of these countries with respect to the rights of Romanian immigrants to stay and work. At least in the first decade, the Romanian migration was highly masculinized, with men representing 88 percent of Romanian international migrants between 1990 and 1995. With the lifting of restrictions on free movement within the Schengen Area in 2002, the share of Romanian migrant women gradually grew to 45 percent between 2002 and 2006 (Sandu 2010). Thus, male migration represented a dominant component of the outward migration for most of the contemporary history of migration from Romania, even if Romanian women are currently known to outnumber men migrants in some Southern European countries, especially in Italy and Spain, where the substantial degree of familialism characterizing their welfare-state policies (Saraceno and Keck 2010) contributes to a constant high demand for domestic work, into which these women are usually channeled (Piperno 2012; Vlase 2013). A complex combination of cultural and socioeconomic factors has been responsible for the gender structuring of migration. First, economic migration epitomized, at least in the early 1990s, one of the riskiest and most adventurous (essentially male) experiences one could undertake because of both the high probability of winding up with informal jobs and the dim prospects of obtaining legal status once migrants exceeded relatively short travel-visa terms. Second, there was a common belief that acted as a deterrent to female migration, namely that women who migrate alone would be lured into the sex industry (Montanari and Staniscia 2009). Whether real or groundless, such local gossip putatively implies a loss of credit by men in their origin communities, as they are thought to be unable to act as real fathers and husbands who are entitled to control the sexuality of their daughters and wives. The failure to properly police women's labor and their sexual behavior from a distance generates a local moral panic and gives rise to contestation and marginalization of these men, with their masculinity under assault. Third, however scarce household resources are, men usually enjoy greater access to them compared with their women counterparts (Vlase 2016). Drawing on this male privilege, men can access resources for travel expenses, which were considerable before 2002, when entry visas were still required for Romanian citizens traveling within the Schengen area (Anghel 2008; Vlase 2016). The ongoing process of migration, however, gradually altered the perceptions of origin communities regarding opportunities in destination countries, contributing to more balanced attitudes toward men's and women's labor migration.

Besides the gendered structuration of migration from Romania, there is also a generational patterning dominated by youth migration and marked by a rejuvenation of migrant stocks over the past few years in popular destinations. Based on data provided by the Spanish National Institute of Statistics for the year 2000, Horváth (2012) shows that Romanians who obtained legal residence in Spain were predominantly young. According to the latter source, one third of Romanian migrants legally residing in Spain were 16–24 years old. This stage in life is usually marked by a high density of transitions associated with adulthood milestones. The similar age structure of Romanian immigration has been reported in England (Culic 2008) and Italy (Otovescu 2012). These observations concerning gender and age structuring in Romanian immigration prompted us to address pathways to adulthood and the performance of masculinities, as they are allegedly affected by migration experiences, pressured or delayed life events and transitions, and the interpretations that migrants assign to these events to forge new age and gender identities. We will further substantiate these contentions through analysis of compelling ethnographic data. More specifically, we try to answer the following two research questions: (1) How do gender- and age-based identities (i.e., masculinity and adulthood) intersect and shape men migrants' adult-male status? (2) How can men migrants resecure their masculine and adult subjectivities upon being challenged by migration and other life events that threaten their manly adult status (e.g., divorces, job losses), resulting in a lack of age-appropriate life transitions that serve to validate one's respectable masculine status (e.g., heterosexual marriage, parenthood, and residential independence, i.e., homeownership)?

Data and Method

The empirical data for this study stem from a research project titled *Migrants' life courses: dealing with uncertain, highly destandardized biographies in Romania*. Within this framework, the research team collected 40 biographical interviews with Romanian migrants, both men and women, who have spent more than five years abroad for work purposes and who returned to Romania either on a permanent or temporary basis. For the purposes of this chapter, we have selected 12 interviews with men originating from the lower working class, in their 30s and 40s and with similar profiles, to observe and interpret patterns in the formation of their adult life stages and masculine performances in relation to their lived migration experiences. Although class is not explicitly referred to in the interviews, our selection of migrants from a similar class background is motivated by evidence that its "structuring absence" plays a major role in the formation of gendered selves (Skeggs 1997). Thus, we try to control for it to be able to capture migration's influence on men migrants' progress toward adulthood. Men's narratives serve as strategic tools to provide meaningful accounts of their fragmented biographies (Riessman 2008). I also consider them resourceful means whereby one can illuminate the tensions and uncertainties underpinning the structural plots of participants' life stories. These tensions are relevant proof of individuals' narrative engagement with cultural scripts on normative adulthood:

> *Although hegemonic discourses on the nature and meaning of adulthood continue to exist, these examples of protest reveal the way in which master narratives are in constant states of tension and renegotiation, as individuals do not blindly internalize them but rather engage with them.* (Hammack and Toolis 2014: 50, emphasis in original)

The interviews were conducted according to a protocol that specified that migrants were first informed about the scope of the study and invited afterward to narrate their life experiences as they remember them, starting with whatever they believed relevant. Subsequently, interviewers guided informants toward specific life events and transitions preceding and following migration, their sequencing, the feelings they attached to them, significant others involved, the meanings they derived from their experiences, and assessments as to whether, and to what extent, their narrated life stories match their aspirations before migration.

Our purposeful sample consists of participants recruited with the help of team members' contacts within large social networks—including professionals, relatives, and friends—ensuring an initial mutual trust between researchers and participants, mediated by these common social ties that brought them together. Interviews took place at participants' homes or other places that they chose. The interviewers ensured that interview situations were never uncomfortable or awkward by avoiding intrusiveness through careful arrangement of the details related to time and place to accommodate participants' needs and rhythms. Written informed consent forms were signed by all participants, assuring them of confidentiality.

Some migrants left the country for the first time while underage by evading border controls or bribing border officers at checkpoints. Illegal activities were often reported during interviews, not only concerning entry and exit controls but also in relation to day-to-day living abroad (e.g., theft from shops, driving on public roads without a license, exploiting fellow migrants who overstayed their visas by extorting money from them to help them get through border controls without incurring penalties, engaging in informal work). Interviews were fully transcribed, and the transcriptions were coded with the help of Maxqda 11 software. On the basis of a system of codes referring to both a wide range of life events and transitions occurring in migrants' lives, as well as migrants' assessments of their manly adult status, informants were classified within four adult-male status types (explained later) according to the most numerous coded text segments identified in the quote matrix as closer to one of the ends of age and masculine identities.

In this study, men migrants' narratives revealed different patterns of adult-male status resulting from intimate links of various masculinities and age identities. As we will show in the next section, masculinities in the men's sample range from *exacerbated* to *threatened*, according to the meanings conveyed by informants about their manhood acts that emphasized either an enhanced domination or a loss of dominant status. Likewise, men's narratives also reveal their perceived ages on a continuum ranging from *delayed* to *premature adulthood*, revealing that some men migrants in our sample were pressured by migration. The four adult-male status types resulting from the combination of the two axes of age and gender identities (i.e., premature adulthood/exacerbated masculinity, delayed adulthood/threatened masculinity, premature adulthood/threatened masculinity, and delayed adulthood/ exacerbated masculinity) serve as an analytical guide to illustrate how men migrants perceive, although not always unambiguously, their age- and gender-based performances. Migrants are knowledgeable actors, aware of the presence of hegemonic narratives of masculinity and adulthood against which they position their own narratives. Without perfectly matching any of the types mentioned earlier, these personal narratives can feature, to a higher degree, one pattern. Moreover, inner tensions are common in men migrants' narratives, as in some life domains in which certain men point to acute senses of prematurity derived from experiencing life events and transitions specific to adulthood at early ages. In other life areas, the same migrants doubted their maturity or even denied the possibility of ever achieving adulthood, given their failure to meet certain conventional markers of adult status (e.g., marriage, parenthood).

Men Migrants' Progress Along Manly Adulthood Trajectories

If we agree that masculinity is plural and hierarchical, and that adulthood is not fixed but rather fluid and contingent on both achievement of conventional social qualifiers (e.g., marriage, parenthood, full employment, independent living) and psychological maturity, then we can better understand the contradictory locations of men migrants who position themselves differently on these two inextricably linked identity axes. Figure 9.1 shows the main traits of informants whose narratives suggest different locations on the masculinity and adulthood axes.

Furthermore, I will provide illustrative examples that flesh out the four patterns describing uneven progress along manly adulthood trajectories in which men find themselves amid a long migration career throughout which they have faced different life events and transitions that have shaped

| | | Self-assessed adult status ||
		Premature	Delayed
Masculinity	Threatened	Swift transitions to marriage and parenthood, certifying achievement of adult status, as well as substantial earnings during migration but bad management of savings, while at the same time, acknowledgement of masculine crises, especially when confronting local hegemonic masculinity narratives upon return, in both public and private encounters (financial insecurity upon return, inability to influence others and obtain deference).	Migration intersects with work, education, and family trajectories, leading to many fragmentations, e.g., school interruptions, romantic break-ups and pains, regrets, ongoing self-doubt over individual achievements, and a low propensity to plan family and work/career outcomes. Such fragmentations threaten both masculinity and the pursuit of adulthood.
	Exacerbated	Early adult transitions and traditional ordering of life events pursued during migration (e.g., marriage, homeownership in home country, parenthood), seekers of opportunities to increase income involving crime, highly agentive actors, orientation toward family protection, breadwinners regardless of current marital status.	Postponned adult achievements during migration, with an emphasis on playful manhood acts that reveal a mischievous boyhood identity, high concern for masculine leisure activities (e.g., riding motorcycles, playing computer games), interrupted work histories, problem with authority figures, reliance on partners' incomes.

Fig. 9.1 Men's performances according to their position on the masculinity and adulthood axes

their senses of manhood and adulthood. With few exceptions, migrants in our sample have experienced nonlinear processes of moving from adolescent to adult life stages, with life transitions marked by discontinuities and repeated life events (e.g., remarriage with the same or different partners, reenrollment in school after migration). The ways in which life events and transitions to adulthood are reflected in participants' narratives convey understandings of their masculine identities, while migrants' manhood acts also indicate age patterning since all these acts are virtually boyish or mature expressions of selves.

Premature Adulthood/Exacerbated Masculinity

This type is epitomized by a few sample cases (04_M_43, 18_M_45). Informants' code is made up of two-digit numbers indicating their order in the sample of the total of 40 interviewees, followed by gender symbol (M for male), while the last information regards informants' age. Both informants belonging to this pattern come from similar family backgrounds (fathers were truck drivers, mothers worked in agriculture) and migrated soon after completing vocational schools, although they made the transition from school to work before migration. The narratives of these informants stand out clearly as they are full of accounts of bold manhood acts through which the storytellers aim to provide an image of themselves as goal oriented and heroic in their ability to sacrifice for the achievement of adult male markers, such as building their own homes in their home country, marrying, becoming fathers, and providing for their families. They consider migration both as an important accelerator of their progress toward adulthood and as masculinity leverage, thanks to their abilities to creatively combine various jobs and enhance money-earning activities, both formally and informally, while benefiting from rich social ties and enjoying a good reputation within their social networks:

> *Operator: If you were to remember the moment when you felt that you had become an adult, when did this transition to adulthood happen? What marked this transition for you?*
>
> *Interviewee: Do you know when? I think it was '89 ... yes, in '89, I was 17 years old… something like that, because you could see everyone… In '90, just after the revolution, you saw that they have all become wealthier, they were leaving, and that's when I started making my own money. (04_M_43)*

While working in Italy, I was the kind of person who wasn't satisfied with the 1000 euros or whatever the monthly salary that one [employer] was giving me. I was the person who sought to earn as much as possible. I was either imposing myself on the employer, or, if I failed to impose my way, I was changing jobs. Wherever I went, I was offering [skills], but I had expected the same in return. Even if I was Romanian or a foreigner, if I am giving you something, you must give something in return too. I did training as well. I have a firefighter qualification in Italy under the Ministry of the Interior. I can get a job as a firefighter in Romania too... a qualified firefighter. I have forklift training, and medical first-aid training... I've done several trainings for qualifications. They are split by categories. And I changed my jobs from unskilled work, to cooker in kitchens, restaurants, I worked in aluminum industry, in a furniture factory, in construction. I've nearly tried jobs in all the branches of the industry in a row. I didn't stick to a single domain. I got involved in all of them... I went where the payment was better. That was my goal. As years went by... they go by anyway, I have to do something. And so I did. And when I left Italy, I left it not because I didn't earn well enough. I was getting good money there. I was employed on a high-level skill category, I was responsible for an entire department, but I left due to family reasons. My children were here [in Romania]. My boy was about to start primary school, then my daughter also came and she had to commute. When I was returning from my godparents', I was coming home every three months [of absence], and I said that with the 500–1000 euros, I was sending them monthly, maybe I can earn just as much in Romania as well. Maybe not 1000, but 500 I can manage to earn back home. (18_M_45)

Money becomes an important asset that provides them with a sense of power and control necessary to demonstrate their masculinity and gain approval as a real man. The narratives also show that in the deregulated market that sprang up upon the collapse of communism in Romania, some young men engineered international thefts and petty crimes, as they had few opportunities to accumulate money and gain financial independence:

Operator: How were you choosing your countries of destination?
Interviewee: From friends. So, someone went to Austria to steal perfumes. So, these were the times back then. I'm not ashamed of anything I've done so far: "Let's go there to steal perfumes!" You took whatever you found there in the stores and sold them to Bulgarians. I came back home. I stayed for a week, and I left with N. I spent a weekend home. On Monday morning, I went illegally to Italy, and I got there through Croatia, Yugoslavia, and... after a day and a half, I was in... Italy. And then I stayed in Italy without visiting home, as I got there... let's say the first week I got there was rougher. I went to my sister, where

I had a bed to sleep in. [...] After a week, I found work, and I kept that job for eight years. In an orchard. [...] After five years, I... came home for the first time. That's when I got the papers. Otherwise, you could not go back to Italy if you were coming home. However, I got my papers, and I came home. But I did not stay. The first time I [returned, I] stayed for a week. And then I started to come [regularly]. I used to come, I started a business in transport, but still kept my job there in agriculture. Being [involved] in agriculture, it was different. You could leave when you wanted. It wasn't like in a factory. And I started back then, during that time with visa over-stayers, in 2003, I was doing two rides per month. But I wasn't staying home. I was coming home on Sundays, getting to Romania on Monday, and by Thursday, I was heading back to Italy. And so on. I was doing this commute twice a month. And I made good money out of these visa over-stayers back then. (04_M_43)

Criminal activities for financial accumulation are themselves a marker of exacerbated masculinity that is underpinned by young men's shared understandings of expectations that society places on them. Such understandings—culturally negotiated and internalized during their early socialization—usually include ways to prove success (financial gains and material possessions are often a measure of it), show physical strength, and take risks. When men are deprived of resources and lack legitimate means to demonstrate their masculinity, their claim to manhood is incomplete, and they might, therefore, resort to unconventional or criminal behavior to restore their sense of manhood. There is, however, an important caveat they should be aware of: To avoid thwarting their journey toward adulthood—entwined in their manhood acts—young men need to desist from criminal behavior in the short run and use their financial resources wisely to ensure future access to conventional ways of proving their proper male adulthood. After becoming financially independent, whether from legal or illegal money-earning activities, settling down and starting a family usually is an important step in gaining full adulthood and respectable man status. Parenthood causes these young men to face the necessity of turning away from crime if they want their children to benefit from their parental support and not be excluded or stigmatized because of their fathers' conduct.

Operator: So, this is the major event of your life: becoming a father?
Interviewee: Yes. That's when I thought about him, that I didn't want him to be alone. Because of what I used to do, I didn't sleep at home at night. And if I were to stay two to three years in prison and he would end up alone—I said "Stop!" and that was it. (04_M_43)

The men in this subsample of premature adulthood/exacerbated masculinity adopt the pattern of marriage, followed by parenthood transitions, a few years after migration, once their financial situations improve. Their ability to earn money and independence from their parents' financial support is central to their concept of adulthood. They emphasized that migration enhanced their opportunities to earn more, while these earnings enabled the realization of their sense of having a meaningful life that includes orderly life events (e.g., marriage and parenthood) and that demonstrates their adult-male status. Throughout their long years in destination countries, these men remained oriented toward definitively returning to their home country, a project they nurtured through savings and investments in their origin communities (e.g., building their own houses, buying properties). Although these men are not immune to life events that can potentially affect their masculinity, adulthood, or both, they resolutely, at least in the discourse, recoup their threatened identity. For instance, a divorce is not seen as disturbing their life trajectory or affecting their sense of manhood, as in the case of 04_M_43, who gained custody of his four-year-old son. Not being able to look after his son while working full-time, the single father decided to send the son to his mother in Romania and continue working and saving for his planned business back home, where he plans to return upon his son's enrollment in primary school. A deep sense of moral duty toward family/children support is present in both of these sampled cases, and although uncertainty is present and acknowledged in both narratives, it is also dealt with in agentic ways:

> *Operator: How do you see yourself, for example, in 10 years' time, at 53?*
> *Interviewee: I never thought about it. What I am doing now [for a living] is something I can live off quite well. That's why I made a plan for the future, and I also planted a hectare of nuts because you never know. Let it [grow] there because in 10 years' time, it will pay out [bear fruit]. I bought a few hectares of land for the same thing, for the future. But you don't know what will happen to the land, but we're still trying to work it. I also planted half a hectare of plum trees. We are producing what is popular nowadays. If anything changes, we will try to change ourselves as well. (04_M_43)*

Men in this group tend to have multiple skills, formal and informal, technical and social, as well as investments in concurrent entrepreneurial activities (e.g., one man manages several enterprises simultaneously—running a bakery, a pig farm, and a car-rental service, as well as leading a construction team), providing these men with resources to handle unforeseen life circumstances through effective planning. Their wide work experience gained as migrants in various (male) domains (e.g., construction, industry, transportation) and a highly entrepreneurial profile upon their return single them out from the other cases. Also, unlike men in the fourth category, these men's references to leisure or recreational activities are present in their discourses only in respect to their past life stage (i.e., before adulthood), and they are often full of self-criticism toward their immature spending habits or behavior.

Delayed Adulthood/Threatened Masculinity

This subgroup contains three sample cases: 19_M_49, 26_M_39, and 27_M_30. Although they are different ages, they are similar in respect to their present life outcomes, which are partly the result of fragmented trajectories in either family, education, and/or work domains. These fragmentations intersect with and are shaped by their long migration careers. As an illustration, I soon will introduce the youngest informant of this subgroup, 27_M_30, and his tortuous pathway to adulthood during migration and his return. He left high school to migrate. He viewed migration as a way to escape his parents' authority and gain autonomy and financial independence. His subsequent work trajectory and romantic career in Italy led to a reassessment of this first decision. Frequent job changes in Italy with no upward mobility and an unstable romantic relationship that ended after five years, in which he felt betrayed, added further volatility to his adulthood achievements and illustrated the serious limits of his planful abilities. The turning point in his unaccomplished pathway toward adulthood seems to be the dissolution of his romantic relationship, when he saw his life plans torn down and decided to return home and pick up where he left off a few years back. He reenrolled in high school with a plan to pursue a university degree while working in a factory:

> *Operator: What kind of high school did you attend?*
> *Interviewee: Mechanical.*
> *Operator: Four years?*
> *Interviewee: No, no, I didn't finish it because I left.*
> *Operator: Since high school?*

Interviewee: Yes, yes. In fact, I am still studying for it nowadays, I'm working hard... for the mistakes I did back then.
Operator: The mistakes from high school?
Interviewee: Yes, because I abandoned it, and I chose to go abroad. I was telling myself: "I'm not going to do anything with it anyways"—that's how I was thinking back then—"I should better go and work."
[...] I wouldn't go again. I would definitely finish my studies because it is somewhat frustrating [to study] at this age. I mean people don't understand that you aren't necessarily stupid if you have 10 grades or 8 or 7, or 11 [grades], or you didn't graduate high school or you didn't pass your High School Graduation Exam. Because, you know, somebody asks you, "Hey, did you pass your High School Graduation Exam?" "No, I didn't." But they won't let you explain why, how, when...which are the mistakes. It is not always fair, but diplomas are more important these days. (27_M_30)

His new romantic partner seems to play a major role in his new attitude and plans for the future, as he tells it:

Interviewee: Pff... I think my current girlfriend changed my life a lot, in a good way. Since we've been together, I have changed a lot as a person, but I also changed my way of thinking, I would say. The people around me and I started to accomplish a few things. I told you, I got my driving license late, but not because...because of her persistence, so to say.
Operator: She motivated you to do things?
Interviewee: Yes. Nobody ever told me. Nobody ever insisted to tell me why I needed a driving license. And she told me, "Go try. You are 30 years old. What if you're going to have a family someday? What will you do? Will your wife drive your child if you need to go somewhere?" And I said "OK. Let's try!" Of course, I tried. I took it without any problem. Good. Afterward, "Go to school. Finish this!" (27_M_30)

He acknowledges that he is late in accomplishing conventional life outcomes in education and work. At the same time, his partner's encouragement regarding his lack of a driver's license questioned his manhood while threatening his chances of becoming a real husband and father by social standards, according to which, men should have a higher socioeconomic status and manage practical and technical aspects of private life. This excerpt also demonstrates that late-adulthood achievements also can interfere with masculinity, preventing men from acquiring the ability to be a good father and husband, and even suggesting the uncertainty of such ontological possibilities. Being a man returnee is often associated with some success during migration, which is proven in the home community through some standard assets (e.g., homeownership, owning a car, and entrepreneurial skills). In turn, the lack of such masculine trappings of success threatens men's adult status by lowering their marriage prospects, residential independence, and economic mobility. Our informant's perceived gap between social expectations and his current achievements led him to adjust his self-assessment about his age and gender identity:

> *Operator:* Do you see yourself becoming an adult in the future, and what would adult life mean?
> *Interviewee:* Adult life for me? ... I don't know what to say. To be prepared to work all your life.... To have a job, a full-time [job]. I don't know. To be supportive of the ones around you. Also like that, unconditionally. I don't know... to have a family. I still don't think I would be ready to get married.

Premature Adulthood/Threatened Masculinity

Unlike the preceding type, the informants clustering in the premature adulthood/threatened masculinity type (11_M_42; 05_M_43, 14_M_46, 17_M_33) do attain social qualifiers of adulthood (e.g., marriage, fatherhood) relatively early in their lives, and migration seems to speed up this growing-up process, but a sense of disempowerment and displacement of their masculine selves is conveyed when life outcomes are evaluated against the expectations and realities in their home countries. One informant captures this feeling when recalling the moment of migration that he believes marked his transition to adulthood:

> *Interviewee:* I was in a hurry, and I took life head on, and that's why I regret that I didn't wait for the other stages.
> *Operator:* Are you referring to your going abroad to Serbia?
> *Interviewee:* Yes.
> *Operator:* That was the first job you ever had?
> *Interviewee:* Yes. (17_M_33)

Another informant acknowledges that his first day in another country marked the beginning of his maturity, but such maturity and honest work did not translate to an enhanced male status as signified by valuable markers such as money:

Interviewee: Starting day one. Starting day one. That's when growing up begun. I kept thinking, "If I wouldn't have left, I wouldn't have grown up. I couldn't have done it. And not only in Spain. When I left abroad for Belgium for the first time."

Operator: Already since then?

Interviewee: The moment I went away from home, it was already a different world.

Operator: What was different?

Interviewee: Well, when you leave your mother's and your father's home, you are left alone. You need to handle things by yourself. And you handle things the way you learned back in your home country. In life, in your childhood, at your mother's home. You either step over everything in order to have a good life, or you work and you earn your life…And I chose to work. I could've done deals, to make money, but I wasn't interested in that. […]

You could see the world differently, with different eyes, you could see… everything with different eyes. Absolutely everything. And after a year, after I went, I think the first time I returned home was after two years. Everybody home was already thinking, "You became arrogant and slier," and I don't know what else. "You don't know where you came from anymore." But I was seeing everything with different eyes. Everything.

Operator: Can you give me an example?

Interviewee: I can't say. But it's different. It can be seen in all Romanians that come back. The Romanians back here don't understand them anymore. They all say: "You don't remember where you left from; you think you are superior" and whatnot. But, in fact, Romanians [migrants] are different. Their eyes [and perspectives] open differently. And then you come back to your country, and nothing is good anymore. You have the feeling that nothing is going right. It's like you can't accept it. (05_M_36)

The dissatisfaction upon returning to the home country has to do with a feeling of displacement that includes both a different perception of old realities by the migrant whose experiences abroad changed his perspectives on his home country, and an attitude of rejection that non-migrants display toward their migrant countrymen when the latter impose their point of view. Their personal feelings of inadequacy and uneasiness in their home country threaten men migrants' masculinity since they cannot convincingly exert influence on local daily routines, as their opinions are met with suspicion and resistance, instead of praise and consent.

Threatening situations concerning masculinity are found emanating not only from public (male) resistance against migrant men's ideas and behaviors but also from relatives (especially brothers), who can oppose men returnees' masculine ways of handling their own affairs. One man returnee from this group was married while earning his university degree, then decided to migrate before completing his master's degree because he couldn't provide for his newly established family. Being unable to buy or rent a satisfactory home, he was living in student housing on campus, relying on his parents' financial support while working part-time for low wages. This living arrangement prior to migration was not sufficient proof of proper masculinity since he could show neither financial independence nor acceptable residential status. His subsequent migration career did not result in major improvements to his adult-male status either. His family trajectory was dramatically impacted during migration, causing him lots of pain because of two divorces and his stated failure to become a father. Concerning work, although he mentions unprecedented income derived from entrepreneurial activities in Italy, he also regretfully says he was unable to realize male achievements, such as owning a house, under local standards of masculinity because of his inability to properly manage his finances and spending, blaming this on his leisure lifestyle abroad. Thus, he questions his adult manhood by echoing both his (non-migrant) brothers and his current partner's dissatisfaction and criticism regarding his inability to manage money.

> *Operator: Do you think you were a role model for them [younger brothers]?*
> *Interviewee: For a time, yes. Lately, no, because their role model transformed, I mean their desire to see a role model has transformed. As long as this financial aspect didn't depend on me or them and it depended on parents, they saw me as a role model of getting good grades, of dressing nicely, clean … Now, since I began attempting to start my own activity, there are moments when… like that. There are moments when I end up asking them: "Hey, lend me some money." They don't see me as a role model because they have the feeling they are doing better. With the little money they have, they manage to ensure continuity. For me, this job is more fluctuating because I either got used to Italy and to spending more, or it is just how I am, and I like to feel good. […] 14 years [in Italy] probably took their toll. It is exactly that period when you become an adult, when you learn to save money or to spend it. Well, I probably developed that since during that period I had a lot, I spent a lot. I oftentimes argue with the girl I am currently in a relationship with, as we are not married, whatever. It's a colleague from… so, she keeps scolding me. This morning, there was a great… scolding, of about an hour, regarding money. Sometimes I do realize that I might also have a problem. (11_M_42)*

For men in this subsample, migration appears as a trigger or as an accelerator of adulthood since it provides migrants with a sense of maturity and enables their full transition to conventional adult-status achievements (e.g., marriage, financial and residential independence), but their return causes them to face different threats against their masculinity. They become contested and marginalized in their home country since their material and symbolic assets are not sufficient to elicit other men's or family members' deference.

Delayed Adulthood/Exacerbated Masculinity

The final subgroup refers to men migrants whose adult achievements are postponed and rendered uncertain during migration, while their age identity interacts with masculinity and shapes their manhood acts, resulting in a mischievous, playful boyhood, rather than the attainment of a mature manhood. Informants 08_M_34, 21_M_32, and 25_M_39 are closer to this type. They are currently in their 30s. Regardless of their marital status, their progress toward adulthood lacks what social narratives of adulthood contain, as reflected in their personal narratives. Informant 08_M_34 acknowledges that his (male) initiation into migration as a masculine act was done through learning bad things first:

> *Operator: Out there, how did you feel about the adaptation process, at the beginning, in respect to the new culture, different people, foreign language?*
> *Interviewee: Fine. I have first learned the foolish stuff. (08_M_34)*

This informant married when he was 24 years old and migrated soon after marriage because he couldn't raise a family while living with his grandmother, which was his residence before getting married. He recalls that his arrival in Spain was followed by hard times, as he didn't find any work for seven months, during which he was torn between the desire to return home out of despair and the reluctance to take this step out of fear of being judged as a failure. During his migration career, he became a father twice, but despite such social adulthood markers, he does not self-identify as an adult.

> *Operator: If you think about it, when exactly do you think you became an adult?*

Interviewee: Never.
Operator: [laughs]
Interviewee: ... Never...
Operator: So, you think you haven't grown up?
Interviewee: Not yet.

Throughout the migration years, this man's slow progress toward adulthood shaped his manhood acts, which emphasized an accentuated masculinity mold in a boyhood concept marked by his interest in leisure activities and spending to display masculinity:

Operator: How was it trying to adapt to a new country, with other people, with another language?
   Interviewee: Fine. Initially I learned the foul language...
   Operator: Really? And when you didn't have work [to do], what did you do?
   Interviewee: Oh... what didn't I do? I played on the PlayStation, I smoked weed, I grew plants—what else did I do? I don't know... I looked for iron. I made up to 200 euro from [recycling] iron.
   Operator: Did you use money for other things, except a house?
   Interviewee: Yes. Cars. About 15 cars. I changed them every year. For each one, I paid at least 1000 euros.
   Operator: Did you buy land or anything of the sort?
   Interviewee: No.
   Operator: You didn't invest in this?
   Interviewee: Only in mobile phones.
   Operator: In mobile phones?
   Interviewee: In PlayStations [laughs]. In computers. (08_M_34)

The other two men in this group are not married but in stable relationships after other broken relationships during migration. Out of the two, participant 21_M_32, ended his relationship because he didn't want to be bossed around by his ex-girlfriend's father at work and wanted to keep his money separate and decide how to spend it, as proof of his masculinity. Informant 25_M_39 still struggles with adulthood achievements, while clearly stating that he does not perceive himself as an adult. His statement also can be interpreted as a negotiation and resistance against local hegemonic narratives of adult masculinity since his prior internalization of social expectations has been discarded in light of migration experiences that enabled him to balance norms and expectations of origin and destination societies:

Interviewee: I wanted to be married at 20 years old. I wanted to have a child at 24 years old, probably about three by 30. Now, I am soon 40, and I don't have any of that. On the other hand, I don't know... I am very content with my life.
Operator: Do you think migrating contributed to that?
Interviewee: You should know the migration opened my thinking horizon a bit. I don't know... I felt very good in another country, I came with... they are more evolved than we are. We are, at an overall level, quite far behind, not like in the West or other countries I've been to. We are still... I don't know. I came with an extra baggage of knowledge, of experience. But it helped me. It probably helped me to be more optimistic, more relaxed. (25_M_39)

This excerpt indicates how personal narratives depart from hegemonic narratives of adulthood. Yet the storytellers preserve a sense of adult-male status by framing their experiences transnationally, in a broader sociocultural context encompassing narratives of both home and host countries. 25_M_39 started a new relationship upon his return and dreams about becoming a homeowner and a father someday. When asked about his worries and concerns for his future, he simply stated that he is most afraid of a motorcycle crash and the expenses that it would incur. Detailing his passion for riding motorcycles is allegedly a way of asserting his masculine self, while his disproportionate concerns about crashing add more ambiguities regarding his progress toward adulthood, as he acknowledges:

Operator: Are there things that frighten you in life, regarding the future? Do you see a certain aspect in a somewhat fearful way?
Interviewee: I am afraid not to crash my motorbike and—not to have enough money to fix it [sneer]. That scares me the most. It can be laughable, but my passion is to... I love motorbikes. I am currently very frightened by the idea of repairing my bike, I mean a major repair after a crash of 2000 euros, for example. (25_M_32)

Although this informant is unemployed and most of the time lives off his new partner's wage income while occasionally contributing his own income from informal work, his masculinity does not appear threatened by his uncertain economic status and unstable income, since he retains a sense of superiority over most other men migrants whom he has met and/or worked with. His masculine leverage is discursively produced by downplaying physical strength's relevance to hegemonic masculinity. While emphasizing knowledge and recreational activities as central to his man identity, he also resists deference and the reproduction of submissive work relationships on construction sites:

I knew my rights, I know my right to work ... it is written very clear, in a conduct rulebook: First of all, you do not lift the bags all by yourself. I took the example of my Italian colleagues, who didn't show off and didn't want to prove anyone anything; most Romanians wanted to prove what slaves they were. "What a slave I am. How many things I will do for little money." Then they played with two bags to carry on their backs. They did these stupid contests on who can carry more bags, and now they are on injected medicine. I feel sorry for them, but this is the way of things. You don't have to prove anything to anybody in my opinion. You need to prove it to yourself. So then, yes, they have medical issues. Generally, back issues. They're in construction—knees, back [are affected]. So far, I don't have any [of these issues]. The only issues I have [are] my knees, I have them ... from the ski track. (25_M_39: 251)

Conclusion

This chapter illuminates the interplay of masculinity and adulthood as affected by the long migration careers of young men about to make life transitions marking their path toward adulthood and mature manhood. As highlighted by other scholars (F. Osella and C. Osella 2000; Liu 2010), migration affects the progress toward adulthood and masculine performances of young men migrants, but the directions of such influences may be contradictory and do not necessarily converge to create mature manhood. The present research contributes to efforts in understanding these migrants' achievement of adult-male status by documenting the different, sometimes opposing, trends in masculinity and adulthood and their interplay in shaping uneven progress along the two identity axes under scrutiny.

The narratives of adulthood and masculine performances that make up the core of our empirical analysis substantiate the four distinct patterns of manly adulthood identified within our sample of Romanian men migrants who migrated in their youth. Their migration careers intersect and shape their work and family trajectories, while their ensuing life outcomes—measured through economic, residential, and family-status criteria—serve as social benchmarks against which men migrants position their masculinity and adulthood. In addition, their planful competence is seriously undermined. Despite prior plans to stay abroad for very limited periods, usually one or two years, these men migrants ended up staying more than a decade in host countries. Moreover, the context of transnational living complicated their choices, affecting their pursuit of stable relationships, upwardly mobile professional careers, and homeownership as ultimate indicators of independent/adult status.

Independent migration is subject to rules concerning minimum ages for being granted the right to travel and work abroad. Some men migrants bend the rules in their search for better work prospects. Migration can become, in this case, an extreme avenue for asserting one's masculinity through the embodiment of courage and strength, and by taking risks, including illegal activities. Upon establishing lives abroad, some men migrants overcompensate in trying to act in masculine ways beyond the limits set by their peer groups (e.g., using concurrent skills to earn more, participating temporarily in criminal activities, managing several enterprises simultaneously), while for other men migrants, late achievements toward adulthood or negative life events during migration (e.g., repeated separations, frequent job losses) undermine their masculinity and threaten their manhood. The ways in which adulthood and masculinity intersect suggest great variation in the interplay of men migrants' adulthood accomplishments and masculine performances. The four adult-male status types illustrated earlier were based on the analysis of men's narratives, reporting not only their biographical data but also the significance assigned to their experienced life events and transitions. The analysis revealed tensions and ambiguities in gender and age identities that men migrants sought to solve by referring to transnational cultural frameworks when they felt that their personal narratives did not match the prevailing master narrative of mature masculinity. Informants' narratives illuminate the complexities of interactions among migration, adulthood formation, and masculinity in the construction of manly adulthood in men migrants whose migration takes place in their youth or early adulthood. By acknowledging that age categories and gender identities are not fixed but subject to permanent social and cultural constructions by agents involved in social interactions embedded in larger socioeconomic and cultural contexts, this research outlines the intragroup variations in manly adulthood among men migrants in their middle adulthood (30s and 40s) by addressing subjective definitions and culturally embedded representations of their journeys toward adulthood and masculine performances shaped by long migration careers.

References

Anghel, Remus G. 2008. Changing Statuses. Freedom of Movement, Locality and Transnationality of Irregular Romanian Migrants in Milan. *Journal of Ethnic and Migration Studies* 34 (5): 787–802.

Anthias, Floya. 2012. Transnational Mobilities, Migration Research and Intersectionality. *Nordic Journal of Migration Research* 2 (2): 102–110.

Bauman, Zygmunt. 2000. *Liquid Modernity*. Cambridge: Polity Press.

Carrigan, Tim, Bob Connell, and John Lee. 1985. Toward a New Sociology of Masculinity. *Theory and Society* 14 (5): 551–604.

Cohen, Deborah. 2006. From Peasant to Worker: Migration, Masculinity, and the Making of Mexican Workers in the US. *International Labor and Working-Class History* 69 (1): 81–103.

Cohler, Bertram J. 1982. Personal Narrative and Life Course. In *Life Span Development and Behavior*, ed. Paul Baltes and Orville Brim. New York: Academic Press.

Connell, Raewyn W., and James W. Messerschmidt. 2005. Hegemonic Masculinity: Rethinking the Concept. *Gender & Society* 19 (6): 829–859.

Culic, Irina. 2008. Eluding Exit and Entry Controls: Romanian and Moldovan Immigrants in the European Union. *East European Politics & Societies* 22 (1): 145–170.

French, Henry, and Mark Rothery. 2008. 'Upon Your Entry into the World': Masculine Values and the Threshold of Adulthood among Landed Elites in England 1680–1800. *Social History* 33 (4): 402–422.

Gallo, Ester. 2006. Italy is Not a Good Place for Men: Narratives of Places, Marriage and Masculinity among Malayali Migrants. *Global Networks* 6 (4): 357–372.

Gherghina, Sergiu, and Sergiu Miscoiu. 2013. The Failure of Cohabitation: Explaining the 2007 and 2012 Institutional Crises in Romania. *East European Politics & Societies* 27 (4): 668–684.

Hammack, Phillip, and Erin Toolis. 2014. Narrative and the Social Construction of Adulthood. In *Rereading Personal Narrative and Life Course. New Directions in Child and Adolescent Development*, ed. Brian Schiff. Wiley.

Horváth, Istvan. 2012. Migrația internațională a cetățenilor români în străinătate. In *Inerție și schimbare: dimensiuni sociale ale tranziției în Romania*, ed. Traian Rotariu and Vergil Voineagu. Iași: Polirom.

Liu, Shao-Hua. 2010. *Passage to Manhood: Youth Migration, Heroin, and AIDS in Southwest China*. Stanford: Stanford University Press.

Mary, Aurélie A. 2013. Re-Evaluating the Concept of Adulthood and the Framework of Transition. *Journal of Youth Studies* 17 (3): 415–429.

McKay, Steven C. 2007. Filipino Sea Men: Constructing Masculinities in an Ethnic Labour Niche. *Journal of Ethnic and Migration Studies* 33 (4): 617–633.

Monsutti, Alessandro. 2007. Migration as a Rite of Passage: Young Afghans Building Masculinity and Adulthood in Iran. *Iranian Studies* 40 (2): 167–185.

Montanari, Armando, and Barbara Staniscia. 2009. Female Migration in a Changing World. Eastern Europeans in Central Italy. *Espace, Populations, Société* 2: 227–241.

Nayak, Anoop. 2006. Displaced Masculinities: Chavs, Youth and Class in the Post-Industrial City. *Sociology: The Journal Of The British Sociological Association* 40 (5): 813–831.

OECD (Organisation for Economic Co-operation and Development). 2015. International Migration Outlook. http://www.oecd-ilibrary.org/social-issues-migration-health/international-migration-outlook-2015_migr_outlook-2015-en

Osella, Filippo, and Caroline Osella. 2000. Migration, Money and Masculinity in Kerala. *The Journal of the Royal Anthropological Institute* 6 (1): 117–133.

Osella, Caroline, and Filippo Osella. 2006. *Men and Masculinities in South India*. London and New York: Anthem Press.

Otovescu, Adrian. 2012. Identity Features of the Romanian Immigrants From Italy. *Journal of Community Positive Practices* 12 (3): 441–461.

Panagakis, Christina. 2015. Reconsidering Adulthood: Relative Constructions of Adult Identity During the Transition to Adulthood. *Advances in Life Course Research* 23: 1–13.

Piperno, Flavia. 2012. The Impact of Female Emigration on Families and the Welfare State in Countries of Origin: The Case of Romania. *International Migration* 50 (5): 189–204.

Qureshi, Kaveri. 2012. Pakistani Labour Migration and Masculinity: Industrial Working Life, the Body and Transnationalism. *Global Networks* 12 (4): 485–504.

Riessman, Catherine K. 2008. *Narrative Methods for the Human Sciences*. Thousand Oaks, CA: Sage.

Sandu, Dumitru, ed. 2006. *Locuirea temporară în străinătate: migrația economică a românilor: 1990–2006* [Living Abroad on a Temporary Basis. The Economic Migration of Romanians: 1990-2006]. Bucharest: Open Society Foundation.

———. 2010. *Lumile sociale ale migrației românești în străinătate* [Social Worlds of Romanian Migration Abroad]. Iași: Polirom.

Saraceno, Chiara, and Wolfgang Keck. 2010. Can We Identify Intergenerational Policy Regimes in Europe? *European Societies* 12 (5): 675–696.

Schrock, Douglas, and Michael Schwalbe. 2009. Men, Masculinity, and Manhood Acts. *Annual Review of Sociology* 35 (1): 277–295.

Shanahan, Michael J. 2000. Pathways to Adulthood in Changing Societies: Variability and Mechanisms in Life Course Perspective. *Annual Review of Sociology* 26: 667–692.

Skeggs, Beverley. 1997. *Formations of Class and Gender: Becoming Respectable*. London: Sage.

Stoica, Cătălin A. 2004. From Good Communists to Even Better Capitalists? Entrepreneurial Pathways in Post-Socialist Romania. *East European Politics and Societies* 18 (2): 236–277.

Thomas, William, and Florian Znaniecki. 1920. *The Polish Peasant in Europe and America*. Boston: The Gorham Press.

Vlase, Ionela. 2013. Women's Social Remittances and their Implications at Household Level: A Case Study of Romanian Migration to Italy. *Migration Letters* 10 (1): 81–90.

———. 2016. *Le genre dans la structuration de la migration*. Iași: Institutul European.

Open Access This chapter is licensed under the terms of the Creative Commons Attribution 4.0 International License (http://creativecommons.org/licenses/by/4.0/), which permits use, sharing, adaptation, distribution and reproduction in any medium or format, as long as you give appropriate credit to the original author(s) and the source, provide a link to the Creative Commons license and indicate if changes were made.

The images or other third party material in this chapter are included in the chapter's Creative Commons license, unless indicated otherwise in a credit line to the material. If material is not included in the chapter's Creative Commons license and your intended use is not permitted by statutory regulation or exceeds the permitted use, you will need to obtain permission directly from the copyright holder.

CHAPTER 10

Conclusion: Setting Up an Agenda for Life-Course Perspective in International Migration

Bogdan Voicu and Ionela Vlase

Life-course perspective has gained momentum recently in social sciences (Alwin 2012). The flourishing and maturation of longitudinal studies, particularly panels—as well as the availability of computing power to make such analysis possible, plus rapid societal changes in demographic processes and patterns—have led to a growing and unprecedented interest in human lives, specifically their trajectories, the impact of life paths on one's biography, and the institutionalization of life-course patterns (Elder et al. 2003; Wingens et al. 2011). Such an interest is consistent with postmodern diversification of lifestyles and de-normalization of education and employment trajectories, coupling, family, and parenting stages, in which life events and transitions are no longer clearly sequenced.

B. Voicu (✉)
'Lucian Blaga' University of Sibiu, Sibiu, Romania

Romanian Academy, Research Institute for Quality of Life, Bucharest, Romania

I. Vlase (✉)
'Lucian Blaga' University of Sibiu, Sibiu, Romania

© The Author(s) 2018
I. Vlase, B. Voicu (eds.), *Gender, Family, and Adaptation of Migrants in Europe*,
https://doi.org/10.1007/978-3-319-76657-7_10

In the introductory argument to this book, we asserted that personal biographies become social locations to create contexts in which one's agency unfolds. Migration adds to the story as an essential process to shape life courses. By changing geographical locations, one simultaneously also changes the structure of social ties, family relations, employment patterns, and, quite often, educational careers. Migration itself is a career that can be imagined as a long sequence of decisions about migrating or *not* migrating, about destinations, and about lengths of stays. As life course is a dance to the music of time (Allan and Jones 2003), migration also is a perpetual state of temporariness, a never-ending succession of movements, including remigrations, return migrations, circulatory movements, and spells of staying (Engbersen et al. 2010).

Migration also creates an even broader context in which age norms of origin and host societies must be negotiated across borders, and this may cause further tensions for migrants seeking to make meaningful choices regarding their family and work careers, as well as other life outcomes. Age norms vary across European countries with respect to behaviors such as entering adulthood, changing residency, entering the labor market, becoming a parent, and so on. Exposure to foreign age norms may lead to acculturation processes, with immigrants adapting to newly discovered norms and mixing them with values from their earlier socialization, in their countries of origin, as illustrated by Anca Bejenaru's chapter in this book. Migrants' exposure to new cultural and social environments in host countries may be conducive to challenging taken-for-granted assumptions about the appropriate age to make life transitions and assume new social roles.

Several chapters in this book also show that migration forces individuals to face and deal with sometimes-competing normative expectations about various behaviors. Migrants often discursively engage in a process of deconstruction of the meaning of certain life transitions in an attempt to make sense of their fragmented biographies and gender identities. The stories migrants tell to create meaningful lives through narratives are of key importance in contributors' inquiries in this book. Narrative appears as a means for agency, as illustrated by Ana Maria Preoteasa's chapter, because in the process of narrating, people become actors. Their voices enable them to make choices, create new possible alternatives, and assign meaning to their lives, all unfolding against the backdrop of prevailing cultural schemes that organize both our lives and our ways of recollecting lived experiences.

Each chapter in this book documents ways in which migration is intertwined with life pathways and tells the story of how migration shapes, and is shaped by, work, family, and educational pathways. Examples come from a variety of migration flows (Poles in Ireland; Romanians and Moroccans in Italy; and Spanish, Portuguese, and Italians in Switzerland), destinations (Spain, Italy, Ireland, and Germany), countries of origin (Romania, Morocco, Poland, and Spain), and return migration and/or remigration destinations (Germany, Spain, Italy, and Ireland).

The aim of this summary is to point out the principal, common features that arise from the diversity of topics addressed by this book's chapters. The task would seem to be a conundrum, given the heterogeneity of approaches and methods. However, life-course perspective acts as a unifying framework, as a general paradigm that puts human life at the forefront and leaves migration in the background. International migration provides a huge natural experiment (Dinesen 2013) that allows for observing and explaining social processes and the relationships that connect them, independent of any kind of geographical mobility.

Attempts to set up an agenda for life-course perspective in migration studies might seem trivial. Life-course perspective already *is* a mandatory part of international migration studies. Furthermore, international migration is simultaneously shaped deeply and acts as a melding tool for life course.

This book provides plenty of examples in this respect, taking readers on a journey to examine both turning points and trajectories; to consider work, family/parenthood, education, and (chains of) migrations decisions; to go from qualitative to quantitative methodology; and to address coping with present uncertainties, while dealing with rewriting uncertainties from the past and projecting representations about others in the future.

Most chapters focus on life trajectories. Migrants are seen as active producers of life sequences, which are partly determined socially. They move from one social role to another in a fluid way, in search of emancipation (see the chapter by Ana Maria Preoteasa), employment security (see the chapters by Alin Croitoru and Justyna Salamońska), or family integration (see Anca Bejenaru's chapter).

Turning points are also salient in migrants' life courses. Ionela Vlase's research provides information on patterns of male transitions to adulthood. Once they become parents, young male migrants in this study decided to desist from petty crimes and present a proper masculine presence to their offspring. The same type of story can be found in Bogdan

Voicu's chapter. Using quantitative data, he shows how turning points such as marriage, divorce, separation, parenthood, and widowhood have slightly different meanings for international migrants living in Germany compared with German natives. One also may consider turning points from the perspective of past trajectories, as Claudio Bolzman and Giacomo Vagni do in their chapter on retirement and later life. The perspective allows for decrypting long-running impacts of past work and family events, which seem to shape migrant post-retirement situations in a slightly different way, compared with natives.

The book brings together chapters using both qualitative and quantitative methods. Concerning qualitative approaches, many chapters are based on data collected through life-story interviews, a well-established data-gathering method used in social sciences (Poirier et al. 1983). This method is particularly valuable in migration research because it provides a way to give migrants the opportunity to deconstruct/reconstruct/reshape their biographies, reflect on past life events, and project future life changes to meaningfully connect their past, present, and future in relation to different cultural and socioeconomic structural contexts from both sending and receiving countries. The analysis of such data includes comparing cases or following conversations between cases (as in Justyna Salamońska's chapter). Beyond the method itself, the usefulness of the qualitative approach resides in its principal strengths, to be retrieved in any field, without any migration specificity. It calls for depicting rich images, with details that allow for observing the intricate relationship between various processes and phenomena. In the case of migrants, the qualitative approach allows contributors in this book to observe how migration decisions intervened as turning points in the work, education, and family trajectories. In turn, the quantitative approach adds to this composite picture the capacity to compare large numbers of individuals. The chapters in this book that are based on quantitative data provide ways to depict life courses by using either descriptive statistics (as Claudio Bolzman and Giacomo Vagni do in their chapter) or fixed-effect models used on panel data (as in the chapter by Bogdan Voicu). In both cases, the common link to qualitative approaches is the longitudinal perspective.

In all chapters in this book, migrants are either followed over long periods of time and interviewed repeatedly (see chapters by Bogdan Voicu and Justyna Salamońska), or else interviewed once, with recollections of past experiences combined with their present situations, sometimes with projections about the future. Time is brought in as an essential element to be considered for both personal agency and the social location in which it occurs.

Work and employment, family-related personal events, education careers, and changes in migration status come into play as specific themes in each chapter. Despite the stress of specific life domains, their intertwining is so strong that each chapter ends by either describing a mix of sequences that include all mentioned life domains or considering turning points from all these domains. For instance, Alin Croitoru's examination of gendered employment trajectories in the case of international migrants offers a perfect example in this direction. Women and men trajectories are described as parallel aspects, but all are actually shaped by permanent references to coupling and parenthood and/or decisions on recurrent education trajectories. Levels of job (in)security are reflected in recollections of past employment and hopeful projections for the future.

The nexus of family, work, aging, and educational careers on one side, and migration on the other, is addressed in all chapters and becomes the red line of the book. Transitions to parenthood in women migrants' family trajectories are addressed by Anca Bejenaru, whose informants reported struggles and uncertainties regarding their decisions to become parents. Parenthood in the case of labor migrants also may raise questions as to how one can pursue economic goals and maintain work connections and continuity of work history. Furthermore, work trajectories of Eastern European migrants in Western countries cannot be fully grasped apart from life circumstances and decisions regarding family and friendship ties, as well as shifting contexts of opportunities at home and abroad, as Salamońska illustrates.

Gender is seen as a mediating variable in almost all chapters, manifested in gendered roles and life courses. Gendered roles are also an outcome of life trajectories. As Francesca Vianello reports in her chapter, gender norms suffer changes as an effect from life trajectories under migration conditions. Such embeddedness again stresses the need to consider time as a crucial element in any explanation, intrinsic to formulating causal interpretations. Consequently, the life-course perspective becomes a mandatory method in migration studies.

The changes elicited by international migration are easy to observe under standardized life-course conditions. Nowadays, de-standardization increases diversity, so one may find it more difficult to grasp the consequences of migration. The chapters in this book focused on this mere distinction, documenting inflexions in life trajectories, with migration the suspected cause, and providing evidence of different impacts on turning points for migrants and natives. On the one hand, most chapters told the stories of migrants, depicting their lives as a succession of personal events, career-related decisions, education stages, and migration stays. On the other hand, migrants and natives are compared. Both perspectives use a longitudinal approach, with the latter perspective allowing for inferences on causal relationships, given the use of non-migrants as a control group. Causality is, however, not fully proven, given the restraints of the control group on natives and a failure to include stayers (i.e., non-migrants from countries of origin, as opposed to natives who are seen as non-migrants from host societies).

Beyond causal determinacy, there is a clear emphasis on the mechanisms that trigger supplemental effects from migration on life courses, as well as life courses' effects on migration decisions. All chapters explicitly or implicitly refer to coping with uncertainties in relation to choices that are structuring personal life trajectories and their sequencing. Uncertainty is usually related to present situations. For migrants, it means coping with precarious work circumstances, as well as fitting into existing dual contextuality, which is a source of axiological uncertainty. De-standardization of life courses elicits additional lack of clarity, related particularly to future pathways. In the absence of a clear normative pattern to follow, one must figure out a potential future from a broad range of choices. Given that many people are in the same situation, the respective condition becomes socialized, with individuals exchanging ideas and attitudes about how they will approach their own futures. Liquidity of migration, understood as a perpetual temporary state in relation to geographic mobility, becomes a crucial part of the alloy, with potential remigrations or return migrations adding to the complexity, increasing uncertainty. Projections also are oriented toward migrants' own past. Recollections of events that led to initial migrations, or to postponing initial migrations, often refer to dealing with precariousness in personal situations or in the society of origin as a whole. Self-interpretations of past decisions and life events depict migrants' journeys as pathways toward integration and adaptation to existing structural opportunities and constraints, in search of self-fulfilment.

People are switching from one social role to another, depending on what suits them best, according to information and opportunities they have, and on their own scale of preferences. This is the story told by migrant interviewees of different origins and life stages in the qualitative chapters of this book. The chapters underline a search to cope with uncertainty and increase adaptation and integration. In many ways, this is a book on adaptation, but adaptation is not seen in the host society but rather the social location provided by past life courses and foreseeable future pathways. This implies, in most cases, integration into the host society, while often also maintaining connections to the nation of origin.

Individuals become subjects and active agents of change for their own multidimensional nexus of pathways. They live in between societies, dealing with uncertainties related to their liquid careers as migrants, and they experience the contemporary de-standardization of life courses—affecting both family and parenthood, employment, and educational routes. There is a continuous reshaping of the structural opportunities and constraints they face in daily life. Despite increased heterogeneity when compared with normative life trajectories of the past, the sequences documented in this book continue to be socialized. Social norms, although more flexible, continue to govern the formation of a broad range of patterns that serve as models for agency. Choice is more varied, which actually increases agentic options and boosts the role of life courses in creating social locations.

Such variety in pathways is not a particular *appanage* of international migrants. Migration decisions are made all the time by natives, including stayers, who simply decide not to migrate, but such a decision is never definitive. With different probabilities depending on various personal traits, one may simply choose a different spatial location at a later point in time. Liquidity of migration applies to non-migrants as well, and their decision to stay is far from constituting an advantage, a privilege, or an endowment. It acts as a simple agentic distinction that leaves open the door for generalizations, starting with studying migrants. Studying migrants from a life-course perspective adds value to such endeavors, allowing for a more general understanding of humans and societies amid their growth. It allows for transferring conclusions from migrants to stayers and vice versa.

Future research directions should include prompting researchers to become more engaged with life-course perspectives in migration studies. At the same time, researchers from this field may more easily communicate with researchers from other related fields since the life-course approach invites examination of connections between various societal structures and individual choices across a wide range of realms, such as work and education, gender and family, and aging and well-being. Therefore, we expect smoother communication between researchers from social sciences in general, indicating that studying migrants is confined not only to examining a peculiar group of individuals but also to assessing resilience in social explanations regarding people and societies under the stress of major life changes.

References

Allan, G., and G. Jones. 2003. Introduction. In *Social Relations and the Life Course*, ed. G. Allan and G. Jones, 1–12. Palgrave Macmillan.

Alwin, D.F. 2012. Integrating Varieties of Life Course Concepts. *The Journals of Gerontology, Series B: Psychological Sciences and Social Sciences* 67 (2): 206–220.

Dinesen, P.T. 2013. Where You Come From or Where You Live? Examining the Cultural and Institutional Explanation of Generalized Trust Using Migration as a Natural Experiment. *European Sociological Review* 29 (1): 114–128.

Elder, G.H., Jr., M.K. Johnson, and R. Crosnoe. 2003. The Emergence and Development of Life Course Theory. In *Handbook of the Life Course*, ed. Jeylan T. Mortimer and J. Shanahan Michael. New York, Boston, Dordrecht, London, Moscow: Kluwer Academic Publishers.

Engbersen, Godfried, Erik Snel, and Jan de Booman. 2010. 'A Van Full of POLES': Liquid Migration from Central and Eastern Europe. In *A Continent Moving West. EU Enlargement and Labour Migration from Central and Eastern Europe*, ed. Richard Black, Godfried Engbersen, Marek Okólski, and Cristina Panțîru. Amsterdam: Amsterdam University Press.

Poirier, Jean, Simone Clapier-Valladon, and Paul Raybaut. 1983. *Les récits de vie: théorie et pratique*. Presses universitaires de France.

Wingens, M., H. Valk, M. Windzio, and C. Aybek. 2011. The Sociological Life Course Approach and Research on Migration and Integration. In *A Life-Course Perspective on Migration and Integration*, ed. M. Wingens, M. Windzio, H.D. Valk, and C. Aybek, 1–26. Dordrecht: Springer.

Index[1]

A
Adulthood, 3, 9, 19, 21, 48, 57, 94, 98, 108, 112, 152, 179, 182, 186, 189, 195–202, 207–222, 228, 229
  delayed, 213–215, 218–221
  normative, 206
  pathways to, 205
  premature, 209–213, 215
Agency, 3, 4, 6, 8, 10, 19, 21, 23, 102, 104, 198, 212, 228, 231, 233
Aging, 68, 69, 84, 85, 183, 198, 231
Anderson, B., 94, 97, 171
Andersson, G., 147
Anghel, R.G., 95, 96, 204
Apitzsch, U., 177
Aspirations, 18, 47, 57, 61, 154, 155, 162, 163, 172, 173, 183, 200, 202, 206
Atkinson, R., 150
Attachment theory, 145, 151, 165
Aydemir, A., 55

B
Baetică, R., 143, 164
Bahna, M., 175
Bakermans-Kranenburg, M.J., 146
Baláž, V., 96
Bauman, Z., 200
Baumrind, D., 143, 144, 153
Beaverstock, J.V., 50
Belsky, J., 146
Berry, J.W., 141, 146, 147
Bertoli, S., 176
Bettio, F., 94
Bijwaard, G.E., 176
Birman, D., 141
Bîrsan, M., 173
Borjas, J.G., 95
Bowlby, J., 145
Boyle, M., 42, 44, 51, 55, 61
Bozkurt, O., 55
Bradatan, C.E., 148, 149
Braun, V., 150

[1] Note: Page numbers followed by 'n' refer to notes.

© The Author(s) 2018
I. Vlase, B. Voicu (eds.), *Gender, Family, and Adaptation of Migrants in Europe*,
https://doi.org/10.1007/978-3-319-76657-7

C

Caces, F.E., 96
Calvo, R., 176
Carrigan, T., 199
Castells, M., 171
Charles, M., 94
Chen, Z., 142
Child birth, 6, 9, 15, 16, 20, 24–27, 31–34, 97, 111, 112, 117, 142–143, 147, 156, 158, 160, 161, 164, 178, 184, 228, 231
Childhood, 3, 19, 98, 142, 145, 146, 148–156, 163, 165, 179, 181, 188, 200, 202, 216
Chiswick, B.R., 42, 45
Clarke, V., 150
Class, 8, 50, 72, 118, 144, 149, 152, 164, 173, 179, 185, 197, 200, 205
Cohen, D., 197, 198
Cohler, B.J., 201
Community, 9, 42, 131, 152, 155, 178, 182, 186, 196, 215
Commuting, 173, 180, 188, 189
Connell, R.W., 199
Conradson, D., 42, 44, 48, 53, 56
Constantinescu, M., 96
Construction sector, 44, 46, 47, 52, 57, 61
Context, 3, 6, 7, 9, 16, 18, 19
  childhood, 152
  migration, 156–158
Cowan, P.A., 142
Culic, I., 203, 205
Cumulative disadvantages, 68, 69, 82, 85
Currie, S., 44, 45

D

d'Albis, H., 143
Daly, M., 176
Damelang, A., 171
de Haan, M., 147
Dependency, 4, 9, 19, 33, 68, 100, 102–104, 107–108, 111, 134, 197
De-standardization, 3, 6, 7, 231–233
Diaconu, L., 98
Discourse, 179, 186, 187
Divorce, 3, 6, 15, 17, 20, 24, 25, 27, 30–33, 178, 187, 196, 212, 230
Ducu, V., 175, 176
Duncan, S., 94, 97
Dustmann, C., 95, 96

E

Eade, J., 48
Easterbrooks, A.M., 142
Eastern European countries, 185
Economic conditions, 175
Economic crisis, 25, 41, 43, 46, 51, 56, 57, 60–62, 107, 117, 119–121, 124–127, 129–131, 133–135, 154
Economic remittances, 175
Education, 2–5, 8, 9, 21, 25, 27, 31, 34, 42, 53, 54, 56, 75, 80, 94, 95, 97, 98, 102–104, 108, 109, 111, 118, 119, 122, 123, 143, 149, 154, 156, 157, 161, 163, 171–173, 175–177, 179–188, 190, 196, 201, 213, 214, 227–230, 232, 233
  career, 178, 189, 231
  system, 174
  trajectory, 178
Elder, G.H., Jr., 172
Elderly, 7, 9, 69–71, 81, 83, 85, 100, 101, 156, 175, 179, 183, 184, 188
Embeddedness, 231
Employment, 185, 189
European Commission, 143, 164
Eurostat, 143, 164, 186
Evans, B.C., 148

Evans, K., 96
Evans, M., 95
Exhausted migrant effect, 70

F
Falicov, J., 142
Family, 2–10, 46, 47, 51, 52, 55, 57–61, 171–182, 184–190, 227–231, 233
  care, 176
  prospects, 176
Favell, A., 41, 47, 50, 57, 58, 61, 171
Feminization of migration, 175
Flexibility, 7, 108
Fluidity, 10, 16, 17, 22–24
Forde, C., 49
French, H., 196

G
Gallo, E., 197
Garapich, M., 48
García, F., 144, 164
Gardner, K., 2, 42, 48
Gauld, R., 174
Geist, C., 174, 176
Gender, 2, 5–10, 25, 31, 117, 119, 122, 123, 127–129, 133–135, 172, 175, 228, 231, 233
Gherghina, S., 203
Ghorashi, H., 176
Ghosh, J., 175
Glick, J.E., 149
Goldberg, W.A., 142
Gracia, E., 144, 164
Green, J., 172
Gurak, T.D., 96

H
Haas, A., 171
Hall, C.M., 42, 61
Hamilton, E., 111

Hammack, P., 201, 206
Hărăguş, P., 97
Harris, E., 149
Health, 68–71, 79, 80, 83–85, 197
Hegemonic masculinities, 199
Hennebry, L.J., 96
Hernandez, M., 147
Hoerder, D., 182
Hoghughi, M., 143
Horsburgh, S., 174
Horváth, I., 205
Housekeeping, 156, 172, 179, 184, 189
Housing, 78, 186, 217

I
Independence
  child, 147, 157, 161, 162
  financial, 48, 52, 53, 57, 104, 211
Inequalities, 71, 75, 77, 78, 80, 83–85, 103
Institutionalization, 5, 19, 227
Integration, 7, 15, 35, 42, 45, 71, 94, 96, 146, 229, 232, 233
International student, 175, 178
Ireland, 41–62
Isolation, 57, 79, 126, 182, 187

J
Janzen, R., 141, 148, 150
Johnstone, M., 176

K
Kaczmarczyk, P., 41
Kâğıtçıbaşı, C., 144, 152
Kahn, J.R., 147
Kaplan, H.B., 142
Karp, J., 142
Keck, W., 204
Keller, H., 144, 165
Kennedy, P., 42, 48, 51

King, R., 42, 48, 174
Kirchkamp, O., 95
Kofman, E., 171
Krings, T., 41, 43, 62
Kulu, H., 147

L

Labor market, 3, 5, 6, 41, 42, 45, 47, 49, 50, 54, 56, 60, 61, 84, 94–96, 98, 102, 107, 109, 111, 112, 117, 119, 120, 122–125, 131, 133, 154, 174, 175, 203
Latham, A., 42, 44, 48, 53, 56
Le Bianic, T., 45
Lee, E., 176
Lersch, P.M., 176
Lessons learned, 185
Life satisfaction, 5–7, 15–21, 23–27, 30–34, 80
Liquid migration, 17, 22–24, 32, 232, 233
Liu, S., 196, 197, 221
Living conditions, 7, 33, 68–71, 78, 83, 85, 96, 129, 179, 189
Local culture, 185
Lutz, H., 95

M

McGoldrick, M., 147
McKay, S.C., 196, 198
McLeod, J., 42
McManus, P.A., 174, 176
Madden, V., 145
Mahler, S.J., 175
Malyutina, D., 96
Manhood, 9, 195–198, 200, 202, 207, 209, 211, 212, 214, 217–219, 221, 222
Marchetta, F., 176
Marchetti, S., 175

Marcu, S., 176
Mărginean, I., 173
Marital status, 7, 16, 25–27, 30, 31, 33, 34, 94, 176, 185, 218
Marks, 145
Marriage, 6, 7, 9, 15–17, 20, 21, 24, 27, 30–34, 97, 106, 111, 126, 143, 148, 156, 164, 173, 178, 187, 188, 190, 200, 205, 207–209, 212, 215, 218, 230
Mary, D., 201
Masculinity, 196–202, 204, 205, 207–212, 214–222
  exacerbated, 209–213, 218–221
  threatened, 213–215
Melzer, S.M., 176
Mental health, 79
Messerschmidt, J.W., 199
Migrant
  caregivers, 175
  networks, 49, 50, 52
  women, 175
Migration
  career, 4, 15, 22, 117–119, 129, 131–134, 182, 183, 208, 217, 218, 221, 222, 228, 233
  wave, 188
Milewski, N., 147
Miscoiu, S., 203
Monsutti, A., 196
Montanari, A., 204
Moscardino, U., 144, 146, 164
Motivation for migration, 174
Muresan, C., 97, 143, 164
Mussino, E., 147, 164

N

Narrative, 185
Naturalization, 71
Nayak, A., 200

INDEX 239

Neagu, G., 174
Nedoluzhko, L., 147
Nesteruk, O., 145
Ní Laoire, C., 42, 48
Nisic, N., 176

Popescu, R., 149
Precariousness, 8, 9, 70, 78, 117, 120, 123, 124, 126, 127, 129–131, 133–135, 135n2
Preoteasa, A.M., 174

O
Occupational mobility, 74, 75, 85
Ochocka, J., 141, 148, 150
Oleinikova, O., 176
Oppedal, B., 146
Osella, C., 196, 197, 221
Osella, F., 99, 196, 197, 221
Otovescu, A., 205
Otto, H., 144, 165

P
Panagakis, C., 201
Parenthood, 3, 4, 7, 9, 25, 30, 31, 184, 229–231, 233
Parenting, 4, 9, 141–149, 151, 153, 154, 156–164, 227
Parenting practices, 143–145, 153–154
Path dependency, 68, 84
Pathways, 2–5, 23, 110, 177, 178, 205, 229, 232, 233
Patton, M.Q., 149
Performance of masculinities, 205
Perrons, D., 94
Personal development, 189
Personal events, 15–18, 23–25, 27, 32, 33, 35, 231, 232
Pessar, P.R., 175
Petroff, A., 174
Pfau-Effinger, B., 94, 97
Piperno, F., 171, 175, 204
Pitkänen, P., 171
Poland, 42–56, 58–61

Q
Qualitative Panel Study, 43
Qualitative research, 175
Qureshi, K., 95, 99, 196, 197

R
Reasons for migration, 172
Retired migrants, 7, 67, 69, 70, 72, 75, 77, 79, 83–85
Return migration, 4, 7, 8, 22, 50, 51, 53, 55, 59, 60, 69, 75, 86n1, 93, 94, 96, 97, 100–104, 106–109, 111, 112, 122, 132, 133, 135, 148, 158, 171–173, 176–178, 181–186, 188–190, 195, 210, 212, 213, 218, 220, 228, 229, 232
Riessman, C.K., 206
Robila, M., 144, 145
Robinson, C., 55
Rooth, R.O., 176, 181
Rothery, M., 196
Ruhs, M., 97
Ryan, L., 96

S
Saarela, J., 176, 181
Saccheto, D., 95
Saldana, J., 172
Sandu, D., 96, 203
Saraceno, C., 204
Sarkisian, N., 176

Schierup, C., 94
Schrock, D., 196, 198, 199
Schwalbe, M., 196, 198, 199
Scott, S., 42, 50, 51, 61
Scrinzi, F., 95
Self-fulfillment, 232
Self-realization, 48, 56
Separation, 15, 20, 24, 27, 30–33, 230
Şerban, M., 96, 148, 171
Serbin, L., 142
Shanahan, M.J., 200
Sharma, N., 149
Shelley, T., 95
Sherman, J., 149
Siouti, I., 177
Skeggs, B., 205
Skills transferability, 45, 61
Sobotka, T., 147
Social
 capital, 78
 location, 3–5, 7, 10, 228, 231, 233
 network, 17, 22, 24, 25, 31, 33, 35, 231
 norms, 18, 19, 22–24, 228, 233
 role, 2–4, 6, 200, 201, 228, 229, 232
 values, 17, 19, 21, 228;
  postmodernism, 6, 35;
  traditionalism, 6, 8, 17, 21, 24
Socialization, 19, 128, 145, 202, 211, 228, 233
Social-learning theory, 146
Spain, 185
Staniscia, B., 204
Stecklov, G., 176
Stoica, C.A., 203
Strategy, 176
Strozza, S., 147, 164
Student, 179–181
Sundström, E., 97
Svensson, L.G., 45

T
Takala, T., 171
Temporariness, 228, 232
Thomas, W., 196
Thomson, R., 42, 43
Thornton, H.P., 95
Thorogood, N., 172
Toolis, E., 201, 206
Training, 71, 75, 83, 94, 108, 111, 173, 183, 187, 210
Trajectories, 2, 6–10, 67, 71, 75, 78, 83–85, 178, 227, 229–233
Transitions, 1, 2, 4–7, 9, 15, 18, 32, 68, 197, 227–229
Transnational, 2, 16, 17, 33, 70
 commuting, 189
 dual contextuality, 18, 22, 232
Trevena, P., 44
Trickett, E.J., 141
Tudor, E., 96, 145
Tufiş, C., 145
Turning points, 229–232
Tyldum, G., 171, 172, 175

U
Uncertainty, 2, 4–7, 16–18, 21–25, 31, 33, 34, 232
Undergraduate students, 176
Unemployment, 34, 54, 70, 94, 95, 107, 118, 120, 123, 126, 127, 129–131, 133, 190, 196, 200, 203

V
van Doeselaar, S., 176
van Ijzendoorn, M.H., 142, 145, 146
Verashchagina, A., 94
Vianello, F.A., 95, 96
Videon, T.M., 149
Vlase, I., 96, 148, 171, 175, 204

Voicu, B., 96, 145, 148, 174
Voicu, M., 97
Vulnerability, 9, 15, 16, 18, 20, 23, 24, 33, 34, 111, 120, 126, 134

W

White, S., 56, 59, 146
White-collar, 48, 49, 56, 61
Widowhood, 3, 15–17, 24, 25, 27, 30, 32, 33, 35, 230
Williams, A.M., 42, 61, 96
Williams, C.C., 95
Williams, F., 97
Willis, J., 172

Work
  career, 4, 8–10, 43, 45–50, 54, 55, 57, 58, 61, 67, 83, 84, 118, 123, 124, 127, 131, 133–135, 183–185, 228, 231, 232
  conditions, 8, 44, 120, 123, 126, 174, 197
  experience, 8, 44, 47, 56, 58, 93, 99–102, 112, 178, 185, 213
  flexibility, 120, 123, 124, 127, 131, 135

Z

Znaniecki, F., 196

CPSIA information can be obtained
at www.ICGtesting.com
Printed in the USA
LVHW07*1711030618
579426LV00006B/9/P